STAY IN LANE

Truck drivers are the silent majority of a huge industry without whom the country would literally grind to a halt. To other road users they are more often presented as the menaces of the motorways, just the chaps who take up the space the rest want to themselves. Here, for the first time, they have a voice. *Stay in Lane* is the only book *for* truckers — written by the man who perhaps knows them better than they do themselves — and *by* truckers. Here are his, and their, unexpurgated views on the things that matter to them most:

● **roads ● docks ● police and the law ● the press ● business ● clubs and festivals ● top-rated places to eat, play and stay**

All the fun and all the flak of life on wheels is here, interspersed with over 100 jokes and anecdotes, plus cartoons by Bernard Cookson.

If today's trucker *really* wants to stay in lane, he can't afford to leave home without it.

STAY IN LANE

THE BANDAG TRUCKERS' GUIDE

FRANKLYN WOOD

Quiller Press
London

Also by Franklyn Wood

Cola Cowboys

First published in 1987 by Quiller Press Ltd
50 Albemarle Street, London W1X 4BD

Illustrations by Bernard Cookson
Designed and produced by Linda Wade

ISBN 0 907621 85 6

Set in Linotype Univers
by The Design Team, Ascot, Berkshire
Printed and bound by R. J. Acford, Chichester

CONTENTS

'It's the transport manager — he was so bloody slow signing the consignment note I hadn't time to hang about!'

FOREWORD

This is a book for truckers, the men behind the wheels of the HGVs which keep the country running. Its purpose is to reflect their views and, as far as it can, give their side of the story.

It is by no means a complete book because it is impossible to cover all aspects of road transport in one edition. But proudly we can say that it is the only book available which truly reflects, usually in their own words, the *drivers'* opinions of life on the road — more than 700 are quoted.

Though there is a great deal wrong with the services provided for British truckers, some people are at least getting it right and others are getting it half-right and improving.

The purpose of this guide is to highlight those who, by common consent of HGV and commercial drivers, are doing the right things at the right prices, and those who are moving towards that end. No café, truckstop or park appears in this edition unless it has been personally recommended by at least one on-the-road-daily driver; some of the services are recommended by droves of drivers, as you will see.

Nobody has been permitted to buy space or advertise in this book. The only way a name can appear in these pages is when a driver tells us about it in writing. So we ask for your further co-operation and help by filling in the postcard at the end of the book and mailing it to us. And please print *CLEARLY* — you are writing to a friend, not the boss or the VAT man.

But the book isn't just about food and accomodation, vital as those are to a good life on the road; it is about you, your lives, problems, belly-aches and your fun — so tell us more about them as well.

Franklyn

THE OPEN ROAD

For Allah created the English mad — the maddest of all mankind!
— *Rudyard Kipling*

Every HGV driver knows that 'M' is for motorway — and 'M' is for madness. But just what kind of madness? The notorious motorway madness that causes multiple crashes in bad weather is a recognised, accepted and much commented upon phenomenon. Almost, in fact, vaunted by the media — they bring out their black types and put on their solemn voices to report it. And truck drivers who spend

most of their lives on motorways, and earn their livelihoods by following the blue routes on road maps, know all about it. A modern trucker lives day by day with danger under his bonnet, and other people's lives depending on the nimbleness of his clutch foot and his accelerator and brake foot — that is the condition of Driving-UK today.

But that kind of madness apart, there seems to be something about Britain's M-roads which induces in ordinary, pleasant citizens an insanity which makes them reckless, or turns ordinary, intelligent people into gibbering simpletons who do not know their lefts from their rights, or whether they are coming or going.

IT'S THE WAY YOU TELL'EM

A time and a place

The driver was struggling under the bonnet of his broken-down bus, rummaging with his hand in the tool-box. His Clippie asked: 'Do you want a screw-driver?' He answered: 'Leave it out, love. We're 40 minutes late already.'
Terry Bates, *Plasmarl, Swansea.*

Wrong way Charlies

There is a definite 'insanity factor' and the proof of it is in the fact that more than 8 per cent of the United Kingdom's registered HGV drivers frequently meet other vehicles — cars in particular — travelling the wrong way down motorways, dual carriageways or around roundabouts and driving head-on at them.

Translate that 8 per cent to people, to feet on the pedals and hands clutching the steering wheels, and it means that, at one time or another, 27,000 HGV drivers have met 27,000 motorists eyeball to eyeball in a head-on crash situation, often at speed, when the motorists have merrily taken the wrong turning and driven blithely into, at best, a heart-stopping fright or, at worst, disaster.

In compiling this book we questioned 5,000 HGV drivers and discovered that, though people do all sorts of other incredible things on motorways, this is by far the most prevalent and persistent folly; in the section of our questionnaire which asked, 'briefly describe something unusual or bizarre you have experienced or seen on the roads,' the answer in reply after reply was, 'Met another vehicle driving the wrong way on the motorway/dual carriageway/roundabout.'

The wrong-way Charlies happen all over the country and cover all sections of the community from Jaguar to Robin three-wheelers drivers. You can meet them anywhere, any time. **John Martin**, of Clacton, met three in one hour near Ipswich. You may not, like Mr **Beaumont**, of Speke, Liverpool, be driving on the M6 over Shap and meet a police car coming at you the wrong way — to be fair, the police car was running alongside a wrong-way Charlie trying to pull him over — but that doesn't minimise the shock.

Russell Hart, of Ashill, Norfolk, was quietly rolling round the south ring-road at King's Lynn when he caused great aggravation by squatting dead in the middle of the road preventing anybody overtaking him. Those behind flashed him and blasted him with their air-horns, but they couldn't see what he could: an elderly lady driving down the wrong carriageway looking everywhichway except straight ahead. She was irate when she had to stop, and furiously demanded to know where they had put the entrance to the town — and demanded that he should get out of her way.

Oh yes, you can get into serious trouble for being in the right. A Humberside driver received a blistering ears-bend from an old lady for going the right way down a one-way system when she was going the wrong way. 'Back up,' she demanded. And acidly asked, 'Have you no manners?' She took his number, the name of his company, and reported him for grave discourtesy.

Why oh why?

The questions to be asked are: Why does it happen? How can it happen?

Well, most of you know how and why.

Sitting high in a truck cab, in splendid isolation, with a near bird's-eye view of the antics of the travelling public, police and ministry officials, you get a different perspective and realise that the roots of the madness are in Whitehall, Westminster and the offices of highway authorities up and down the land. For a country like Britain, the roads are, to use the drivers' most common description, diabolical. And the regulations are worse.

There is a state of chaos on the roads of Britain, but it cannot all be placed at the door of the government; Big Business, the sector which has most to gain from efficient roads, is itself often a major contributor to the bedlam.

So we have begun this book with a belly-ache. But that is because *you* are writing it. I may be putting down the words but they are your thoughts, your ideas, your complaints and your suggestions. Do you ever listen to yourselves talking? Perhaps you have talked because you think it is time that drivers had a voice in what is happening on the roads.

IT'S THE WAY YOU TELL 'EM

You'll never walk alone

The football fans' car was in a bad shunt on the motorway on the way home after the match and Paddy cracked his skull. When they rang, the emergency services instructed: 'Support his head until the ambulance arrives.' The ambulancemen found them clapping and singing in unison: 'Pad-dy's head...Pad-dy's head.'

D. Davis, *Ystalyfera, South Wales*.

A few salient facts emerge from the extensive survey we did for the book:

While road transport is increasing all the time, facilities and services for trucks are, in many cases, declining dramatically.

Safety regulations and new laws, quite often, actually increase the dangers and hazards on the roads. Take the 40 mph speed limit on all roads other than motorways and dual carriageways. To the general public that may seem an eminently sensible safety rule: but there isn't a modern truck which is built to cruise at so low a speed, so the driver is constantly dodging up and down the gear box to maintain his steady speed. He is, in fact, obliged to drive his articulated vehicle in a manner it wasn't intended to be driven.

IT'S BIZARRE

Thank you, officer

Clutching the steering wheel, a very old man in an even older car was motoring happily down the hard-shoulder of the M6. A police car pulled in front of him with its 'STOP' sign lit. **Graham Whitehead**, of Swinton, Manchester, watched the old man conscientiously stick out his hand, signal a right, pass the police car and pull back on to the hard-shoulder still bumbling merrily along.

The tachograph, until the change on 29 September 1986, for five years had imposed a great strain on drivers having to rush to keep within their tacho time limits. Safety and caution often went out of the window in order that the driver should keep to the legal restrictions of his tacho card.

Six axles are now universally recommended both for safety and to ease the wear and tear on roads. Yet the law states that you must compress your three-axle trailer, say a fridge box, and three-axle tractor to a maximum overall length of 15.5 metres. That makes the unit unstable and allows the trailer to push the tractor about all over the road. Apart from that, there is no room for adequate fuel tanks so your capacity is reduced and you are pulling in more often.

Side guards are compulsory on any 38-tonner but not on a 32-tonner: yet there is far more space between axles for a car to run under on a four-axle 32-tonner than on a six-axle 38-tonner.

Rear fog lights seem another marvellous safety factor. But at the same wattage as brake lights they dazzle a following truck driver and they can completely obscure the brake lights.

Those are a few random examples off the top of the head. There are many more examples and many worse.

Planners as often as not create more disruption than than they cure — and curing planners' mistakes creates even greater chaos. Maybe by the year 2001 they will have sorted something out. So if you can keep trucking until then, you might be all right.

Second class citizens

You carry 84 per cent of all consigned goods in Britain. Many of you argue that it is nearer 100 per cent because everything that comes off the railway, canals or aircraft ends up in a truck or van for delivery. Consigned goods means everything everybody sends and everything everybody receives — it is that important. More important is the fact that you carry 99.3 per cent of all food consumed in the country. A pretty important job. Yet, for some inexplicable reason, you are regarded as, and treated like, second-class citizens.

IT'S BIZARRE

cleanliness is next to gormlessness
Our CB contact, **King-of-the-Road**, from Edinburgh, pulled into the car-wash. The brushes were whirling and the water jetting and a man was riding through on a push-bike.

It isn't like that on the Continent, as everybody who drives overseas knows. But on this tight little island, tight little minds keep the truck and its driver at arm's-length — preferably the jib-arm on a Cole's crane length. Why, you are not considered fit enough to eat with the travelling public in motorway services, Little Chefs or Happy Eaters — though, in the view of many of you, you wouldn't feed dogs in some of them. And all but 100 per cent of you think that motorway services proprietors make Dick Turpin look like an 18th-century Bob Geldof; in your view, those who run services on the motorways are 20th-century licensed highwaymen.

Crazy charges

And that takes us back to madness and planning — and are the two synonymous? The Department of Transport licenses and approves the plans and operations of motorway services. And it also licenses — franchises — the emergency services which are allowed to operate from the service areas. How many members of the public realise that often trucks have to pull off motorway service areas and park on the hard shoulder in order to get service from their regular, contracted emergency services? They have to do it to avoid the exorbitant charges of the franchised operators.

So the operation of a so-called service actually creates a serious hazard and turns the hard shoulder into a breakdown repair area because it was planned that way.

But, of course, they planned the M25...

At that point the conversation and rational thought usually come to an abrupt stop — like traffic at the Dartford Tunnel or at the M3 interchange in the morning, or at the A12 junction queueing to get on, or... well, you name the place, or maybe think about it while you are in the tail-back at South Mimms.

We asked in our survey for your best jokes and, you've guessed it, motorways and planners were high on the list.

While we are on the subject of jokes, let us get one out of the way: it is the classic trucking joke and it is claimed to have happened everywhere. And everybody claims to have met a fella who actually saw it happen. But, alas, the only place where it can be proved to have happened is in the old Clint Eastwood classic film, *Every Which Way But Loose*.

The action is in a trucker's café. The trucker is just beginning to eat his meal when a gang of Hell's Angels arrives. Arrogantly the Angels swagger into the café. They surround the trucker's table and begin silently to taunt him. One by one they help themselves to portions of the food on his plate. He takes no notice. Then they steal his bread, his pudding, his coffee. Still he takes no notice. A terrible silence has fallen on the café and the tension is electric. The trucker stands up, says nothing, turns and walks out. His engine roars as he starts up, and he is away.

Smirking, the Hell's Angels' leader scoffs at the café proprietor behind the counter: 'He wasn't much of a fighting man, your tough, hairy trucker.'

Without looking up from pouring the teas, the café owner nods agreement and says: 'He wasn't much of a driver either — he's just run over all your bikes.'

If anybody kids you it happened at Thirsk, or Huntingdon, or The Hollies, say a little silent prayer for Clint and then buy the storyteller a pint for a good try. On the other hand, if he can prove beyond any doubt that it did happen where he says it did — buy him a gallon.

Mind you, if you do like a laugh and you are broad-minded, very broad-minded, you could do worse than spend half an hour with **Dougie Vick**, of Santa Fe Express. He could lay claim to being the Frank Carson of the truckstops. I think that a good night at, say, a T45 Team Club meeting could be an hour of Dougie and Mrs Mary Whitehouse. It would be interesting. You might see some action... she would probably switch off all trucks.

IT'S BIZARRE

's no fun

Flash Hamish was in one heck of a hurry to get to his Christmas celebrations while driving along the road to Glasgow, and very impatient with the line of slow-moving trucks strung out in front of him. **Peter Mack**, from Milton Keynes, watched him dodge and weave up the line ignoring all the flashing-light warnings truckers gave him. Going like the clappers , he overtook the lead truck and ran smack into a snow-drift. He hit it so fast and so hard that they had to dig him out through the hatch-back while the truckers fell about laughing.

But, for a moment, let's go back to the madness — it is difficult to avoid it on the road. Could anything be more insane than changing a wheel in the fast lane of a motorway?

Yet it happens all the time. On a percentage basis, 4 per cent of HGV drivers have had to slap on the anchors because they have almost run into somebody changing a wheel on any motorway you choose to name. They have been Jaguar and Rover owners down to humble mini-drivers. There they stop, with traffic flashing by at 70, 80, 90 mph, brakes screaming, horns blasting, tyres scorching and, with jack and wheel-brace, unconcernedly set about replacing a flat.

If it were an isolated occurrence, then it might be worth an astonished gasp when the tale is told round the bar at an overnight stop. But it isn't a rare event, it happens several hundred, possibly a couple of thousand times a year. Unbelievable! Unbelievable, that is, until the facts are revealed in first-hand eye-witness accounts by those who have had the misfortune to burn off half an inch of rubber, and lose a few years off their lifespans, braking and swerving to avoid jacked-up lunatics in the suicide-lane.

That says a lot about the standard of driving on motorways, but it says a lot more about the training for motorway driving. There isn't any. The HGV driver has to pay £515 for a course, wait until he is 21 to take a gruelling test for a class 1 licence, and then live in the permanent knowledge that his licence — his livelihood — can be removed at any moment for any — any — misdemeanour. He is the only driver on the road who is actually tested on motorway driving. Any wild hot-head or persistent fuddy-duddy with no driving aptitude whatsoever can try, try and try again until they succeed in passing a not very searching test... and then stop and change a wheel in the fast lane of a motorway.

You find that incredible? Well, stop and look at the bizarre footnotes at the bottom of some pages of the book where I have named some of the drivers who have seen this happen.

IT'S BIZARRE

Pride comes before...

The man in the car in front wasn't paying attention to his driving, he was too busy spraying lacquer onto his hair and giving himself a really sharp look. Came a corner and he drove straight through a hedge as **Scott Hillier**, of Leamington Spa watched. He was obviously on his way to meet a girl friend, and she would tell him: 'My God, you look as if you've been dragged through the back of a hedge.'

There are also dangers on the hard shoulder for the unwary. You might pull in and run over a picnic party, or a group of people at prayer. Those combined are number three on our list of bizarre happenings on motorways. Picnics and prayers — you might say that there is something to be said for dying happy and holy if your time has come. But a motorway is hardly the place for either.

Alex Main, a driver from Preston, Lancashire, did a double-take when he saw a family playing cricket on the central reservation of the M6. Naturally, the question must always be asked, did they know it was wrong? Did they know it was against the law? There is always a chance that they didn't. They would have found out pretty quickly had the law turned up. But by then the damage could have been done.

Pakistanis figure prominently in drivers' reports of odd incidents along the M-roads; they seem to have a great love of picnics while watching the fast cars go by. Under the present state of the law, by even mentioning it one could be at risk of being accused of racial prejudice. But better that than have the occurrences go unremarked with the risk that one day a happy family road-side party turned into a massacre.

Perhaps it is a job that could be done by police community relations officers. After all, there aren't many motorways in Pakistan — there aren't all that many brilliant roads, for that matter, so why should they know the rules?

Couple caravanners with picnicking and praying, and assorted foreign travellers and you have a complete cross-section of that strange breed, the hard-shoulder party lover. Where the caravan has rested — on the M1, M6, M69, M4 or any old M — it is time to set up the picnic table and put the kettle on, to judge by the reports HGV drivers make. They stop on busy A-roads too. **Jim McNally**, a driver from Kirkby, Merseyside, was running along the A390 Dobwall to St. Austell at 6.45 in the morning when he ran into an accident. A car and a caravan were upside down on the road. Police and firemen were everywhere. They were sorting out the wreckage and the traffic chaos the crash had caused. Meanwhile, at the side of the road, on the grass verge, sitting round the picnic table and enjoying breakfast, were the family — completely unconcerned.

IT'S BIZARRE

One potato, two potato, three potato, four...

Luck was definitely *out* for the man driving the grossly overladen spud truck. The police pulled in front to stop him, he ran into the back of the police car. Then he lurched into a parked Avenger. His overhang caught and pulled down two bus stop signs and his load spilled into the road. While he was discussing his problem with the policemen, old ladies were scrabbling about the highway filling their shopping baskets with bonzers. And a photographer was taking pictures for the local newspaper. **Kevin Simpson**, of Folkestone, who watched it all, doesn't say whether he lived on free chips for a month afterwards.

A point which comes out strongly in your replies to our questionnaire is that many HGV drivers feel that the police could do worse than set up a community relations operation for caravanners in general. In the HGV driving fraternity there is a — it's difficult to find a suitable word among those used by drivers — let's say, a lack of understanding of caravanners on tour.

Not everybody goes as far as **D.B. Emmerson**, of Dumfries, who says that the funniest thing he ever saw on a motorway was a 300-yard-long caravan — the wreckage of an empty van scattered for 300 yards along the road with the driver blissfully unaware. But he touches an emotional chord in many truckers' bosoms.

All roads lead back to that motorway madness and the truly amazing things that can happen because of it. As in the case of **George Mindham**, from Paisley, who was driving south on the M1 when, in his rear-view mirrors, he saw a car towing a caravan about to overtake. He took no further notice until the car passed him on his nearside — both were moving at a pretty good lick.

IT'S THE WAY YOU TELL 'EM

Dummy hand

Just at the very moment the earth was about to move, the bedside phone rang. So she answered it and he lay back in irritation. 'It was my husband,' she said. 'Hell, don't say he's coming home early,' he expostulated. 'No,' she assured him, 'he rang to say he'll be home very late — he's playing poker with you and some of the other lads.'
Brian Maydew, *West Midlands*.

Since this is allegedly a free society, and the Queen's Highway is free to all who wish to use it — well, free if you discount the £5,000-plus tax and insurance you pay to be on it, and tunnel and bridge tolls, and parking fees at services, but that's another story to be dealt with later — everyone has every right to be on it. In charity, let us assume that they just don't know and maybe 'no picnics, no praying, no cricket and no going the wrong way' could be added to the list of 'don'ts' at motorway entrances. Mind you, it would be a brave man who would venture on to the M1 on a wintry, wet, freezing-foggy Friday night without resort to a silent prayer or two.

There is always the chance that motorway transgressors have been confused. G.K. Chesterton tells us that 'the rolling English drunkard made the rolling English road' and there is a school of thought that, in the same vein, the Department of Transport *Times* crossword solver made the motorway sign-posting system. So who can blame anybody with only a slight command of English, or a naturally nervous disposition, becoming confused. Even policemen can be confused by the signposting on their own patch. **Jonathan North**, a Bourne, Lincolnshire, driver, witnessed a police car — in a hurry and advertising, its occupants peering intently at the road signs — miss its exit from a roundabout, hurtle round again and crash into a car coming out of its junction to join the roundabout.

These are all symptoms of a motor-madness that afflicts a section of the public and causes a fecklessness that can be alarming to those involuntarily caught up in it. And there is yet another manifestation of it: sex.

Sex appeal

Cars used to be sold — or in the case of the infamous Ford Edzel*, not sold — on sex appeal. And turning an ignition key seems to be an astonishing turn-on for a surprising number of travellers of both sexes.

High on the list of bizarre and unusual incidents witnessed by the men in the high cabs are the sexual aberrations of motorists doing it at high speed, sometimes in company, often alone.

Part of the mysterious psychology of motorways is that they seem to produce an irresistable urge to exhibitionism or streaking. Get in the fast lane, peel off and flash seems to be one syndrome; get on the hard shoulder, peel off and streak seems to be the other. Whichever way, it disconcerts the conscientious, serious driver intent on daydreaming his way to his destination.

Mooning, at one time, reached epidemic proportions. By all accounts there were car-loads and coach-loads of students, rugby teams, football fans, schoolchildren and happy loners with their bottoms hanging in the breeze out of open windows or pressed like pancakes against coach windows for the edification and admiration of passers-by. Some bottoms were hung out over motorway bridges, and Telford could qualify as No 1 Cheeky Spot of England — they let it all hang out at Telford. And all of them did it in all weathers. Which could prove that the British are still a hardy race prepared to suffer in the serious pursuit of their aberrations.

IT'S THE WAY YOU TELL'EM

His luck ran out

Hymie, who drove a clothes van from Leeds to Whitechapel, sat in Deputy Dog's looking miserable as sin. 'What's the matter?' the lads asked him. 'Last month my sister dies and leaves me £20,000, two weeks ago my brother dies and leaves me £30,000, this week — nothing, everybody stays healthy.'

Steve Ward, *Ashford, Middlesex.*

***Footnote**: For those of you too young to remember the Ford Edzel débâcle, it was the American Ford Motor Company's biggest disaster. Named after Henry Ford's eldest son, it was, they said, specifically designed with a powerful, macho appeal as a sex and virility symbol on wheels. Potential buyers flocked to the showrooms to drool over the car's exciting lines. But very few had the courage to buy it and be seen flaunting their masculine virility and intentions down Main Street, US — it flopped. A few years later it became a treasured collectors' item. Actually, it looked a mess.

But motorway sex is not confined solely to the British. Naturally, the French had to get in on the act and bring a touch of Gallic insouciance to the pastime. Like the Frenchman observed by **Francis Baker**, of St. Helens. Relaxed in his Renault and drawing deeply on his Gauloise, this amorous Latin was revelling in oral sex with his girl friend (who knows, it might have been his wife) at 60 mph on the M6 near Lancaster. Suddenly the truck took on a definite shudder and he pulled in. A witness remarked: 'He went soft on the hard shoulder.' The lady repaired her make-up and lipstick.

IT'S BIZARRE

where was the pot of gold?
Beattock is a windswept, lonely place and the imagination can run riot, especially at 1 a.m. in a torrential downpour. It was on such a night that **William McWatt**, from Denny, came out of Beattock café with a group of companions. On the way to his truck, one of them stopped dead in his tracks. Ashen-faced he returned to his friends and told them: 'There's a leprechaun sitting on my spare wheel – honest, I'm not joking.' Tentatively they approached the wagon. there on the spare wheel was a midget, a tiny little man, hitching a ride.

Not all near nakedness in cars is necessarily sexually motivated, some is for the laudable purpose of smartness; to turn up at a meeting like a tailor's dummy without a crease or wrinkle. To be sharp and make the opposition look like scruffs. Why else would the businessman seen by **Tommy Beetham**, of Birkenhead, be motoring dressed only in his string vest and underpants, with his pin-striped suit, shirt and tie neatly folded over the back of the passenger seat?

That incident shows a lot about the Rover driver: it shows firstly that he is supremely confident in his driving, he doesn't intend to have a shunt in his vest and pants. If he did and his suit was mangled in the wreckage, how would he get home? It shows secondly a splendid independence of spirit, to hell with the lot of them, what do I care what they think? Thirdly, it indicates a fine athleticism to be able to wriggle and squirm into a suit in the close confines of a car — a healthy mind in a healthy body! But it could show that he has only one suit. Or that he is a plain nutter. In the latter case, tell him: 'Welcome to the club.'

Another vest-and-panter wasn't so self-assured as the Rover man. He was spotted by **J. Fiddes**, a Cowley, Middlesex, driver, standing on the hard shoulder of the M6 having been kicked out of a car by his girl friend. What on earth did her mother/father/husband or whatever say when she arrived home? 'What's that man's suit doing in the back of the car, eh?' That's a turnabout from the traditional bra and panties situation. But that's the liberated woman for you.

Naked Truth

Revelation came to **Ron Hawkins**, of Lambourn, at a set of traffic lights when he was driving out of Reading. He was on the red when he glanced idly down and saw a naked woman in the car alongside. She was wearing a seat-belt but nothing else. And that must have been pretty uncomfortable. By this time the green had come and he'd missed a couple of gear-changes.

So it goes on, the naked truth about the sexual habits of the British on the roads. What a lot a poor car driver misses with only a worm's-eye view of the action. It can all look terribly respectable at window-level from the outside. But Big Brother Breaker, sitting high up in his tractor-unit cab, gets an entirely different perspective.

Is it an M6 speciality? The sexy-six, maybe. A lot of it seems to go on along that highway. **John Howard**, of Penrith, was passed by a couple in a car. In his mirrors they looked like any normal couple behaving normally while out for a fast spin, she was sitting maybe a little closer than usual. But when they sailed past him, John saw the man's trousers and underpants round his knees, seriously impeding his clutch, accelerator and brake operations. And he would have had a bit of a tussle to get to his gear-lever in a hurry.

There is nothing governing this sort of behaviour in the Highway Code or even in the Road Traffic Act. In the name of road safety it might be possible to extend even further the 'Don'ts' signs at motorway entrances to include, as well as 'No picnicking' and 'No praying', 'No nakedness, no flashing, no mooning and no hanky-panky'.

It is doubtful if signs, warnings or even dire penalties would ever stop it. People, alas, are just like that, sex maniacs. There might be a case for the police to introduce mobile sex-therapy units to cruise up and down and counsel offenders could they catch them. The incidents I have recounted are but a few of those reported, there are more to regale you with later, just for your instruction and warning, you understand. However, if such antics offend you, why not do as **Tony Squires**, a Poole, Dorset, driver does:'I just keep my eyes shut when I'm driving, you see so many daft things.'Cynics among you might say: 'Him — and 50,000 others.'

IT'S BIZARRE

> ### Double vision
> 'Driving along near Sandbach Services on the M6, I was chatting to a woman with the CB-handle 'Barbara Windsor'. She asked me to look out of my window. And there she was alongside waving her bra at me. Then she pulled up her jumper and said, 'Now you see why I'm called Barbara Windsor.' 'That is what **Charles Youles**, of Binfleet, South-end, reports — other less fortunate souls have to put up with hump-backed bridge signs.

THE M25

So, as the old advertisements for the *News of the World* used to say, 'All Human Life is Here'. And that means also all human folly; there is a lot of folly incorporated on motorways.

For every mile of diverting incident there are a thousand miles of boredom and aggravation, and hold-ups, road works, and more hold-ups and three-lane jams, and time to think about the folly of the high-and-mighty and the rich-and-powerful who designed and built these 'lifelines of a nation'. The people who designed and constructed them so that they cracked up under the strain almost before the tarmacadam or concrete was dry.

Think of the M25 as it is *now*, and as it has been since the first sections were opened. And you are almost bound to think of it as a nightmare at certain times of the day. Forget that they are going to spend millions in an attempt to put it right, but think of the unparalleled confusion there will be while they are making good the mistakes. It is not a happy prospect. Then ask why they couldn't do it right in the first place.

It takes a politician to make a cock-up; and it takes several politicians to make a perfect cock-up and be proud of it. Who but a group of disorganising geniuses could create a permanent traffic jam in 120 miles of virtually green-field open countryside? Yet they did it. And every truck driver should dip his lights in salute at how well they did it. A masterpiece of cock-up should not go unrecognised.

Claims that the forecasts were wrong aren't true. Some forecasts were right — exactly right.

The Director of Transportation for Cambridgeshire wrote to *The Times* on 27 May 1986, in reply to a prolonged and heated campaign of complaint about the M25. This is what he wrote:

Congested M25

Sir, in the early 1970s I was responsible as superintendent engineer of the South Eastern Road Construction Unit in Surrey, for the design and construction of the M25 motorway from Heathrow to Westerham, in Kent. At that time traffic forecasts were being prepared in my office predicting flows for 15 years hence, namely the mid 1980s.

The traffic forecasts which I recommended to the Ministry of Transport at that time, for the section of motorway from the M3 interchange at Thorpe to Heathrow, were of the order of 100,000 vehicles per day in the mid 1980s. This forecast of traffic required dual four-lane motorway and over the section in question I recommended construction to dual four-lane standards with two hard shoulders (one conventional one and one adjacent to the fast lane) to cope with the traffic requirements across the river Thames.

Unfortunately the minister of the day did not accept the recommendation and the motorway was built to standard three-lane capacity. It is fortunate indeed that land requirements were purchased for the ultimate width and hence the widening of this stretch, which is clearly required as a matter of urgency, can be constructed at a minimum additional cost (I understand approximately 9 million).

It was always envisaged that the river crossings east and west of London would be under the most severe strain. It can be seen therefore that the forecast 15 years ago for 100,000 vehicles per day was correct and has been achieved as predicted.

Yours faithfully,
BRIAN OLDRIDGE,
Director of Transportation, Cambridgeshire
Gloucester Court, Shire Hall,
Castle Hill, Cambridge.

Naturally, all those striped-shirted, white-collared executive gentlemen who appear on sites wearing borrowed wellies and the spare safety helmets which don't quite fit will read this with contempt and dismiss it as provocative, subjective drivel. They will have an answer to every point raised, and it will be a very good answer, you bet. They don't see it from the drivers' viewpoint at cab-level watching a tail-back stretching ahead to infinity. They don't **feel** it like the owner-driver forking out his £3,100 tax and £1,400 insurance, and £600 goods-in-transit — having already, say, poppied up £75,000 for a new fridge unit. In all he will have invested £85,000 to put that unit on the road. And now he is sitting in a ten-mile tail-back with the tacho ticking his hours away. The freedom of the Queen's Highway comes very expensive for him. And he is entitled to beef about it, and beef like hell!

IT'S BIZARRE

pulling the wool over their eyes

Hot, bothered and highly embarrassed, six sweating policemen were discovering how nippy frisky ewes can be. They were chasing sheep all over the M3 as **Richard Hawkins**, from Canterbury, drove by. Maybe their colleagues in Cheshire had been counting sheep, for the two **Cyanide Sid**, of Nantwich, saw were the second lot we have had reported asleep in a police lay-by.

Not that officials and ministry folk were alone in their miscalculations, the Freight Transport Association, the voice of the transport industry as it proudly claims, went a bit over the top about what it called 'the biggest "bypass" in the world,' and motorways in general. In 1985 the association published a map of the road with the following eulogy:

The Freight Transport Association has consistently promoted the many benefits afforded to Britain by the motorway system. In addition to these roads providing the most appropriate track for the rapid movement of goods and services, motorways also bring the environmental benefits of keeping large quantities of through vehicles away from towns and residential areas, where they have no need to be.

The M25 is a spectacular example of this. The ultimate completion of the M25 will provide the biggest 'bypass' in the world, enabling traffic of all types to move either north-south or east-west in Southern England without the need to travel through London. Trials carried out by the FTA have confirmed cost, fuel and driver effort advantages of using the M25 for through journeys. These benefits to road users are matched by the relief provided to London by the removal of considerable numbers of vehicles.

Now that didn't quite come off. And it looks as if the FTA allowed itself to be carried away by the idea rather than wait for the implementation. The 'many benefits afforded to Britain by the motorway system' were at that moment being dug up, bollarded off and castigated daily by Timpson and Redhead in the BBC 'Today' programme. When holes in the road become a running daily news feature on a major radio programme of the day, and a source of exasperation, then something's wrong. It is a situation daft enough to raise a wry smile at a piece of ripe corn by **Nameless**, an Alfreton, Derbyshire, driver: 'There's a big hole on the M1. But don't worry, the police are looking into it.' (No wonder he wants to remain anonymous.) While **Mussolini**, of Chichester, Sussex, lists his most bizarre experience as 'The M25 during rush hours'. (C'mon, Musso, Il Duce's crowning achievement was making the trains run on time. Live up to your CB handle and get that truck moving!)

YES, MINISTER

The M25 was, of course, meant to be the key to the solution of the road problem in England. At a stroke it would wipe out the enormous black spot of London and free the traffic to run smoothly north and south, east and west.

The Transport Minister of the day was John Peyton and his number two was Tarzan, Michael Heseltine. Both subsequently moved on to bigger things and greater political glories in the manner our cartoon suggests. Many of their predecessors had a hand in the planning for the road which had been talked about for political generations, not just years.

It is interesting to look at the list of Transport Ministers for the last three decades and see what they have done for transport, and whether, from a driver's point of view, it has been constructive or

otherwise. The first task is to remember who they are:
*Ernest Marples 1959−64; Tom Fraser 1964−65; *Barbara Castle 1965−68; Richard Marsh 1968−69; Fred Mulley 1969−70; *John Peyton 1970−74; Fred Mulley 1974−75; John Gilbert 1975−76; *William Rodgers 1976−79; Norman Fowler 1979−81; David Howell 1981−83 (No. 2 Lynda Chalker 1982); Tom King, June to October 1983 (No. 2 Lynda Chalker); Nicholas Ridley 1983−86 (No. 2 Lynda Chalker); John Moore 1986 (No. 2 David Mitchell).

What is interesting about that list is how few of them stayed for any length of time. Possibly it is a good thing they don't stay long in the job; those who do seem to inflict the greatest damage on all things on wheels. See the list opposite.

When he wasn't growing grapes in his vineyard in France, Ernest Marples was inventing parking meters and meter-maids. Those who remember the introduction of the sixpenny and one shilling monsters and the beginning of the "tanner-terror" will also recall the fine words and promises which went with them to soften the blow. The money raised from the meters would be used to provide acres of off-street parking and clear the city streets for the moving traffic to run through clear city streets. Like hell!

At least they had the honesty to call the Road Fund Tax a *tax*, even if it is swallowed into the general tax fund and not spent on the roads. The Road Fund Tax is a tax to let you move along the Queen's Highway, parking meters have become a tax to let you stop on it.

IT'S THE WAY YOU TELL'EM

Free-wheeling

Broken down on the motorway, the driver returned from making his emergency telephone call to find his truck jacked-up and a man removing the wheels. 'What the hell d'you think you're doing?' The driver demanded. Without looking up the man replied: 'Don't worry, I only want a couple, you can have the rest.'

John Evans, *Slough, Berks.*

Tom Fraser Tom who?

Barbara Castle Lovely Babs, the fiery red-head who introduced the breathalyser and speed limits.

Richard Marsh Who didn't do much memorable for transport except later to become boss of British Rail, a radio and TV celebrity and later still boss of the Newspaper Proprietors' Association.

Fred Mulley Skip Fred and you won't miss a lot...

John Peyton Gave the go-ahead for the M25 in its present form.

---

*Footnote to list: Lynda Chalker was an Under Secretary of State until she was made up to full Minister. It was after that she got into her car and made rude signs at truckers, through the back window of her car, it was widely reported in the media. Then she was elevated to the heights of the Foreign Office. And their gain was the truckers' loss, curious as it may seem − see next page.

'He won't have time to read that, after all, Bernard, he's only here until they give him a proper job!'

Fred Mulley He's back again but it is still difficult to recall what he did that drivers can remember him by.

John Gilbert Has even less to remember him by.

William Rodgers He was the incumbent when the tachograph was under consideration and plans were laid to introduce it...

Norman Fowler He was in the chair when the tacho became law on 31 December 1981. So it is only fair to link the two together and lay at their joint doorsteps the unholy mess that resulted from the provisions of the Road Traffic Act, 1968, being allowed to run in harness with the tacho regulations.

All the above lot, whatever political party, have three things in common: whatever they did for transport restricted your freedom of action, didn't quite work out as they said it would, and cost you money.

After them came the period of the 'terrible twins' at the Ministry of Transport as listed. And there also comes something of a turn-up for the book in the form of Lynda Chalker. In fact, it is a full U-turn because this lady, during her extended term as number two at the Ministry of Transport, managed to some extent to redeem the follies of a dozen senior predecessors. She proved herself a tough little madam in a very hairy man's world and did what none of her predecessors had ever succeeded in doing: she actually won respect.

She deserves a special note if only because that most experienced of truckers, **Big John Martin**, of Clacton, who, in his time, has had ten trucks of his own, worked for long spells in the Middle East and Europe and generally knows a bit about the game — including grumbling vituperatively about it — was moved to say of the energetic MP for Wallasey:

She's a little diamond. She's the only one out of the whole lot who has shown the slightest idea of what it's all about, and she is the only one who has ever done anything useful for truckers. At least you see her on motorways, and she listens. She put the weight up from 32-tonnes to 38-tonnes, if she'd had her way it would have gone up to 40-tonnes, which everybody knows is pure common sense. For instance, they're building roads in Holland to take 52-tonnes. She put up the speed limit for trucks to 60 mph which everybody knows is common sense on a motorway. She put the hours up to ten hours, spread over. She is the only one of the bunch who has ever done anything practical, sensible and actually useful to truckers on the road. And she doesn't stop at one thing, she's working it out all the time.

The Bald Facts

The HGV driver crawling, dangerously, along an 'other road' at 40 mph with a crocodile of cars, vans, coaches and sundry other 'locomotives' strung fretting and impatient behind him may feel that the ghost of the man with the red flag is still walking in front of his high-technology, with-every-known-safety-device-built-in truck.

Drivers in the crocodile will fume, swing out to make a dash to overtake, swing back in again when they can't make it and furiously ask: 'What the hell is that bloody great truck doing on a road like this?'

The HGV driver will also ask: 'What the hell am I doing here?'

The answer to both questions is that the Department of Transport put the truck on that unsuitable road, if only by sins of omission. Study these figures:

> The International Road Federation statistics of 1983, which are accepted as accurate, revealed that Britain has 2,775 kilometres of motorway.
>
> On the same date, West Germany had 8,080 kilometres of autobahn. And West Germany is about the same size and population as the UK so how about that?
>
> Shamefully, little Belgium, one-seventh the size of Britain, had 1,375 kilometres. Oh dear!

And in Germany, Belgium and Holland, and all points east, the roads are better and the services indescribably better.

It doesn't matter that the year quoted is 1983, what counts is the ratio. We have now got a few more miles of motorway and adequate bypass, but so have the Germans and Belgiums and they are building roads to higher standards. I am not suggesting cutting great swathes through the countryside and laying motorways in all directions. There are good arguments against that which experts expound in the chapter on roads. The man in the crocodile is sure to be in a hurry and desperate to pass, so his temper will have reached boiling point and his thoughts will run along the lines: 'Bloody juggernauts, shaking the place to pieces, destroying the roads — and I'm paying for it out of the taxes I'm clobbered for.'

So another indisputable fact you need at your tongue-tip the next time you are accosted by some bellicose motorist, or maybe a militant environmentalist, is that it isn't a question of being able to afford the roads and services. You have actually paid for the roads you haven't got. And you will keep on paying for roads you won't get. The Secretary of State himself confirmed this. He disclosed that in 1985/1986 you paid in £260 million more than you got out. The phrase was that HGVs contribute £260 million more to the Exchequer than their track costs. And how is this for pure cheek? He also said in the same paper that Vehicle Excise Duty increases had achieved the 'right structure'. All that means is that he has got his sticky fingers in your back-pocket or wallet for £260 million a year *ad infinitum*, and that's all right by him. So goodbye to your profits and your wage increases, they've gone to the Exchequer, and the Chancellor is a very happy man indeed. Tough luck, trucker. In independently published figures, the Society of Motor Manufacturer and Traders says that commercial vehicles pay £500,000,000 more in tax than they cost the road system. Say that aloud to yourself, 'Five hundred million,' and then wonder why you are considered to be a second-class citizen.

IT'S BIZARRE

Unexpected attachment

En route to Plymouth, **Martin Blackman**, of Aldershot, reports, a driver in a rig up front alerted followers to a female 'flasher' in a mack and nobody believed him. But the 'flasher' duly appeared in mack, high-heeled shoes, nylon-stockings and suspender-belt — but the gender was wrong.

TIME FOR ACTION

The Road Haulage Association says: 'The uninformed constant attack upon lorries and the road haulage industry must be answered.'

Ask yourself, isn't it time to get your act together?

It is easy to understand the frame of mind of an Arnold's Transport driver, from Rugby, who answered the question, What he would most like to do: 'Chase a police car down the suicide lane with my horns blasting and lights flashing six inches from *his* bumper!'

There are, of course, ways of dealing with all these situations and methods of easing the pain and frustration they cause. But perhaps the one adopted by **Mark John Taylor**, of Radstock, Avon, is best avoided. He was stopped by police and asked why he was speeding. He told them: 'My wife is getting pregnant tonight, and I want to be there.' Sadly he adds: 'They done me.'

THE ROADS —
MORE OR LESS

The man said: 'I'm not into the kick of building more asphalt.'

And that is surprising considering that his whole career has been building roads and particularly motorways, coupled with vigorous campaigning for a better roadways system; it is also one in the eye for the anti-lorry lobby whose propaganda is that the road haulage industry's main objective is to destroy the countryside and environment.

Brian Oldridge 'went public' with that letter to *The Times* quoted earlier. He literally blew his top when he listened to the BBC programme 'Today in Parliament' and heard Nicholas Ridley,the Transport Minister at the time, tell the House of Commons that his department had been misled by experts' forecasts of the traffic volumes that could be expected on the new M25, and because of that wrong information the poor old Department of Transport had ordered the construction of the wrong road at the wrong time.

Mr Ridley's statement was codswallop. His department had been given absolutely accurate information and forecasts and they had turned them down, flat! Mr Oldridge mentioned no names in his letter of contradiction of the ministry's statement because he doesn't believe in personalising issues. But if Nicholas Ridley had sought the advice of his then close colleague, Michael Heseltine, who was directly involved with the decision at the time, he might have been more accurate.

The stark truth is that governments and ministries bugger-up the road system, not drivers; the Treasury penny-pinches on every conceivable occasion and costs the country billions. And that is a plain fact. No single government or minister since World War Two has understood the roads or transport, and none has ever bothered to try to understand them.

Hitler understood roads, he understood and appreciated them better than most. He built his amazing war machine on autobahns and invented his blitzkrieg technique by moving armies along his four-lane highways. Let us not forget that for a long time, too long, he won. And the cost of stopping him was a prodigious cost to the rest of the world.

'You fool! That's not what I meant by robot policing!'

Then came peace and Konrad Adenauer who worked his 'economic miracle' partly on the roads Hitler had constructed — communications!

Hitler built roads and his successors inherited an economic miracle; Mussolini made the trains run on time and his successors inherited some very pretty stations and a non-stop financial crisis; the British built 'nowt to move owt' and have been foot-slogging ever since to try to catch up.

Now we do have some roads. 'Enough for the time being,' insists Brian Oldridge. But the way we are going they will be at a total standstill by the early 1990s. They will have been 'politicised' into a massive snarl-up from Land's End to John o' Groats and the quickest way from one end of the country to the other will probably be to take leaves out of Dr Barbara Moore's and Ian Botham's books and do a charity walk.

Brian Oldridge knows what he is about. He is chairman of the County Surveyors Association and No 2 Big-shot in the Institute of Civil Engineers, which is a world-wide force. He does virtually nothing else but study roads and he knows that the present roads —

A funny thing happened...

A helping hand can cost a lot of energy, as **M. Taylor** discovered driving down from Scotland. A cattle van overturned and its cargo of piglets escaped. Mr Taylor stopped to help the driver and diving, ducking, leaping and chasing over the road they got a good number of the wriggling escapees back in the box. But with 60 little pigs squealing and running everywhichway over an adjoining field they had to give up. So they only half-saved the bacon.

---

motorways — are working to only a fraction of their capacity. He knows too that the reason is rank bad, appalling driving, mostly by private motorists.

Yes, he concedes that one per cent of HGV licence-holders are 'cowboys' and as bad, if not worse, than the worst private motorists. And it is a singular fact that the one per cent comprises mostly tipper drivers. Reflect on that: they are a crazy, ill-disciplined bunch, the tipper men and they give the rest a bad name.

IT'S THE WAY YOU TELL'EM

Stripe me
The helpful trucker leaned from his cab window to tell an old man struggling to cross a traffic-jammed street: 'There's a zebra-crossing 50 yards up the road.' And the old geezer wheezed: 'I hope it has more success than me, I've been trying for half an hour.'
Herbert Johnson, *Peterborough*.

Driver bovver
The problem, according to Mr Oldridge, is that when man or woman climbs into the driving seat of a car they become utterly, recklessly *selfish*. Of course, a man in a car has been a standard joke for decades: the meek little chap who turns into a rampaging, tyrannical, macho Rambo the instant his toe taps an accelerator pedal... And a woman's brains are popularly thought to fly out of the window as soon as she flicks, or forgets to flick, a blinker at other traffic.

Well, the joke isn't all that funny because it is partially true — in many cases, very true.

Those who watch the roads for a living know that nobody will willingly use the centre lane in rush-hour conditions, and stick in it. Everybody is afraid to move back into the centre lane in case they cannot get out again. Nobody uses the slow lane even when the road is as clear as Pendine Sands on a freezing December night.

It is all a question of attitudes and the delusion that motorways are made up of slow, medium and fast lanes.

Flight Control
Now let us look at some rather startling facts about motorways themselves: every centimetre of a busy motorway carries 1,000,000 tonnes of traffic weight travelling at an average of 60 mph every working day.

To make that a bit clearer: that is the total weight that travels along a stretch of busy road every day, so it must run over the stated centimetre in lanes one, two or three; it crosses each centimetre at a maximum of ten tonnes per axle, but the cumulative weight it carries in 24 hours is as quoted.

If all three lanes were used properly, that would be 333,000 tonnes per lane. As it is, some lanes get infinitely more wear than others. They would all last longer if they were properly used. The maximum average speed obtainable on a busy road, flowing freely without impediments is between 50 and 60 mph — that is what has been proved to be the 'natural' speed of the road.

America has unwittingly proved a point for traffic engineers.

Every Brit who visits America, and every European more so, is amazed to find virtually all American drivers sticking religiously to the 50 mph speed limit. It is not the American image we have been educated to expect.

Yet they do it. It all began as an energy conservation programme when the oil crisis first struck. Then they found that they actually got there quicker driving slower in all those motor-maniac cities where walking became redundant years ago and schoolchildren, when asked what their two feet are for, reply, 'Clutch and accelerator'.

To save Britain from snarling-up completely in the 1990s, Brian Oldridge believes the only answer is electronic control of all traffic. He explains:

> Every aircraft that flies over Britain, takes off and lands at a British airport, is electronically controlled from the minute it appears in our skies; the pilot responds to electronic instructions and cannot get anywhere without them. Every train that runs on a railway line is electronically controlled, the drivers answer electronic signals. Traffic in all our cities is electronically controlled. Only on the roads outside and on motorways do we allow *laissez-faire* travelling. The motorist gets in his car and does what he wants, when he wants and how he wants with scant regard to others.
>
> The answer is electronic control, when the motorists stay in lane, are instructed by signal which lane to be in, what speed to travel and what actions to take. They will be monitored and those who transgress will be filmed and get an automatic ticket sent on to their address. This way we will use the roads to their full capacity, keep the traffic moving, cut out hold-ups, save money for everybody, privately and from public purse, and drastically reduce accidents.

He wants a mandatory system backed by the full force of the law. But by no means is Mr Oldridge a repressive, authoritarian figure; nobody believes more in the freedom of the road than he does. All his working life has been spent assuring the freedom of the road and freedom of movement for the millions. He simply wants to keep it free and moving for everybody.

Is it such a tough proposal? We all willingly obey traffic lights without giving them a second thought; most of us stop at halt signs and are thankful they are there. In fact, very few of us break the traffic laws as they are, provided they are self-evidently sensible.

'Do this and we will not need to think about building many major new roads until the turn of the century,' he maintains.

Uppermost in his mind is money. The eternal, never-ending fight for cash to keep us all circulating and making money is the road planner's problem.

One mile of new motorway costs £40 million.

One mile of electronic control of an old motorway, with signals every half-kilometre, will cost £120,000.

Over in Holland they have done it. They have set up an 'experimental' stretch of electronically controlled road covering 80 kilometres. In other words, 50 miles of experiment, that would get you quite a long way up the M1 out of London, and it is only an experiment.

But the Dutch take their transport seriously.

IT'S THE WAY YOU TELL'EM

Monkey business

At the safari park, the gorilla was becoming embarrassingly randy and the crowd was giggling. The driver on a day's outing opened the cage door, pushed his wife inside and said: 'Now try telling him you've got a headache.'
Silver Wheels, *Penkridge, Rugeley, Staffordshire.*

Now back to the 'monitoring' business. Up in Manchester, Assistant Chief Constable J.D. Phillips, the area traffic controller, has more urban motorway on his patch than anybody else in the UK, and a fat headache it is for him.

His problem has been that all his motorways converge on a two-lane bottleneck over the ship canal at Barton Bridge. This is where the traffic comes to a halt until it spills out on the opposite side with a great glug. Now they have announced plans to widen it, but it should not have been there in the first place.

Mr Phillips says: 'It is impossible to police the motorways. What we need, is a complete system of electronic policing.'

At this moment of writing Mr Phillips does not know Mr Oldridge, but the man who runs 'em is in total agreement with the man who builds 'em.

Manchester police 'motorway control room' is a masterpiece of display. A huge electronic map showing the whole motorway system and keeping tabs on everything that happens. But it doesn't *control* anything. All it does is to enable the Manchester police to watch while the disaster situations develop and then take fast, urgent action to sort out the mess they were powerless to prevent.

Mr Phillips, with his team, wants to be there *before* the action and not to arrive afterwards to clear up the mess. That is why he demands electronic control.

It is coming. There is no doubt about that. It is coming because it *has* to come — or we can all stay at home or buy a new pair of walking shoes.

24

THE PLASTIC JUNGLES — OR MOTORWAY SERVICES

We are still on the motorway and make no excuses for it since M-roads are a dominant part of most drivers' lives. Meanwhile, here is a message for Trust House Fortes, Ross, Granada, Rank, Roadchef, Welcome Break, Blue Boar, Kenning and any other caterer on the motorway system.

340,000 HGV drivers think your services are execrable.

Now that is a pretty serious state of affairs. It is serious for the image-conscious purveyors of plastic finery and, according to the drivers, plastic food; and serious also for the Department of Transport which licenses the sites to the operators and once again seems to have fallen flat on its aspirations to serve the needs of the motoring public.

For, despite the attitudes of some areas of officialdom and

'He's the manager!'

caterers, HGV drivers are fully paid up, qualified and legitimate members of the motoring public, and also have some claim to be actual members of the general public. Though often they are treated as undesirables, and very unpleasantly so.

The motorway catering industry is good at defending itself. So it ought to be, it has been under scathing attack so very often in its short history. Before the yelps and squeals of outrage arise from the service providers, as they surely will, they ought to ask themselves four questions:

1   Do we really, in our heart of hearts, want truckers in our service areas?
2   If and when they come, do we really make them welcome?
3   Do we give them a fair deal on prices?
4   With our hands on our hearts, can we say we treat them well — except at the pumps where they might be filling up with a hundred quid's-worth of fuel?

And the man who answers yes, yes, yes, yes, will go down in the truckers' books as a hypocrite. He will have only himself to blame.

A simple glance at the service areas is proof enough of caterers' attitudes to truckers: truck-trade accommodation is crude and lamentable compared with even the poorest of that provided for the carriage-trade. All the marketing has gone into those sites attracting family and business motorists, the mothers-and-childrens rooms, the fancy names for restaurants — almost as imaginative and tempting as the descriptions on the menus — and the posh gents in black coats and pin-stripes. A whole new trade has evolved for the trucking trade: down-marketing and up-pricing. Somewhere along the evolutionary line of these plastic palaces, the trucker has remained stuck in an historical perspective as a man covered in oil and grease or even mud, dust, hay, oats, bran and reeking of horse-dung.

Maybe I can say that whatever you think about motorway services, you also think about Little Chefs and Happy Eaters — and it's enough to curdle the milk in the ice-cold dispenser.

Oh yes, there is one thing. I can quote the *Which?* magazine report which actually said that some motorway food and services were getting better. They also said that walking into Kenning's was like 'entering a time warp'.

I can also say that Little Chefs and Happy Eaters don't want you, and make no bones about it, because you take up four or more private-car spaces and you are slow eaters. 'They would sit here while they waited out their tachograph breaks. We could lose half a dozen or more customers in that time. No, truck drivers are poison to me,' said the man. At least he's honest and you know how you stand with them. As if you didn't know already.

Anyway, in case you need it ever, here is a list of all available services and a map of where they are, courtesy of *Commercial Motor* Magazine. Keep it in case you need to avoid them.

Motorway service areas

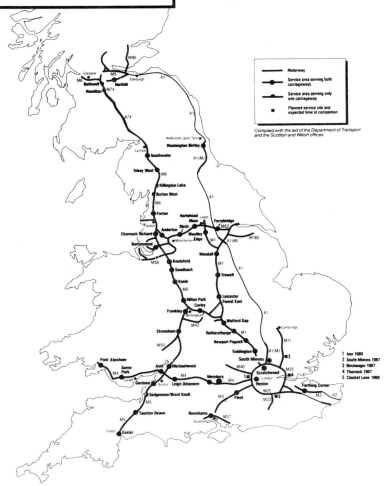

Reproduced by kind permission of Commercial Motor magazine.

GUIDE TO SERVICE AREAS

FACILITIES

Service area	Operator	Overnight £	Meal voucher	HGV spaces	Showers	Shaving point	Separate rest room	Separate eating
M1								
Scratchwood	THF	3.50	No	190	No	No	No	No
Toddington	Granada	5.00	150	190	Yes	Yes	Yes	Yes
Newport Pagnell	THF	3.50	No	85	No	No	No	No
Rothersthorpe	Blue Boar	none allowed	–	40	No	No	No	No
Watford Gap	Blue Boar	5.00	1.50	150	Yes	Yes	No	Yes
Leicester Forest East	Welcome Break	3.00	1.00	180	No	Yes	Yes	Yes
Trowell	Granada	5.00	1.50	80*	No	No	No	Yes
Woodhall	THF	3.50	No	80	No	N/A	No	No
Wooley Edge	Granada	5.00	1.50	80*	No	No	No	Yes
M2								
Farthing Corner	Rank	3.00	No	70	No	Yes	Yes	Yes
M3								
Fleet	THF	3.50	No	55	No	No	No	No

Service area	Operator	Overnight	Meal voucher	HGV spaces	Showers	Shaving point	Separate rest room	Separate eating
M4								
Port Abraham	Roadchef	3.50	1.00	20	Yes	Yes	No	No
Sarne Park	THF	3.50	No	20	N/A	N/A	No	No
Aust	Rank	3.00	No	100	Yes	Yes	Yes	Yes
Leigh Delamere	Granada	5.00	1.50	160*	No	No	No	Yes
Membury	Granada	5.00	1.50	100*	Yes W'bd	Yes	No	Yes
Heston	Granada	5.00	1.50	100*	Yes W'bd	Yes W'bd	No	Yes
M5								
Frankley	Granada	5.00	1.50	70*	No	No	No	Yes
Strensham	Kenning	3.00	1.00	140	No	No	No	No
Michaelwood	Welcome Break	3.00	1.00	128	No	Yes	No	Yes
Gordano	THF	3.50	No	150	No	No	No	No
Sedgemore (Brent Knoll)	Roadchef	3.50	1.00	30	No	N/A	No	No
Taunton Deane	Roadchef	3.50	1.00	130	No	Yes	No	No
Exeter	Granada	5.00	1.50	60*	No	No	No	Yes

29

Service area	Operator	Overnight	Meal voucher	HGV spaces	Showers	Shaving point	Separate rest room	Separate eating
M6								
Corley	THF	3.50	No	175	No	No	No	No
Hilton Park	Rank	3.00	No	70	No	No	Yes	Yes
Keele	THF	3.50	No	150	No	No	No	No
Sandbach	Roadchef	5.00	1.00	140	Yes	Yes	No	No
Knutsford	Rank	3.50	No	50	No	No	Yes	No
Charnock Richard	THF	3.50	No	60	No	N/A	No	No
Forton	Rank	3.00	No	70	Yes	Yes	Yes	Yes
Burton West	Granada	5.00	1.50	20*	No	No	No	Yes
Killington Lake	Roadchef	5.00	1.00	25	No	No	No	No
Tebay West	Westmoreland	4.00	2.00	80	No	Yes	No	No
Southwaite	Granada	5.00	1.50	120*	Yes	Yes	No	Yes
M8								
Harthill	Roadchef	3.50	1.00	100	Yes	Yes	No	No

Service area	Operator	Overnight	Meal voucher	HGV spaces	Showers	Shaving point	Separate rest room	Separate eating
M27								
Rownhams	Roadchef	3.50	1.00	140	Yes	Yes	No	No
M61								
Anderton	Kenning	3.00	1.00	500	No	No	No	No
M62								
Ferrybridge	Granada	5.00	1.50	58	Yes	Yes	No	Yes
Hartshead Moor	Welcome Break	3.00	1.00	180	No	Yes	No	Yes
Birch	Granada	5.00	1.50	120*	Yes	Yes	No	Yes
Burtonwood	THF	3.50	No	300	No	No	No	No
M74								
Hamilton/Bothwell	Roadchef	3.50	1.00	100	Yes	Yes	No	No
A1(M)								
Washington Birtley	Granada	5.00	1.50	80*	No	No	No	Yes

THE LAW I — LEAST SAID, SOONEST MENDED

The first thing to say about the law is — you could stay in bed.

The next thing to say is stay on the right side of it or it will cost you plenty. But *how* to keep on the right side is the problem, often you will feel that you could use a tame itinerant solicitor travelling in the cab with you. Sometimes there is no answer to the law: such as the time when Mr **P. Newell**, of Willenhall, West Midlands, travelling alone, was stopped by two officers. He sat in regal solitude in his cab while they perambulated round his truck doing their customary inspection. Then one approached the cab and asked: 'Are you the driver of this vehicle?'

And **Dave Roberts**, of Hull, when driving in really mucky weather, in the middle of a torrential downpour with mud, spray, fumes and surface debris flying in all directions and obliterating everything in sight, was pulled in by a super-conscientious Ministry of Transport inspector who bravely ignored the conditions and walked round the rig completing a detailed inspection. Soaked to the skin, he approached the cab and stern-facedly complained: 'You've got a very dirty number-plate, that's illegal.'

Those two individual experiences will strike a chord with many drivers, and they raise serious issues, as well as a contradiction which will show up starkly in the chapter on the police. They illustrate the law in operation, and also how the law is *perceived* by an ever increasing number of HGV drivers. Most of it is only talk, but that perception ought to begin to worry those in authority outside the industry. It already worries those in the industry more than enough: directors, operators, managers and drivers alike.

There is a lot of law. Law has been heaped on transport to the extent that every vehicle that turns a wheel on the road is down on its axles overladen with law. So much so that the law comes at every driver from all directions and in a dozen guises; and now, lamentably and in contradiction of all British concepts of law, in disguises such as the silent check.

Contemptuously, drivers dubbed the tachograph 'the spy in the cab', now the 'spy in the cab' is augmented by the 'spy in the concealed car' — ministry men lurking by the roadside secretly noting truck numbers and the times they passed and cross-checking with census points and tachograph records.

Clever? A cunning deterrent? Well, that all depends how you look at it and from which side.

'Are you sure I'm going to get a fair hearing, mate?'

A dog's life

For a change, let's look at it from the drivers' point of view. Who gave the Department of Transport the right to label every truck driver as a potential law-breaker looking for a villainy to perform? Who gave them the right to wage guerrilla warfare on the transport industry in motion? Who was it who was permitted to label 400,000 certificated and licensed people going about their legitimate businesses as congenitally irresponsible, anti-social and dangerous, a group in need of constant surveillance and outwitting?

Somebody did. And somebody else is making sure that the reputation sticks whether deserved or not. Admittedly, there are cowboys: those lads who fiddle the tacho with a wodge of chewing gum or a sliver of sponge-rubber, but the tacho isn't all that easy to cheat without being discovered. If it is, then the Department of Transport is to blame. There are the ones who run grossly over time without a care in the world, they take a big risk and pay a huge

33

penalty if caught. There are the wild ones who overtake in the fast lane on motorways and travel three abreast — until a police car looms unexpectedly into sight.

Cowboys bend and break the rules. And as a rule they are as much despised by genuine drivers as by the public for giving the trade a bad name. They are an infinitesimally small percentage of all drivers.

A driver has to make his living, and to do that he has to keep his nose clean and that means keeping his licence clean. The days of the big fiddle are long gone. There used to be tanker drivers who grew rich by keeping fuel in the delivery pipes, up to 20 gallons, then filling up their jerry-cans in a quiet country lane; and the ones who made an art out of kicking the tank with steel-capped boots to get a convincing ring as they dropped the dip-stick into the tank — but not far enough in to touch the bottom.

But look at the modern tanker, it is metered to the last fraction of a litre.

The days of 'it dropped off the back of a lorry' died when the engineers designed trailers up to a thief-proof standard — and what about containers and box-cars? Don't those who constantly talk about 'fiddles' ever really *look* at modern rigs?

So it's a dog's life where the law is concerned you tell me, in a deluge of moans, groans and heart-rending wails of agony. God, you can go on a bit about it. There is no clearer instance of the old adage 'give a dog a bad name' than the transport industry in general. Alas, that 'bad name' permeates the benches of the Palace of Westminster, local county halls and magistrates' courts alike.

Like punks and rockers, mods and skin-heads, Hell's Angels, black men on the streets of Brixton or Toxteth and gypsies anywhere, truckers are 'perceived' as potential anti-social beings intent upon wrong-doing at the drop of a jack-handle.

IT'S BIZARRE

Animal crackers — or vice versa

G. Seltock, of Leighton Buzzard, which is an appropriate name in the case, was staggered to see a chicken driving a car. It was a man in fancy dress. But it was real enough for **Buster**, of Spalding, when he rounded a blind bend and found his way blocked by an elephant. And **Daffy Duck**, of Sandown, Isle of Wight, ran into a herd of cows on the main road, unaccompanied at 3 o'clock in the morning. **Chris Smith**, of Bettws, thought it unusual to see a stuffed camel at the side of the road, while **Brian** Saville, of Burstall, came across three cats fighting on a zebra crossing. Up at Scotch Corner, **J. Aylett**, of Blyth, found himself in a flap when a load of 5,000 chickens tipped over. The whole damned country is one giant zoological gardens, it seems.

That may indeed sound extreme, but sadly it is the truth. And it is a truth known and often stated by a vast majority of people who earn their livings by turning a commercial wheel to the benefit and prosperity of the rest of society.

The social implications of this state of affairs are profound: in any other sphere of life, when the law is considered to be oppressive, unreasonable — in the true and proper sense that no jury of twelve honest, true and *reasonable* men or women would convict on it — and unfairly applied or, conversely, not applied so that it becomes held in contempt, then that law is deemed *bad law* and efforts are made to repeal and adjust it.

Much of the law in connection with the transport industry and those engaged in it is thought, by those who have to live by it, to be plain bad law which is unfairly and unevenly applied, and not even understood by those administering it.

In this chapter I will examine a few instances: there is no possibility of going into great depth on the subject since it is so massive. But first let us look at the overall situation.

Actually, nobody really knows the exact overall situation, so nobody can accurately judge it.

A funny thing happened...

In his television programme Clive James showed a series of TV commercials for a Swedish motor insurance company. In one, a man in a telephone kiosk is booking his insurance with his newly aquired car parked outside — a massive tree falls on to the motor. In another ad, a woman is in the insurance office with her Volkswagon seen through the plate-glass window, a van reverses into it, brakes hard and a huge boat flies out of the back and crushes the Beetle. **A. Taylor**, of Letchworth, lived through a similar experience. He drove behind a police recovery vehicle with a car on top and followed by a second police car. They stopped at a junction. As the recovery truck pulled away, the car shot off the back and crashed onto the bonnet of the police car.

HOW MANY TRUCKS ARE THERE?

Statistics pour out from the Ministry of Transport and the licensing authorities; as an HGV driver you are a statistic. But you are also a mystery.

To plan a road system you would think it essential to be pretty certain how many vehicles are going to use it, and how many of those vehicles will be big ones. In this age of the multi-million-pound computer you would also think that it would be possible to press a button and know immediately how many trucks there were on the road — after all, the Swansea computer has been running a long time. Long enough certainly to have ironed out all the initial faults and bugs in the system.

But out of the fairy-tale world of computers and sitting with 12, 14, 18 or 22 wheels firmly on the road in real life, the truth is that nobody really knows how many trucks there are running around the country.

The *Commercial Motor* magazine undertook a survey to try to establish exactly how many commercial vehicles there were working.

What emerged was the information that all official figures could be wildly inaccurate, as much as 30 per cent out. Thirty per cent of what? Thirty per cent of *a lot*.

Commercial Motor discovered that 27 per cent of all those taking out O-licences go out of business in the first six months. Yet that licence remains on the records for five years; which must mean the cumulative effect over five years is enough to distort any statistics. And those who survive the first six traumatic months do not necessarily survive the rest. There is a shocking casualty rate. Bad enough, I would suggest, to warn those with the burning ambition to own their own trucks and run their own businesses: 'Think and think again. Be sure before you put a penny down.'

IT'S BIZARRE

he didn't know whether he was coming or going
He sat patiently behind the big rig motoring up the motorway, his vision obscured by the tilt in front. Then suddenly the big rig pulled out sharply as if to overtake, and at that moment Driver, St Neots heart leapt to his mouth. In front of him was revealed, full-face on, a big tractor unit and he was headlight-to-headlight with it. It was moving at 50 m.p.h. — backwards, being towed by a recovery vehicle.

The little man

Several surprising facts emerge about the operation of road transport which contradict the popular image of it.

The first 'fact' to emerge is that by common consensus there are about 340,000 HGV vehicles operating: it could be more, it could be less. We do *not* know accurately.

The second fact is that it is probably the biggest 'cottage industry' in the country; an industry which ought to thrill Tory politicians' hearts but which doesn't inspire them to do much for it. Out of the approximate 340,000 motors running up, down, around and across these islands it seems pretty certain that 70 per cent are owned and operated by companies with five or fewer wagons; the suspicion is that a great proportion of small operators are owner-drivers who are sub-contractors. But nobody really knows.

So when it comes to a question of law, it means that usually it will be the 'little man' versus the great panoply of the state. The little man cannot afford to fight test cases to get the law fully examined, often he's hard put to afford a solicitor.

And here is food for thought: in how many sectors of our modern society do you find so many individuals willing, anxious even, to commit themselves to a £50,000 to £75,000 investment, a £100-a-week tax and insurance before a wheel can be legally turned or a penny made towards a break-even turnover or a ha'penny profit in the pocket? On top of that, how many private entrepreneurs are there willing to pump an average of 200 gallons and £174 *tax* into their tanks every week simply to be able to go to work?

That doesn't sound like a bloke who is going to go out and look for trouble. To emphasis the strength of feeling on this issue let drivers talk for themselves. I will call them:

THE ANGRY BRIGADE

This list comes straight from the hearts and minds of men with a serious grievance, and at least it will show the powers that be that there is, in fact, a problem. A problem for men like

Alex Ferries, of Glasgow, who demanded: 'Less hassle from police.' Mr **Walker**, of Penrith, who asked for: 'Less harassment from traffic laws.' Mr **D. Cotteringham**, of Ashford, Middlesex, who pleaded for: 'More respect from police.' As did Mr **R.P. Fell**, of Cleethorpes: 'More respect.' While Mr **N. Holmes**, of Melborough, repeated the cry: 'Less hassle from police.' Tom Morley, of Runcorn, diplomatically requested: 'Better public relations between police and drivers.' But **Daniel Macdonald**, of Middleton, was forthright and deeply aggrieved: 'There are no good police, they are all b— .' Whereas **R. Allison**, of South Queensferry, wanted: 'More tolerance from police and wardens.' The harassment allegation arose again with **Kevin Howard**, of Peterborough: 'Less harassment from police, fewer ministry checks.' From Letchworth, Herts, **A. Taylor** asked: 'Get the police off our backs.' While **Andy Berryman**, of Portsmouth wanted: 'Better police.' 'Sack the Ministry of Transport snoopers,' was a Sale driver's plea. 'Less harassment from police and ministry,' said **Kevin Taylor**, of Richmond, Yorkshire. 'More civility from some police forces,' said **Andy McFadyen**, of Bonnyrigg, Midlothian. 'More respect from police,' commented **Davy Patterson**, of Hamilton. 'Less hassle from the law,' said a Norfolk driver. 'Less hassle of truck drivers,' was how a Bolton driver put it. 'Do away with traffic police,' suggested **Colin Pedlow**, of Portadown. **Water Baby**, of Hagley, wanted: 'More considerate police.' Mr **Appleyard**, of Stafford, has a big hang-up: 'The law.' 'Less intimidation by police and ministry,' said **Gordon Clare**, a North Hykenham, Lincs, man. **Colin Roadright**, of Bradford, was disillusioned enough to comment: 'Most police are antagonistic — the rest are bastards.' So it went on. 'Less trouble from ministry and police,' was **Brian Chambers's** observation. He comes from Ruskington. 'Less harassment from the polce,' said **Paul Raymond Smith**, of Ipswich. **W. Hackney**, of Huntingdon, echoed the sentiment: 'Less police harassment.' **Dawn Fox**, a Holbeach driver, was emphatic: 'Abandon the police.' 'Less hassle from police,' said **Steve Newall**, of Leigh. 'Less hassle from police,' said **Steve Hoggard**, of Wigan. To ease the apparent great tension building up between police and lorry drivers, Mr **J. Blunt**, of Wednesfield, suggested: 'Fewer police cars.' From a Northumberland driver came the wish: 'More tolerance from police and ministry.' And **Hayon Elms**, of Chester, asked: 'Let the police leave us alone.' A Scunthorpe driver, **Stewart McClure**, summarised the views of many: 'Let there be less penalising by authorities for small and petty reasons.' The now familiar cry came from **Mike Lambert**, of Ramsey, Essex: 'Less motorway police harassment.' Similarly from **Geoff Mayston**, of Altrincham: 'Less hassle from police.' And the rather sinister observation by **'Drumstick'**, of Edgware (also supported by others) was: 'Less spying by ministry.' For Driver, of Manchester, his hang-up was: 'The attitude of police towards drivers.' More explicit was **Malcolm Hottewell**, a Hexthorpe, Doncaster, driver. he put it this way: 'Less hassle from the Ministry of Transport with checks, etc. — less unreasonable harassment from both police and

37

ministry.' What **R. Hull**, of Macclesfield, wanted was: 'Less stops to be checked by police.' So did **Alan Arrowsmith**, who drives from Sandbach: 'less weight checks, less police checks.' Under his CB-handle, **Oil Baron**, of Stevenage, requested: 'Help from police, not hindrance.' And yet again came those two emotive words. First from **Graham Elgar**, of Headington, Oxford: 'Less hassle from police.' Then from **S. Gallagher**, an Abercrave, Powys, man: 'Less harassment from police and the ministry.'

That is indeed an expression of real anger. Strangely, it is not the full story. Even more strangely, it does not reflect the average driver's view of the police, as I will show you very clearly in the following chapter about the police and drivers.

IT'S THE WAY YOU TELL 'EM

Colour blind

Young Johnny was picking his nose and his mother reprimanded: 'Don't do that, it'll give you red ears.' He scoffed: 'Oh no it won't.' She said: 'Oh yes it will,' and clipped him a backhander across the head.
Scott Hillier, *Leamington Spa, Warwickshire.*

Sharp practice

The van carried the sticker for following drivers to read: 'Be alert!' Underneath was written: 'Britain *needs* lerts.'
Tommy Tantliner, *Wirral, Cheshire.*

What it does show is the average driver's utter disenchantment with the law and how it is operated. When talking about the law, drivers say with resignation and a shrug: 'It's a laugh.'

It is such a laugh that **Stephen Taylor**, of Staines, Middlesex, reported that the funniest thing that had ever happened to him was to be fined £75 at Peacehaven for just tipping the scale over the seven-and-a-half tonnes limit. It was a laugh also for **Jonathan North**, the Bourne, Lincolnshire, driver who, when in a great hurry and despite strong protests, was obliged to submit to a roadside weight-check when he was carrying six tonnes of straw. What is self-evidently lighter than straw, except air?

Those are two niggling, inconsequential incidents (though the £75 wasn't inconsequential to Mr **Taylor**) and not the stuff of great courtroom drama. But, by heck, they take time and cost money, cause bad feeling and, in the second case, bring the law into disrepute — in just the same way as not being allowed to drive your 12-tonnes tractor unit without a trailer attached across a 16-tonnes restricted bridge because you have a 32–38 tonnes tare rate printed on your cab.

Cuckoo Land

This is a familiar scenario to drivers, but unbelievable to the general public. 'It was like playing a game of snakes and ladders and sliding down the snakes all the time,' says **MC**, the Ipswich driver involved.

He had driven empty 276 miles to pick up a load from an

agricultural depot. Driving down a good country road he turned a bend and could see the depot accross the fields. But in front of him was a bridge with a 20-tonnes restriction. Parked by the bridge was a police car. Over the bridge and down the road was a party of officials in deep conclave.

'Sorry, mate,' said an apologetic policeman, 'if you go over that bridge I'll have to nick you, and I can't turn a blind eye because the guv'nor's on the other side with a party of big-wigs. I know you're only 16 tonnes but you are rated 38 tonnes.'

They studied the map for an alternative route: back to the A-road, up to the motorway, come in from the other side.

'Tell you what,' said the helpful policeman, 'there's a short cut, I'll take you part way.'

'I'll be well out of tacho-time,' said **MC**.

'We'll treat it as an emergency.'

At the motorway the helpful police waved goodbye. **MC** carried on, pulled off at the next junction and met a second police car with the inevitable result: 'Tacho, please — you're over time.' They were good. They got on the radio and let him proceed the eight miles to the depot where he found the gates closed.

'Sorry, mate,' said the watchman, 'our time is 4.30. It's worth more than my job to open those gates now.'

He trudged three miles to the nearest phone and his boss screamed: 'What the bloody hell have you been playing at?'

IT'S THE WAY YOU TELL'EM

Missing link
Stopped for having no number plate on his trailer the driver protested: 'It was there this morning.' But the sceptical police officer smirked: 'Well, it isn't there now.' Said the driver: 'In that case, I want to report a theft.'
N. Wallis, *Manselton, Swansea.*

Heavy breathing
How do you know when two elephants have been making love in your back garden?
Your bin-liners have gone.
B. Moorhouse, *Warrington.*

Now that is 'a laugh' just as much as the infamous weigh bridge at Wetherby is. You should know about it in case you have to use it. It is an axle-weighing machine, and if you drive over it one way you get one set of results; if you drive over it the opposite way you get a completely different set of results. Two sets of results from the one ministry machine, and yet people have been hammered unmercifully in court on the evidence based on the results produced by driving over it in the direction that came out worst for the driver.

Compare that with the hullabaloo when the VASCAR speed

detector and Alcometer breathalyser machines were suspected of being inaccurate and thus placing the *private* motorist in jeopardy. They were withdrawn pretty quickly until faults were rectified and they were proven accurate beyond all doubt.

So they brought in the law about maximum axle-loading yet made no provision for *everybody* to be able to comply with the law. How many companies large or small and how many owner-drivers have ready access to an axle-weighing machine? The answer is few, very few indeed.

A funny thing happened...

'I was laughing my head off as I watched a pair of wheels running alongside me on the hard-shoulder,' says **B.R. Gammon**, of Ashford, Kent, 'then the breaker behind me called up and said they were mine.'

Every operator knows that you can come out loaded spot-on to the milligram on your overall maximum weight and have conscientiously checked and cross-checked every aspect of your loading, and then still find yourself tonnes over on one axle.

Of course, the folly is that they have made a fixed rule for a variable content. Like people, cargoes come in all shapes and sizes, and they also come heavier in different parts — it is like trying to compare Samantha Fox and Twiggy.

Common justice would seem to suggest that if a law is made and enforced, the means to abide by that law should also be provided *at a reasonable cost*.

One way to do that would be for those environmentalist groups, like Friends of the Earth, who lead 'the uninformed and constant attack on lorries and the road haulage industry' to do something constructive for a change and supply the machines as a public service. They've got plenty of money to splash about attacking the industry, let them put a bit of it towards helping the industry cure the ills they accuse it of causing.

THE YOBBO FACTOR

Are lorry drivers yobbos? Or is it the barrage of adverse criticism levelled at them, and the law itself, that gives the impression that they are?

If they are yobbos then the man behind the wheel in his £75,000 rig, like **David Seaman**, of Swaffam, driving with a £4.7-million cargo of customer's delicate electronic equipment entrusted to his sole care could prove to be a hyper-expensive hoodlum if he ever chose to behave in the manner which the critics say drivers do.

On the other hand, are the police uniformed yobbos bent on harassing innocent HGV drivers? Or do they also suffer from a bad image because they have to enforce bad law?

The police represent authority, and it is nice to see authority take a tumble now and again. So here are a couple of light little stories in case your resentment is reaching simmerimg point; and to show that we do try to keep a balanced view of the forces of law and order with due sympathy, knowing that they are only doing their jobs to the best of their abilities. Let's take the experience of Mr **Bright**, of Ipswich, whose sympathy was greatly touched when he was trucking down a motorway and carefully observing the actions of a motor-cycle policeman in front of him.

Coming in the opposite direction was a truck going like a bat out of hell, and safe, he thought, from the attentions of the police. However, he attracted the attention of Mr **Bright**'s motor-cycle officer who went into a series of expert racing changes and an abrupt right turn, revving to cross the central reservation, intent on hot pursuit — OK, turn a blind eye to smokie crossing the central reservation, he was a conscientious man doing his duty.

Alas, he sank into the mud up to his axles. The more he revved, the deeper he dug himself into a muddy grave and took the shine off his polished leggings. Meanwhile the offending trucker, oblivious of the mini-drama he had created, was showing a clean tailboard over the far horizon.

That's life — and it is comforting to think that sometimes a policeman is hoist with his own petard. For example, when **Brian Watson**, of Cleveland, was pulled up on the A38, the policeman in his eagerness to get to Brian's lorry forgot to take off his motor-cycle helmet and damned nearly strangled himself on his ear-phone wires.

The drivers' attitude is, serve 'em right, they cause us enough aggro, it's nice to see them suffer once in a while. And officialdom does actually have to suffer a great deal of aggravation in the course of performing its duties.

'Five! If you give me six do I get a free tumbler?'

As Mr **J. Hughes**, of Preston, discovered at the weighbridge at Beattock, on the A74, where a Ford Transit had been pulled in and found to be three tonnes over the top. So much overweight that the tyres had been worn bare on the wheel arches. Angrily the van owner protested to the ministry inspectors: 'Overweight my arse! I had plenty of room inside for a few more bits and pieces.'

Good jokes — but there is an edge to those stories which isn't, perhaps, as entertaining as the anecdotes. In all truckers' tales nowadays there is a strain of anti-authoritarianism and a streak of anti-constabulary attitudes; drivers are becoming sick of authority and it shows in their jokes. Their humour is now a statement of resentment which is perhaps encapsulated in the response of **John Harris**, of Isleworth, Middlesex, that the funniest thing he had seen on a motorway was: 'A motorway smokie running down the hard shoulder chasing my tacho card which had blown out of his hand.'

Really, the moans that do go on, hundreds of them. I now have a suspicion that, like certain ladies who were only happy when they could go to the cinema and have a good cry, you drivers get your fun by going to the truckstop to have a good moan.

So why the moans? It isn't the nature of the business nor is it the character of those who work in it. Part of the fun of the game is the 'crack' you get in it and the laughs you come across. So there must be an explanation.

One explanation is that, unfortunately, there is plenty of cause for complaint.

THE APPALLING IMAGE

The image of the industry worries everybody in it from the multi-national company director in his plush boardroom to the breaker eating his bacon buttie in Rose's A12 café at 6.30 in the morning. And it is an image which has been created largely on the say-so of a handful of cranks, fanatics, self-interested élitists who wish to preserve their own particular interests, and plain nutters who have managed to convince the mass of the sensible and well-meaning public that everything on 14 wheels or more is mad, bad, dangerous and undesirable.

It is an image based usually on wrong information, false facts and flagrant misinterpretations plus the stimulation of fear; one arguable view is that 'knocking the road haulage industry' has become itself a lucrative industry.   So serious is the image problem — and image and law are inextricably entangled — that members of the SMMT (Society of Motor Manufacturers and Traders) subscribed £1 million in 1985 specifically to counter the bad publicity. But a fat lot of good it did. It could not actually do much good, even £5 million would not have had much effect. In one year you cannot hope to reverse the insidious propaganda of forty years.

It is all very simple in reality, the public — and that includes you and me — relishes bad news to the extent that it will not buy or read good news: all the 'good news' newspapers ever conceived have failed abysmally and died. The wife of the great press baron Lord Kemsley formulated a policy of printing 'all the news that's fit to print' and promptly killed off half a dozen of her loving husband's most profitable journals including the massive selling *Empire News* — known affectionately as the 'Impure News' — which used to make the *News of the World* look like *Pilgrim's Progress*.

IT'S BIZARRE

Brass monkeys and other livestock

It was an odd enough sight when **Stanley Hunter**, of Burtonwood, saw a streaker cross the M6 and run up an embankment at Stafford. But it was odder still when **Leonard Biggs**, of Southampton, met his streaker at three o'clock of a freezing November morning.

It has to be accepted as a simple fact of life that bad news sells newspapers. 'Juggernauts' are bad news, so you seldom — *never* — read a good word about them. And those who read bad words often enough eventually become brainwashed and begin to believe them.

But somebody has to plant the seed of an idea that things are bad news. In the case of 'juggernauts', high among the somebodies who plant and nourish such ideas is the organisation Friends of the Earth. The following is an example (a mild one, as it happens, they have published some pretty inflammatory posters and documents in their time) of what they say about lorries:

So What's Wrong with Lorries?

What are the problems with heavy lorry traffic?

Noise

Millions of people in Britain suffer from traffic noise: a 1977 official report showed 40% of Londoners were receiving an excess level. Lorries contribute disproportionately to this problem, especially at night.

Vibration

Traffic vibration can come both via the air or the ground and most of it comes from lorries. The full effect of vibrations on buildings have not been adequately researched. The impact on residents is clearer; up to a third of London householders experience some form of inconvenience on account of the effect of vibration.

Road damage

London's roads are cracking up in a quite spectacular fashion because of the damage of heavy lorries. A fully-laden lorry causes the equivalent wear-and-tear of nearly 200,000 cars.

Any illegally over-loaded lorry does even more damage. The many potholes and dangerous stretches of road surface in London are mostly caused by lorry traffic.

Other damage

Lorries also do damage below the road surface. Sewer and gas main collapses are increasingly attributed to heavy lorries. In 1980, the National Water Council said that most of its £100 million annual repairs then were attributable to lorry damage.

Up on the surface, of course, there is the steady battering of walls, pavements, railings, sometimes of people's homes. And when lorries are involved in road accidents, they are more likely to be serious ones.

Pollution

Heavy lorries run on diesel, and badly-maintained or over-loaded lorries can be a major source of pollution. Unburnt particles in their exhausts can foul the air and spoil our historic buildings. Hydrocarbons from diesel fuel are suspected of causing increased cancer rates in urban areas (see our companion leaflet, *Vehicle Emissions*).

Physical threat

Lastly, lorries pose a visual annoyance and an actual physical threat to people on the street. Some of the problems referred to above come mainly from over-laden foreign trucks or from lorries run by small firms which are 'cutting corners' in their operations. However, even the best maintained vehicles from reputable fleets are resented when they are felt to be in the wrong place at the wrong time.

Even in its mild form, that is pretty emotive stuff; the public will say, I myself would be tempted to say: 'Well, they are *environmentalists*, they are out to *do good*, they're probably right.'

Then the public, like me, would see their associates in this particular instance and begin to wonder if they are, in fact, all that right. I for one would not place all that much confidence in a report issued by the 'Loony Left' of the defunct GLC as Friends of the Earth apparently did:

We are grateful to the GLC for help in the production of this material.

If you would like any further information about CITIES FOR PEOPLE, please do not hesitate to contact us here at:

FRIENDS OF THE EARTH
377 City Road, London, EC1V 1NA Tel:(01) 837-0731

Not one point is substantiated: vibration — 'not been adequately researched'. Road damage — 'the equivalent wear-and-tear of 200,000 cars'. Come off it, mates, I don't believe it. I drive down roads in my car which never see a 38-tonne artic. from one year's end to the next and they have pot-holes you could keep ducks on and that is due to lack of maintenance. Sewers and gas mains — many of them were over 100 years old and rotting away from old age. In my area a lot have now been replaced.

So what has this all got to do with the law?

This is what: the GLC passed the law banning or restricting lorries from London on evidence like this. The Department of Trade tried to prevent that law being enforced but failed to do so in the courts. The GLC died, the law lived on. Yet its value has never been proved and it is a law based largely on prejudice, not fact. The environment does need protecting and by law if necessary, so all power to the elbow of Friends of the Earth. But are they above a suspicion of self-interest in making their constant and insistent attacks of lorries? Maybe not. Societies like Friends of the Earth need money to run on, they become big and expensive to maintain, and to survive they must have targets to attack. Because over the years — many, many years — they have built up such an antipathy in the public mind to trucks and road haulage, it has become an easy, sitting target; and because road haulage is such a visible target it is all the easier to attack.

So the scenario is: find a target to attack to raise the funds; then, to raise public interest, give the media bad news which you can be sure they'll print.

IT'S BIZARRE

Accidental Pot Black champion

Darkness hides a lot of sins. **J. Wood**, of Rugeley, Staffordshire retails the story of driving a 23-foot trailer, reversing to park on the forecourt of a darkened café which was closed for the night, and stopping next to the billiards table. Unaware that he had pushed in the front of the establishment, he climbed from his cab and asked the irate owner where the nearest chip-shop was.

Has anybody ever seen an environmentalist's pamphlet that has listed the fantastic developments in trucks over the years? A pamphlet describing how research and development have turned the old-style truck of a decade ago into what Roger Dennis, Distribution Director of Bass (UK), with 3,000 vehicles on the road, describes accurately as the 'whispering giant'? And stating the astonishing safety factors now built into every truck?

Ignorance creates prejudice; ignorance and misinformation bring about bad law. And the law that concerns you is the tacho...

THE LAW II – THE TACHO

Drivers do not like tachographs.

They did not like them when they were first introduced. They didn't like them for the four years and nine months they ran under the old rules because they created utter confusion.

The law changed on 29 September 1986, and was made a little easier to operate from a tachograph point of view — and still you don't like tachographs.

To prove that you don't like tachographs here are some comments you made in answer to questions about tachographs:

First, a general observation from Mr **T. Cable**, of Ipswich, about the number of times drivers are stopped to have their tacho cards examined: 'Let car drivers be stopped and cautioned as often as HGV drivers are.'

That would cause a row, I'll bet!

Secondly, a very interesting observation from two Middleton drivers which actually points up remarkably the hindrance value of tachographs, and is a tacit acceptance of that fact by the road authorities. These remarks might raise a few eyebrows:

Mr **G.Stockton** says: 'I complain about how the police are a law unto themselves as far as tachos go — i.e. there were no tachos during the miners' strike and the Falklands war. They were ignored and forgotten.'

His Middleton colleague, **Daniel Macdonald**, supports him: 'During the war with Argentina, tachos and speed limits were forgotten.' Quite a few other drivers agree with those statements and it raises a couple of very important questions.

Did the public know about tachos being suspended during those two periods of national emergency? Did Parliament know?

Was the law officially amended during those periods of crisis? If not, on whose order and authority was it suspended?

Two important principles are at stake here:

1   Is the road law subject to political expediency and can an Act of Parliament be suspended without the due sanction of Parliament?

2   Can chief constables suspend the provisions of the road laws and restore them at will?

The other question drivers are entitled to ask is, if tachos, speed limits and weight restrictions (those came into the miners' strike and

'He's out of time on his tacho. He hasn't got a sleeper cab and the law states he must take his rest and ease outside the cab.'

Falklands war as well) impede the effort during crisis times, what the heck do they do during ordinary times?

It is all very confusing as well as being suspicious, and it looks as if the HGV driver is made a Patsy whenever the authorities feel like it.

The enormous strength of protest against the hold-ups and 'intimidations' claimed to be brought about by the tachograph is summed up in a proposal from **Derek Gordon**, of South Shields, who demands: 'Let drivers be represented as a body against all hold-ups and intimidations they have to swallow.'

Thirdly, in our tachograph section, saying 'a lot of drivers don't like the tacho' doesn't carry much weight. The weight comes from numbers and voices raised in anger. So, after the Angry Brigade:

THE ANTI-TACHO TASKFORCE

A. Stewart, Blairgowrie: 'Abolish tachos, return to log books.' **Cruiser One**, Cardiff: 'Get rid of tachos.' **Bob Nicholson**, Workington: 'Remove tachos.' **Water Baby**, Hagley: 'Abolish tachos.' **Mr Appleyard**, Stafford: 'No tachos,' **G. Thomas**, Peckham: 'Scrap the tacho since most police do not know how they work.' **John Cook**, of Edmonton: 'Make the tachograph laws understandable for an everyday man.' **Andy Hall**, Sudbury, Derbyshire: 'Take the tachos out.' **C. Reynolds**, East Herptree, Bristol: 'Take the confusion out of the tachograph laws.' **P. Newell**, of Withenhall: 'Vary the use of tachos.' **Alex Main**, of Preston: 'No tachos — more say in the laws.' **A. Stewart**, Borders: 'Make the rules and regulations simpler.' **J.J. Coleman**, Darlington: 'Scrap tachographs.' **John Shortland**, of Spalding: 'Get rid of tachos.' **M. Peedon**, of Coventry: 'Not such close scrutiny of tachographs.' **Mal Grimes**, of Downham Market: 'Throw out tachos.' **Mark Seymour**, of Hendon: 'Abolish tachos.' **J. Wood**, of Rugeley: 'Vary the tachograph rules.' **Driver**, from Middleton, Lancashire: 'Log books back — tachos out!' **Peter Austin**, of Bramley: 'No tachos.' **Davy Patterson**, of Hamilton: 'Get rid of tachos.' **Andy McFadyen**, of Bonnyrigg, Midlothian: 'Let's have less scrutinising of tachographs, and more civility about it.' **M. May**, of Liverpool: 'Get rid of tachos.' **Flying Fortress**, Lancaster: 'Tachos removed.' **Alan Ball**, of St. Helens, Lancashire: 'Tachos stopped.' **Frank Allingham**, of East Malling, Kent: 'No tachos.' **Arthur Penbridge**, of Llandudno: 'Get rid of tachos.' **P.A. Chapman**, of Dartford, Kent: 'Get rid of tachos.' **W. Hackney**, of Huntingdon: 'Do away with tachos.' **Brian Howard**, Putson, Hereford: 'Get rid of tachos.'

Driver, from King's Lynn: 'Scrap tachos.' **John Russell**, of Luton, was an exception to the general rule on the subject of tachographs. Most other comments were crisp, terse or all but spat out. He said: 'I would like to see the easing of statutory controls on tachographs.'

Those lists of names have exposed three factors causing acute discontent: harassment, the tachograph as the main cause of harassment, and the random enforcement of the law. To those factors add a fourth: how drivers think and feel that the public, as well as authority, perceives them. They feel that they are seen and treated as a bad lot — and who can argue with them?

IT'S BIZARRE

Self-destruct handle

Being lost, **Scania Man**, of Perthshire, jumped out of his cab and ran to ask the driver in front of him for directions. Talking to the driver, he glanced back and was horrified to see his own rig rolling forward to crash into the rear of his helper's tilt. Try telling a man who has stopped to assist you that you didn't know the rig had a faulty hand-brake. 'It was so frightening it was almost funny,' laments Scania Man, 'run over by my own truck.'

No deterrent

While working in Saudi Arabia, Driver, of Ashford, was amazed to find two Arabs syphoning petrol from his car: petrol in Saudi is 4p a gallon, and the penalty for theft is a hand chopped off.

It hurts deeply and rankles incessantly. They ask why they should be thought of like that. They work hard for 24 hours round the clock and don't make a great fuss about unsocial hours, they do a good job, they don't go on strike, they don't run riot like football hooligans, they don't block roads and borders like the French and Italians, they put more into society than they ever take out and the result is that they are thought of as a second-rate group of potential delinquents.

The answer is that they are the victims of the propaganda mill run by organised professional protesters with the major purpose of stirring up fear of and antagonism to them.

When a group of people — all 340,000 of them — get a universal chip on otherwise cheerful, resilient shoulders, it ought to be a matter of very great concern to everybody. And particularly the powers that be. Which, if you haven't already grasped that there is a lot of grief on the road, brings us to the final categories in our tattered, rebellious army of malcontents, the —

THE 'I'M SICK AND TIRED OF BEING RUBBISHED, SO PACK IT UP' CONTINGENT

Mr **Pratt**, of Swindon, encapsulates the general feeling: 'We want to be shown some respect for the job we do and the conditions we have to put up with.' Mr **Mills**, of Ipswich, takes it a stage further: 'The time has come to stop classing HGV drivers as second-class citizens.' **William Hodgekinson**, of Sheffield, sees it further still down the line: 'Why should we be looked on as third-class citizens?' From Penrith, **J.R. Ousby**, demands; 'We want more respect as a professional body of men.' 'Yes,' says Mr **R.P. Fell**, of Cleethorpes, 'more respect.' **Terence Archbold**, of Purfleet, endorses the view: 'It is time they gave us better recognition and respect.' While Mr **S. Mulvaney**, of Audenshaw, asks for: 'Better attitudes.' **Susan Stringer**, of Blackley, Manchester, states simply and strongly: 'The job is not appreciated.' The resentment about attitudes comes out in Kirby driver, **Jim McNally**'s insistence: 'We should be treated like a professional body of men.' And in **J. Fiddes**, of Cowley, remonstration: 'We need to be treated with greater respect.' It is an advantage to see ourselves as others see us. **Ron Berghout**, of Puttershoek, Holland, is a regular visitor to Britain. He says with puzzlement and concern: 'Lorry drivers in England don't get any respect. They are much better regarded and treated on the Continent.' Travel broadens the mind, so they say. It has broadened the outlook of **Ian Elliot**, of Bournemouth, who observes: 'We ought to be treated as professionals — as on the Continent.' And also **Stephen Taylor**, of Staines, who goes one stage further: 'We expect to be treated as human beings as lorry drivers are on the Continent.' Those views are echoed by **Driver**, Bolton, who also objects to sub-human treatment: 'I would like to see drivers treated as human beings.' There is great pride in the job in the trucking world, and a regard for skills. **Clive Nuttall**, of Rawtenstall, puts it this way: 'We want to be recognised as professionals and be treated accordingly.' Professionalism is also a sore point with **Ian McLachlan**, the Dalbeattie driver: 'We must have more respect as a professional body.' And Mr **H.S. Jeffrey**, of Wigan, agrees: 'Better respect.' This is endorsed by Mr **D. Cresswell**, of Basildon: 'There must be greater recognition of truck driving being a skilled, professional job.' And adding his weight to the argument, **Drumstick**, of Edgware, says: 'There must be recognition as a skilled trade.' **Richard Mills**, of Boston: 'Treat us with more respect.' In the same vein, **Paul Bonney**, of Huntingdon, demands: 'Give us status as a professional body.' And finally, with great simplicity, and all the more forcefully for that, under his CB handle, **Drifter**, of Macclesfield, says: 'There ought to be recognition of our usefulness.'

And at the back of the straggling column —

THE 'LET'S SORT THIS MESS OUT ONCE AND FOR ALL' REARGUARD

The lads who know that the law, rules and regulations are such an unholy mess that the officials who formulated and drafted them cannot themselves understand the half of what goes on.

At this point let us stress that it is not just the lads on the road who are baffled, bemused and bewildered by it all. It is also the top bosses, the manufacturers, officers of road haulage associations, directors of national and multi-national companies and men of proven managerial expertise and calibre.

No wonder **Tom Cook**, of Spalding, demands: 'Simplify working hours.' **P. Pegler**, of Hartcliffe, Bristol, laments: 'Rules and regulations must be made simpler.' Mr **J. Johnson**, of Denton, Manchester, pleads: 'Less red tape.' Driver **E. Tearle**, of Ramsgate, wants: 'Fewer and simpler regulations.' In darkest Maidenhead, Mr **D. Sherrington**

49

seeks enlightenment with: 'A revision of motorway rules, and a revision of regulations.' There are some, many, in fact, who would say to that: 'God forbid, don't let them get an official brain with an official pen in hand anywhere near the rule book — it's baffling enough as it stands.' They would go along with Mr **D.J. Wiffen**, of Aveley, who asks simply: 'Reduce restrictions.'

Others just want assistance. Like **Colin Standferd**, of Ipswich, who asks: 'Give us better facilities with help from the government.' And Mr **A.A. Parker**'s plea from Helsby is: 'Let them show more consideration for HGV drivers.' A common complaint is pin-pointed by Lowestoft driver, **M. Smith**, who says: 'There should be a better understanding of truckers' use of the road.' Understanding is also required from traffic wardens, according to **L. McDonald**, of Forfar, and **Arthur Hughes**, from Liverpool, who asks for: 'More consideration from traffic wardens.'

Traffic Wardens. They come in for an incredible amount of stick which is understandable because they meet lorry drivers in close contact on alien ground and few know how to interpret the 'unloading trade goods' provision. Some do use their loaves, says **DW**, of Walton, but often in exasperation he will tell them: 'If you're going to put a ticket on it, warden, get writing.'

Meanwhile, **Frank Jones**, of Rugeley, says: 'Traffic wardens! Send them all back to Japan.'

IT'S BIZARRE

A rose by any other...

The *Buckingham Advertiser* reported: 'The Chief Constable will be accompanied by Chief Inspector G. Bollard, of the Traffic Division.'

Au lait! CAP this for cheek

Malcolm Apsey, from Weymouth, was privileged to see the Common Agricultural Policy in action on the M1. A French truck pulled on to the hard-shoulder, the driver climbed from his cab carrying a container, vaulted the fence into a field and proceeded to milk a cow. If you prefer lemon in your tea, go to Spain.

TACHO, TACHO...

The big hope at midnight, 29 September 1986, was that things would be much better. They would not be perfect but they would be an improvement.

The big question was would *they* let them be?

To remind you, that was the date when the tacho rules changed and Great Britain got into step with the Common Market about how to use that 'alien' device, the tachograph, which had been forced on us by the EEC in the first place. At that magic moment in time, four years and nine months of muddle and confusion was meant to go out of the window and a new era of liberal enlightenment was meant to dawn.

The answer is that it did get better — for the simple reason that it could not have got much worse. So thanks be for small mercies. The rigid rule, putting the industry into a strait-jacket, had been relaxed and a degree of blessed flexibility allowed back. So there was relief and the industry scratched itself with pleasure like a woman does who has just taken off an over-tight girdle.

Some drivers were succinct about the tacho's unpopular history: 'Diabolical!' Others were rather more savoury: 'What have we been buggering about at for five years? Wasting my life, wasting thousands of man-hours and millions of pounds trying to work a poxy, impossible system dreamed up by some crappy civil servant with his arse on a posh leather seat in a swivel chair in a London office which everybody on the road knew could never work. It's like a registered docker, if it's ever seen to work, it's a miracle.'

That driver was a little irate, he was worried about his time. He had been sitting in Park 72, at Felixstowe docks, waiting from twenty past two in the afternoon until ten past seven that evening to pick up a container, and wasn't best pleased about it; and Felixstowe is one of the better (the best even) docks where they don't actually have registered dockers.

The vital thing was, and is, to remove the unnecessary irritations of the tacho system. One of those irritations is that if there is a checkable system in a lorry cab, open to be checked at any time, far too many officials will be tempted to randomly check it at any time. And they do.

I know the A12 road particularly well and one of my 'consulting drivers' sets out every Sunday from Clacton-on-Sea to drive along it. The time and the place are important: Clacton is a busy seaside resort and it shares its main approach road with both Harwich and Felixstowe. On Sunday the holiday traffic pours down. Being Sunday, on his way to the M25, my informant sees on average only fifteen other HGVs among the thousands of private cars. Inevitably, every weekend for a year, one of those trucks has been in a lay-by with a police car in attendance. It is a game for the police, a bit of Sunday sport to break the tedium. But that poor bloke in the truck is probably on his way to catch a boat at the docks. And what do the police say when they pull in the trucks? They say: 'Routine check, driver.'

And because they know that they are being a deliberate nuisance without due cause or apparent reason, they often attempt to justify their action by seeking out every minor fault they can find. Like the ministry men, they go into a conference out of earshot of the driver to discuss what they can possibly hang on him. That happens all the time, and we all know it happens. And it doesn't only happen in Essex.

To get the situation into some degree of proportion, go back to that question I raised about an ordinary private motorist. Imagine the outcry if a company rep, an office worker, an executive, a company director or a housewife going about their daily business were subjected to random stops to be told, 'Just a routine check, driver', and then held up for an hour, maybe more. God knows, there has been protest and outcry enough at the mere suggestion of random breath-tests outside pubs.

Now, of course, it should be better because the rules are better. In all fairness it should be said that some degree of common sense has been used at last to relate the rules to actual conditions on the road. There is more than a spark of hope in the new regulations. In fact, it is a little flame of hope for drivers in that at last the weight of opinion has budged the leaden hand of authority.

Before going into detail about the new rules, which are EEC rules, let us say that formerly the interpretation of the rules has been wholly a British problem; a sort of new 'English disease' in which officialdom had tried to run old British laws and new EEC rules at the same time and the poor dumb trucker had been caught between. The effectiveness and benefits of the amended rules will depend upon how the British authorities decide to interpret and implement them. On the track record, that could be a problem.

The Continentals have taken a different standpoint using the rules to curb transgressors and cowboys and not to impede the whole industry. The interpretation in Europe is liberal compared with that in the United KIngdom. What matters now is how the rules since 29 September 1986, work. If confusion arises it could be because of the interpretation of the rules as applied before that date, so an occasional reference to the rules laid down before September 1986 will help to clarify the situation.

In brief, a lot of the problems which arose previously stemmed from the fact that two sets of rules were being applied simultaneously: the British Road Traffic Act, 1968, and the EEC regulations. For all practical purposes, since September 1986, only the EEC rules apply.

There are two exceptions to this but they need not concern the average HGV driver carrying out normal haulage business.

The constant plea from drivers is: why can't they make the rules simpler and write them so that they can be understood by the driver on the road? The answer is that the rules are written by lawyers for lawyers and in a style and language which only lawyers will fully understand.

Enforcement

At this point two words become paramount, and they are: emphasis and purpose. Both are a cause for concern to drivers on the road. So the *emphasis* will lie in the interpretation of the law, and the interpretation will depend on the *purpose* of the law. So what exactly is the purpose of the law as expressed in the four crucial papers:

The Community Drivers' Hours and Recording Equipment (Exemptions and Supplementary Provisions) Regulations 1986.

The Community Drivers' Hours and Recording Equipment Regulations 1986.

The Drivers' Hours (Goods Vehicles) (Modifications) 1986.

The Drivers' Hours (Harmonisation with Community Rules) Regulations 1986.

Who says those papers are crucial? The Department of Transport does. But if you, a driver whom they most concern, were to obtain them from HM Stationery Office, the betting is that they would be meaningless to you. But back to the purpose of the law. Is it to facilitate the free and unhindered movements of goods by hauliers honestly and properly engaged in that business? Is it to safeguard the interests of drivers of HGVs, their customers and the public? And if it is all of those things, where does it actually say so? Where does it spell out the benefits to society? Where does it stress the advantages to the community at large — as apart from the Community with a capital C?

What is spelt out is the emphasis to be placed upon *enforcement*: that is spelt out by the Community and by the Department of Transport.

Rightly or wrongly the Department of Transport gives the distinct impression that their interest is primarily in enforcement to the letter of the law. It all depends on the manner and approach used: certainly the ministry has a duty to pursue and prosecute wrong-doers, but it has no mandate, no status nor any writ to persecute the rest.

The Council of Ministers dwelt a lot on enforcement and demanded ways of improving it; anybody who talks to the Department of Transport knows that their minds and enthusiasms are concentrated upon that aspect of the law. They think about it so much that it gives cause to wonder whether they think about it to the exclusion of everything else. There is a militancy about Transport Ministry attitudes to transport that means that an HGV driver

IT'S BIZARRE

Sleeper-cab beauty

Paul Taylor, a Bradford driver, recalls the friend who finished his journey early and parked in Northampton cattle market at two o'clock in the afternoon. 'Great,' thought the friend, 'a quick kip, a meal at five o'clock then out for a night on the town.' At five he wakened, ate, dressed in his fancy gear and at six o'clock set out for his night's adventures. The town was deadly quiet. A couple of trucks were pulling out. He asked the drivers where they were going. 'To work, you pratt,' they answered, 'where do you think we're going at six in the morning? And why are you all dressed up like a dog's dinner?'

running entirely legally must often consider a civil servant with a chit of authority a far greater traffic hazard that a drunken driver. The driver behind the wheel is the enemy. And if he or she ever wins a skirmish, it is sure to be a Pyrrhic victory.

Philippa Edmonds, whose company we deal with as a typical transport company in another chapter, was picking up one of her trucks one Friday evening when she was stopped by the police. Everybody in transport knows the famous Friday syndrome; the police see a truck lateish on Friday and say to themselves: 'Ah, late Friday evening, bet he's running illegally, let's give him a turn.'

IT'S BIZARRE

When retribution comes at two leg-power

On his way from Fiddler's Ferry power station, **Bryan Pritchard**, of Cannock, took his coffee break and casually tossed his slops out of the window. To his horror they caught a passing cyclist full in the face, The man rode into a ditch. Thinking discretion the better part of valour, Bryan quickly moved off. Then he came to a Halt sign with a steady stream of traffic travelling along the other road, there seemed no way he could percolate out into the nose-to-tail flow. But he did, fast as a Williams-Honda off the grid at Brand's Hatch — in his mirror he saw a furious man dripping coffee dregs about to climb into the cab. 'I made it in the nick of time,' says Bryan.

But Philippa was not running illegally and the police were annoyed. At the end of an intensive examination they could find no fault. Then they told her: 'You drove over a red light.'

They did not know that she was being followed in her own private car by a friend who had volunteered to take her home after she had parked the truck and who witnessed the whole event.

The case was thrown out by the magistrates. But the price of innocence on a completely trumped-up charge was £717.

The rules are infinitely better than they were and do indeed allow you much more flexibility, so be thankful for that.

But it is clear that they will not fit some of the circumstances you, as a working driver, may meet in the course of a day's work. Thus it is equally clear that you may find yourself unwittingly, unwillingly and unavoidably breaking the law in circumstances beyond your control. And if you don't break the driving laws you may find yourself unavoidably breaking another law.

To give an example of this: if you meet a traffic jam or are delayed by a major pile-up on a motorway or on an urban clearway and placed in a position where you cannot stop or park legally, you may be forced by circumstances outside your control to break the driving laws.

Even though the new rules do benefit drivers more than the old ones, it is still a heads I win, tails you lose situation.

Referring back to the *old rules*, there are two significant changes to them which make life easier:

1   The British rule of a 5½-hours' limit on overall work or — in the other phrase used — continuous duty has been scrapped.

That was the rule which caused more problems than any other.

2   The British rules of different compulsory breaks for 'large and non-large' vehicles and different maximum driving times have also been scrapped.

THE RULES ARE:

1   You are allowed four-and-a-half hours' driving time. And driving means *time behind the wheel controlling the vehicle*.

That can be done in one block with a 45-minute break at the end. Or in shorter periods *with breaks in between* but the breaks must be of *not less than 15 minutes*.

During those breaks you *must not carry out any other work*. But *waiting time* and time spent on a *ferry* or *train* in motion

'That lot was new laid when I left the depot — but there were roadworks on the M1!'

while you are not driving your own vehicle is *not regarded as other work*.

To simplify even more: for every 4½ *hours accumulated driving time* you must have 45 minutes break. If you took the shorter breaks option you could, for example, drive for 1½ hours, break for 15 minutes, drive for another 1½ hours break for another 15 minutes, then drive for the final 1½ hours and break for another 15 minutes. The point to watch is, if you took, for example, two 20-minute breaks during the 4½-hour period, you could *not* just stop for an extra 5 minutes at the end to make up the 45 minutes. The final break would also have to be 15 minutes.

2   The *daily limit* you can drive is 9 *hours* with 10 *hours* twice a week.

These driving hours coupled with the required *rest periods* are what will concern most HGV drivers. And this is where it can become complicated. It is best to look at it over a period of a fortnight.

Hours are based on a *fixed week* which is from *midnight Sunday* until *midnight the following Sunday*.

The *fortnightly limit* for driving is *90-hours*.

The *weekly rest period* is *45-consecutive hours*. This rest period can *overlap* from one *fixed week to the next*.

For drivers on a regular five-day week there is no problem at all. But, of course, not many drivers are so lucky and the problems and complications arise for the others. So it goes like this:

The rest period can be *reduced to 36 hours minimum* if taken at the driver's or vehicle's normal base.

The rest period can be *reduced to 24 hours minimum* if taken elsewhere.

But in either case the rest time *lost* must be compensated *before the end* of the *third week following the week* in which it happened. This *compensation* must be given *en bloc* and attached to another *rest period* of at least *eight hours*.

And there is a point to bear in mind about that eight-hour period which will emerge during the next few paragraphs.

It is compulsory to take the weekly rest after *no more than six daily driving periods*. And the maximum driving time for those six driving periods will be 56 *hours*, which is four 9 *hour* sessions and two 10 *hour* sessions.

There are concessions and changes for drivers travelling by ferryboat or train, but these will be dealt with later. Meanwhile, let's look at the *daily rules* and those chiefly concern *daily rest*.

3   *Daily rest* takes in the vexed question of *spreadover* and spreadover affects the rest period.

The daily rest period is *eleven consecutive hours*.

This can be *reduced to nine consecutive hours* on no more than *three times in any one week*.

If you reduce your rest time then you will have to take an *equivalent* period of rest *before the end of the following fixed week*.

Please note particularly that compensations for *daily rest* reductions take place the *following week*, and those for *weekly rest* are *spread over three weeks*.

IT'S BIZARRE

Not much relief...

The driver of the truck parked in the lorry park near **John Russell**, of Luton, was too tired, too idle or too desperate to get up and go. So he peed from the door of his truck, slipped, fell and had to be taken to hospital for injuries. Not too serious, we trust, only a broken leg or something trivial.

But there is a further provision which is exceptionally useful though it can be subject to different interpretations by different authorities:

> The daily rest period can be split into *two* or *three separate periods*, but one of those must be at *least eight hours* and they must *total at least* 12 *hours*.

This means you can take 2 *two-hour breaks*, or a *one-hour* and a *three-hour break* coupled with the *eight-hour break*, making the total of *twelve hours* and you could work like that day in, day out without incurring any reductions in rest times. That would be your working day and there would be no need to compensate the following week — and it would give you a *sixteen-hour spreadover*.

Now let's look at the rule that:

> The required *daily rest* has to be taken in 'each period of 24-hours'.

That means that if you have a spreadover of *more* than *thirteen hours* a reduction in the 11-*hour daily rest* has automatically happened and it will have to be compensated.

If we take an example of three working days it becomes clearer how this applies:

> On *Monday* you start work at 7 o'clock in the morning and finish at 8 o'clock in the evening. So you've done a 13-hour day.
>
> On *Tuesday* you start work again at 7 o'clock in the morning but finish at 6 o'clock at night — having done an 11-hour day.

The important point here is that from 8 o'clock Monday evening until 7 o'clock Tuesday morning, you have taken your *eleven-hour rest*.

> On *Wednesday* you start work at 6 o'clock in the morning and work through until 9 o'clock at night. So you have done a 15-hour day.

The night before you had a *twelve-hour break* from 6 o'clock Tuesday evening until 6 o'clock Wednesday morning — *but that does not cover you*. The way it works is this: you take the *time you finished* and work back 24 hours to fix the 24-*hour period*. That makes it 9 o'clock Tuesday evening so you will have taken only *nine hours rest* and the missing two hours will have to be compensated.

'Make it simple,' you plead (and so do I) but I'm sorry, friend, there is no way of making it simple. Sometimes I feel that if you try to simplify it, you only add to the complications. It is a complex set of regulations and in all honesty all you can do is to try to understand them as best you can.

Another point to remember is that you can take your daily or weekly rest in the cab providing there is *a bunk* and the vehicle is *stationary*. If you have no bunk you have got to get out of the cab and lay your weary head elsewhere... with luck she might be very beautiful.

Now *stop*! *Emergencies*!

Oh the fun and the misery that is going to be caused by emergencies.

They say that the provision for *emergencies* has been *extended and clarified*. So it has on paper, but will anybody tell the police forces and regional ministry people exactly how it should be worked?

> so long as road safety is not jeopardised, and in order to allow the driver to reach a suitable stopping place, the driver may depart from any of the provisions of the Regulation to the extent necessary to ensure the safety of persons, of the vehicle or of its load. The driver is required to indicate the nature of and the reasons for his departure from the provisions on his tachograph chart.

That is a good bit of law. It is a beautiful piece of law, in fact; it is full of sense and is clearly designed to help — now it all depends on what the mutton-heads do when they get their fingers on it. You and I know that it will not work out like that in practice. What you, the driver, will see as an emergency the mutton-heads will see as you trying to dodge the column.

All I can suggest is that when the occasion arises you insist: 'I was working to the emergency provision as laid down in the Regulation and I have complied to the letter with that provision.'

IT'S BIZARRE

Market forces in operation

Two drivers who work with **Alan Hopkins**, of Redditch, stopped overnight in Newcastle-under-Lyme, Staffordshire, town centre — very good parking. There is very good beer in Newcastle too so they went out on the town for a few jars before going to bed. Crack o' dawn they heard a commotion outside but paid no heed. At 8 o'clock they wakened, looked out and found the weekly street market in full swing all around them. They had to sit there until 4.30 in the afternoon to wait for the stalls to be taken down. The boss was not amused so he applied market forces of his own — three days, suspension.

Regarding *ferry-boats*, which affect a lot of drivers nowadays:
The rest period can be interrupted by *one interruption*.
The part of the rest taken on land must be taken *before* or *after* the part taken on the boat or train.
The period between the two portions must be as short as possible and may *on no account exceed one hour* before embarkation or disembarkation with customs formalities *included in the embarkation or disembarkation operation.*

IT'S THE WAY YOU TELL'EM

Hot seat
She was a gorgeous hitch-hiker. As she crossed her shapely legs she murmured suggestively: 'I'm sitting on something all you truck drivers love.' Angrily, the driver snapped back: 'Hell, you've squashed my Yorkie Bar.'
J. Wood, *Rugeley, Staffordshire.*

That can only have been written by a man in an office who hasn't got off his backside and been to a port for years — one hour for customs! My god, think of the joy and pleasure if only that were so at any British port.

During both *rest portions* the driver must have access to a bunk or couchette.
The interrupted rest period must be increased by *at least two-hours*.
Finally, the only part of the Transport Act 1968 that is retained continues the 10-hours driving and 11-hours duty rules for vehicles of not more than 3.5 tonnes GVW and some specialist classes — but these won't affect the class of drivers who will read this book.

I have written this section using lots of italics and indented paragraphs not because I think you are an idiot but solely to try to make it easier to find the particular point which concerns you at a particular time.

What I do most seriously counsel you about is the stepping-up of *enforcement*. That comes direct from the horse's mouth: I talked to very high officials in the Department of Transport and I can assure you that they are planning rigorous enforcement. They have mustered what can only be described as 'assault groups' which will conduct special purges at ports and specially selected key points around the country; small armies of inspectors will be gathered together and special courts will be set up to deal with offenders.

Rightly or wrongly, that is the plan: rightly or wrongly, the law is what I've written about it; you can be in no doubt about my views as an impartial observer on certain aspects of the law and in particular its application. In some cases it is plain idiocy.

But you will do yourself no favours by not knowing what the law is and how it affects you, and you will do yourself less favours by falling foul of it.

Attack Stupidity

Here are a few more points to note with, alas, the caution that there is probably damn all you can do about them.

— There is a strong feeling that you are allowed a 5 per cent leeway on overweight because of the inaccuracy of ministry weighing machines — well, maybe you are, but don't count too much on it.

— There's aggravation that you can leave your depot spot-on as to weight limit and then be fined for being overweight on one or other axle. Well, you can and there is little you can do.

— Off the motorway you are down to 40 mph, so in the case of practical, sensible and *safe* motoring you are at risk of being nicked most of the time — aren't you?

It is safe to say that there is not a modern truck made which is designed to motor in top gear at 40 mph or under. So to keep to that speed the driver is obliged constantly to juggle with his gears or travel a gear or two down: both driver and truck are being put under acute strain to keep to an artificially imposed limit. That cannot be considered safe.

In that contentious and suspect report from the Cranfield Institute referred to in the chapter on the press, the principle cause of overtaking-accidents was overtaking at the slower speeds. For the uninformed, speed is automatically the killer, it conjures up pictures of mayhem on the roads — yet the Cranfield investigators listed the safest cars for overtaking as the fastest.

Just think what would happen if all truck drivers decided to keep to the official speed limit. The country would be completely snarled up in a matter of minutes; all the secondary roads throughout the length and breadth of the country would be virtually impassable.

But good sense, or even common sense, is no answer — nor even is safety. Forty mph is the law and if you go faster you are breaking the law.

If the laws are stupid, as a majority of experienced drivers consider them to be, the answer is to change the laws. The only way to do that is for every lorry driver in the country to sit on his or her MP's back until the member's axles creak and groan under the weight of complaints and protests. Equally importantly, sit on your Euro-MP's back because the laws come out of Brussels. But that is the impossible dream, the majority of workers in the transport industry are too busy earning a living to find an effective voice. It is difficult to organise collective action from the solitude of a moving truck cab.

Not all authority is antagonistic to HGV drivers, there are the notable and powerful exceptions: Mr Brian Oldridge, Roger Birch, Chief Constable of Sussex and former chairman of the Chief

---

A funny thing happened...

'They were two good-looking girls hitching a lift by the side of the road. Then I saw they had great balls and chains round their ankles — they were hitch-hiking for charity,' says **Willie Carson**, the Kirkintolloch driver.

'It was my fault,' says **Peter Robinson**, of Colne, 'at a junction I pulled out a bit late in front of a silver-haired old lady driving a Triumph Toledo, she must have been at least 70. I couldn't believe my eyes when she gave me the V-sign.'

Constables' Association Traffic Committee, James Anderton, Chief Constable of Manchester, and his Traffic Controller, Assistant Chief Constable J.D Phillips, all speak highly of lorry drivers and openly commend them wholeheartedly.

Powerful men, whose job it is first to sort out the mess the Treasury has created on the roads, then clear up the mess and the carnage when it all goes horribly wrong.

The Treasury? Very much the Treasury. That is where the chaos and crisis on the roads begin. The roads and the law are entwined, more especially breaking the law.

Some Qs & As

Meanwhile, here are a few pointers in reply to questions most commonly asked. To get them right we asked **Denis Summers** who was in the Traffic Department of Avon and Somerset Police for twenty-six years, a Class 1 instructor at the police driving school for ten years, on patrol motor cycles, cars, coaches and HGV vehicles. Now he is a consultant and senior lecturer and the North Devon and North Cornwall examiner for the Institute of Advanced Motorists for all vehicle groups from motor cycles to HGVs. He has published *HGV Law Guide* and *The Conveyance by Road of Dangerous Substances*.

1. Yes, it is damned stupid that you cannot drive your tractor and trailer unladen over a weight-restricted bridge, though you are well below the restricted weight limit, when you have a higher tare rating printed on your vehicle. It is daft, but it is the law. You cannot even take your tractor alone.
2. No, you cannot be summonsed for speeding on the evidence of your tacho card alone. The police have to produce other evidence as well.

The only time a disc was used to prove a speeding offence in Britain was when it was accepted as evidence because the defence did not challenge it. Discs can be used to *support* cases of reckless driving to suggest speeds at the time of impact. Enforcement Officers collate discs and licencing authorities send out sharp reminders to operators whose vehicles continually show extra high speeds. Abroad, discs are used for speeding offences and on-the-spot fines.

Q Am I legally obliged to pay motorway service area parking fees?
A Yes. The areas are franchised and operated by private caterers, so you are parking on private property.

Q What is my legal responsiblity if my employer asks me to do work likely to infringe road traffic laws?
A If you take out an unroadworthy vehicle, YOU will commit the offence and your boss will commit the offence of permitting. If you break the tacho laws, it is down to you. If you are sacked for refusing to do either, your only recourse is to the Industrial Tribunal.

Q If I lose my HGV licence through disqualification, can I appeal to the Transport Tribunal to get it back?
A No, the TT deals with operators' licences. The Traffic Commissioner in the area you live deals with the issue, suspension and re-issue of HGV licences. You can appeal to him; if he refuses, then you can appeal to the magistrates' court.

Q Can a Ministry of Transport examiner stop me to examine my vehicle?
A NO, only a police officer or traffic warden *in uniform* can actually stop vehicles. If you are parked in a lay-by, then a ministry examiner can examine your vehicle.

IT'S THE WAY YOU TELL'EM

What's in a name?
Stranded by snow, three drivers, two mates running in tandem and a stranger, sought refuge in the nearest B&B cottage and found it was run by a deaf old lady. She wanted to know where they came from but couldn't hear a word they said. The first driver took a salt cellar from the table, tapped it and tossed a pinch on the fire. 'Och,' said the old dear with a gleam of understanding, 'Saltburn.' The second man followed suit...and so did the stranger. He challenged: 'You try telling her I come from Cockermouth.'
Fat Harvey, *Leigh, Lancs.*

Q Do I have to take out my tacho disc when I finish my tour of duty each day?
A Yes and No; it is very unclear. If you have no responsibility for the vehicle after you finish duty (if you leave it at the operator's yard and go home until the following morning) then you take it out. If you are out tramping, say for a week, then the legislation requires the tacho to be kept running continuously.

Q What are the limits to dimensions to indivisible loads carried under a 'Special Types Order'?
A Weight, 152400 kgs; width, 4.3 metres; length, 27.4 metres. Above that, special authorisation is required from the Department of Transport. (Sunters of Northampton moved a 221 ft. load, and Econofreight pulled 647 tonnes, a British record.)

Q What are the rules about outlining my cab in lights?
A As many as you want providing that two side-parking lights are fitted, one each side of the front of the vehicle. Maximum power of other lights must not exceed 7 watts, and red, blue and green lights are forbidden.

Q What power do I have to stop the police searching my cab, and what power do they have to search and confiscate my possessions?
A The only power the police have is to enter your cab and look at your records — your tacho or log book (which doesn't count now); apart from that, they work on their ordinary powers of stop and search.

Q Where can I find out about the traffic law if I do run into trouble?
A The 'bible' used by police and solicitors is *Wilkinson's Traffic Law*. You might find a copy in your central reference library, ask them.

IT'S THE WAY YOU TELL'EM

No help needed
Helpfully, the passing breaker called what he took to be a stranded truck on the roadside. 'Engine gone?' He queried, and the answer was no. But he persisted and asked: 'Tyre down?' And the answer came: 'Don't need to — she's willing.'
Tony Squires, *Poole, Dorset.*

GIVE A DOG A
BAD NAME...

Look at these headlines and extracts from newspaper reports. Study them carefully, they all appeared on the same day:

'Lorry drivers "a major menace"' *Dundee Evening Telegraph*
'Lorries overtaken — in safety' *Edinburgh Evening News*
'Fast-lane lorries "are a menace"' *Daily Mail*
'Menace of "hell drivers"' *Daily Mirror*
'Curb the hell-drive truckers!' *The Sun*
'Truckers branded a road menace' *Western Daily Press*
'Lorry drivers' safety crown slips' *Glasgow Herald*
'Truckers branded motoring menace' *ITN Oracle*
'Inquiry spotlights lorry "menace"' *Yorkshire Post*
'Fast cars "safest" in overtaking' *The Times*
'Lorry driver "menace" in overtaking' *Daily Telegraph*
'Driving of lorries criticised' *The Guardian*
'Fast lane trucks "are a menace"' *Today*
'Lorries menaces of fast lane — survey' *Aberdeen Press & Journal*
'Lorry drivers "a menace", says inquiry' *East Anglian Daily Times*
'Mighty menace of fast lane lorrymen' *Daily Record*, **Glasgow**
'Lorries a "menace"' *The Journal*, **Newcastle**
'Lorries biggest menace, claims inquiry' *Western Mail*, **Cardiff**
'Road hogs' *Evening Leader*, **Wrexham**
'When lorry drivers are a danger' *Oxford Mail*
'Lorry drivers spotlighted as major menace' *The Scotsman*
'Danger of fast lane lorrymen' *Aberdeen Evening Express*

As you will probably remember those headlines which appeared on Monday, 7 July 1986. Vast national coverage was achieved. You may have fretted or fumed at your inability to answer back as your name was blackened. It is a perfect example of how, if the dog has a bad name already, you blacken it still further. The technique is simple: you bend the facts to suit your own purpose and you distort an 'expert's' views.

The expert in this instance, Mr Don Harris, of the Cranfield Institute of Technology is researching overtaking techniques by all *motorists* and he was shattered by the furore he discovered could be created as the result of an innocent telephone call. He also discovered that it is far easier to get a sensation into the media than it is to get a retraction or correction.

Don Harris's research is legitimate, honest and sincerely well-intentioned for the benefit of all drivers, including HGV men, and not intended in any way to smack them in the teeth. His objective is to *try to ensure the safety of the driver on the road* — TO SAVE THE DRIVER'S LIFE. One life saved is his reward, because he doesn't get any money out of this.

Harris and his colleagues are psychologists — they are 'shrinks' of a sort but no psychiatrists. And they work at Cranfield because the technologists and scientists at the Institute — the metal bashers, as it were — decided that they had engineered the risks out of the automotive trade, machinery, roads, electronics — the lot, to the best of their scientific ability but still accidents happened. They concluded that machines do not cause accidents by themselves, the people who drive them do. So they brought in the psycologists to try to sort out the problems of the people who run the machines. A cushy job, you think? Most of you reading this book wouldn't get out of bed for the money they're paid.

So how did they come to 'knock' HGV drivers? It all began on Friday, 4 July 1986.

A reporter from the Press Association news agency telephoned Don Harris to ask him about drivers' signalling habits, and whether they had deteriorated over the years. He had called because he had heard there was some work in that area going on at Cranfield. There wasn't, but Don told him about the overtaking research programme. He explained that, out of 5,000 incidents observed, 4,700 were private cars, and 300 were lorries, coaches or buses which were all lumped together; out of the total 120 lorries were 'judged' to be potentially dangerous overtakers, while 240 cars were 'judged' the same way: lorries were shown to be very infrequent overtakers in the situations in which they were filmed.

The research was carried out at sites which were selected because they were potential accident sites: 'There would be no point in studying them otherwise,' Harris explained. All the sites were single-carriageway roads. At no time were 'fast lanes' mentioned, yet six of the newspaper reports specifically picked out motorway 'fast lanes' as worthy of special mention. Nowhere in Don Harris's research are the words 'menace', 'road hogs' or 'hell drivers' ever used. The strongest words used are: 'The results suggest that there is cause for concern about the overtaking habits of HGVs, especially in their use of filter lanes.'

Mild as they were, Don Harris's views were controversial, in the manner they appeared in the press they were inflammatory; they could cause immense damage to a whole industry and very great distress to thousands upon thousands of people involved in that industry and to their families as well.

Popular newspapers went over the top with such headlines as 'frights of the road', 'hell drivers' and 'inquiry blasts lorry drivers' though none of those sentiments or words, nor anything remotely like them, appeared in the Harris report. A newspaper like the *Daily*

Telegraph stands aloof from the popular press and proudly claims balance and objectivity in its reports. Yet this is how the *Daily Telegraph* printed the story:

Lorry driver 'menace' in overtaking

The British lorry driver—once respected as one of the safest of road users—has been spotlighted as a major motoring menace by the Government-backed Economic and Social Research Council.

Its inquiry into the perils of life in the fast lane has shown that 40 per cent of overtaking by heavy goods vehicles poses the threat of an accident.

In contrast, the car driver overtakes unsafely far less than five per cent of the time, and the safest "burning up" of all is done by high-performance BMW, Porsche and Ferrari cars.

5,000 on film

Mr Don Harris, research assistant at the Cranfield Institute of tyechnology, where the inquiry is based, said the team had filmed more than 5,000 overtaking manoeuvres on A-class roads in Oxfordshire and Bedfordshire.

"Lorry drivers were definitely much less safe on overtaking." he said. "Dangerous overtaking tends to take place at the lower speeds, between 30 and 40 miles an hour. There is a build-up of frustration at that speed."

He added that the psychology of overtaking sometimes showed irrational thinking. For example, drivers seeing a bend ahead in the road would tend to overtake, whereas they should hold back if they saw an approaching vehicle at the same distance, although both presented equally dangerous possibilities.

On very slender and unsubstantiated evidence the *Telegraph* felt justified in dubbing British truck drivers *'a major motoring menace'* and saying they had been *'spotlighted'* by a Government-backed organisation. To rub salt in the wound they say the lorry driver was *'once respected as one of the safest of road users'* — the only purpose of that phrase is to endorse and justify by sneer and implication the *bad* information contained in the rest of that outrageous introductory sentence. Who are they to judge the standard and quality of the nation's highly tested and qualified lorry drivers? And the SAFE haulage industry?

Perhaps the answer is to say: 'The *Daily Telegraph* — once respected as one of the safest and most accurate of newspapers — has branded itself as a major menace to the truth.' If any British lorry driver had driven his vehicle on the public highway in a comparable irresponsible manner as that in which 'responsible' *Daily Telegraph* journalists composed and published that story, he would have been put inside for five years.

The Freight Transport Association answered the *Telegraph*:

Dear Sir
"Lorry driver 'menace' in overtaking"
You were sold a pup! Your news item on Monday 7 July on overtaking unfairly criticised lorry driver behaviour. It would seem that, in common with many other journalists, your reporters followed and enhanced a Press Association story which itself was incomplete...

Three-quarters of the lorry overtaking manoeuvres which were "judged" to be potentially dangerous were on the same stretch of road. Indeed, all these manoeuvres were "judged" to be potentially dangerous because the lorries in question drove over all or part of a white painted ghost island in the centre of the road. This island was painted on the road to create a third lane for right turning traffic where the road had been locally widened for that purpose. It represented possibly the only opportunity for a slow moving vehicle to overtake.
Richard K Turner
Director of Planning & Information

Don Harris and his associates also issued a statement setting the matter right: —

In a statement to the press, the study's authors wrote, "The reports published in the national newspapers and also in one of the television interviews ... were subject to questionable editing. It was felt that in all the above cases the results were presented in an unbalanced manner which highlighted the overtaking behaviour of heavy goods vehicle drivers while ignoring the potentially greater danger of the overtaking behaviour of car drivers."

That got very little show in the national press.

IT'S BIZARRE

Something to chew on

Kindness comes in many comforting ways: a visiting driver at a site where Mr **Bickley**, of Hednesford, also calls somehow managed to leave behind his false teeth... and somehow somebody on the site managed to find some Steradent in which to keep them until he returned. They keep the oddest things on sites. It couldn't have been in Birmingham, fans of Jasper Carrot will know that in Brum they use only bleach to keep their plastic choppers gleaming.

ONLY FOOLS
— AND OWNER DRIVERS

Trucking gets into the blood because it isn't just a job, it is a life style; if it is only a job, you are best out of it because it will break your spirit and your heart. The Americans call it 'white line fever' and Mel Haggard sings evocatively that 'I'll die with this fever in my soul.' Fevers, of course, produce hallucinations. And an ever-recurring dream for many drivers is: 'My own truck, my own business, my own boss and my own life.'

It is a good dream, an honourable and commendable one — but life isn't quite like that. Of all drivers who set up in business on their own accounts, nearly one third go out of business in the first six months. And after that the death rate makes betting on horses look like a secure profession.

Yet the whole industry is comprised of 'little men' and 'little companies' with fleets of five or under. Though it does begin to look as if the actual owner-driver, the one-man band, is in decline. Nevertheless, owning your own rig is a splendid ambition and a lot of people can and do make it work. But before you take the plunge do first look at facts and the black side of the business.

And those are that by any standards it is a cut-throat game, the rates are too low and the costs are too high.

Next comes the fact that there are too many trucks chasing too few cargoes. You could say that there are too many trucks, full stop. All the newspapers are full of stories about 'over capacity' in the truck-manufacturing industry, which simply means that they are making more trucks than they can sell. So the skids are under giant, multi-billion industries. If you do decide to go it alone it is no use thinking that the problems of Leyland, General Motors, the British, French and Italian governments and all are nothing to do with you, because they are directly related to you and your chances of surviving. When the market is as jam-packed and overcrowded as the haulage industry is, then it is a devil of a job to get a fair and decent return for your labours. In Britain we seem to have reached the not unfamiliar situation that we have an apparently thriving, even booming, industry yet few people are making any money, and a lot more are going skint.

'I know you love that damned truck much more that you love me... but I never expected it would go that far!'

What would worry me if I were about to put a truck on the road is the fact that I know of a number of big companies with immense backing who are in serious trouble: by that I mean not making any money, and not just cutting corners to break even, but chopping off an arm and a leg to stay solvent.

Face it, the rates are too low. You are not going to make a fortune and you are hardly going to make a living on 59p to 65p a mile. True, the rates are much the same on the Continent, where things are supposed to be infinitely better — for instance, in Belgium the official rate is 65p — but they pay nowhere near the taxes you would have to pay and their diesel is under £1 a gallon (converted price). On top of that they have the facilities, the roads, the systems and the co-operation of industry.

Bad Payers

What breaks most people in Britain is getting the money in. In 1985 I watched a friend go bust. He was an exceptionally good, experienced driver who had decided to expand (isn't that what the government wants everybody to try to do?) In a few weeks he was moving eleven trailers a day from his yard, the place was humming, his phones rang and his telex clattered non-stop, they were queueing at his gates. In six months he went broke for £41,800 *because he couldn't get the money in.*

The plague of the little man's life; bad payers, late payers, slow payers and big companies, mighty conglomerates with great City names, who put you at the very end of the list when it comes to settling up. Ruefully, drivers will tell you: 'The bigger they are, the worse they are.'

Even the Confederation of British Industry knows about it; they set up a working committee to examine means of dealing with the problem and they were sympathetic. Talk doesn't put cash in the bank. But a fat lot of good it has done.

A parliamentary Bill was proposed to allow those who wait excessively long for the ghost to walk to charge interest on the amount due to them. Reading this well-intentioned item to a group of drivers unfortunately caused a hollow laugh and the comment from a Birmingham driver with problems: 'We all know the geezer at x, the one who is the world's biggest expert at losing things in his computer. Let's give him a bell and say, "Right, x, boy, from now on we're going to slap 10 per cent on the bill for every day you're late paying out — then we'll sit back and wait *another* three months while he reprocesses the bill with the extra 10 per cent on it — honestly, the people who think up these ideas are out of touch with reality.'

IT'S BIZARRE

Digging for gold
Colin Waters, a 37-year-old con-man from Kingston, Surrey, set up a bogus construction company, hired a gang of workmen from a Job Centre, stole a digger and dug up a stretch of the M6 in Staffordshire. He was trying to convince a bank manager that he had a £1 million contract for drainage work on the motorway. The police found one hole too many on that particular stretch of road. And Mr Waters found himself in the Old Bailey where he was jailed for 4½ years.

The long wait
The saddest thing for a person just starting out is that the valued customer is often the greatest enemy. But that, they will tell you, is business. An experienced driver will know the score first hand, he will have seen it with his own eyes and experienced it sitting on his own backside waiting. Waiting to load, waiting to tip, waiting to clear customs, waiting for papers, waiting for warehouse space — 'waiting, waiting, always bloody well waiting.' It is infuriating enough while you are waiting at somebody else's expense, it can be disaster when you are waiting at your own.

The way it appears to a driver is that he reads glowing accounts of the brilliance of people running and taking over giant concerns; he reads about the 'skills' the 'expertise' the 'get-up-and-go' of the entrepreneurs; he sees on his television the glitter of the advertising, he knows all about the dazzle in the high street up front. But he also knows that at the back door it is diabolical.

Like **Gary Ambler**, of Salford, he may plead: 'God save us from the Little Hitlers at back doors of supermarkets we deliver to, and all the aggro!' But he knows that the power of prayer takes a long, long time to percolate to a tally-clerk's heart — especially if it is his tea-break.

To go it on your own needs a lot of thought — and a lot of money. And both those factors mean time.

The better side of the coin.

For the time being, forget the enormous cost of buying a rig, even a second-hand one, and think only that you will have to tax, insure and diesel it for at least three months before you are likely to see a penny back. Meanwhile you are still paying for your rig and the interest on money you may have borrowed, and keeping yourself.

Pessimism and faintheartedness never got anybody anywhere, but neither did foolhardiness and bravado. Some do succeed, quite a number, in fact, but still nowhere near the number who fail: facts, looked at coldly and analytically, temper optimistic pipe-dreams. It isn't much use saying: 'I'll be working for myself, I'll really graft, I'm willing to work all hours God sends,' because that is impossible. If you cannot make it work in 45 hours a week, you are not going to make it work at all.

For a positive view it is best to look at success and listen to those who have made it work, like the **Edmondses**, of Ashill, Thetford, Norfolk.

Class 1 HGV driver Mrs Philippa Edmonds, who speaks for the company, is blunt about the prospects. She says: 'From the beginning it is three months before you get any money in, five years before you get a foothold and ten years before you accumulate sufficient equipment to be viable enough that if one customer goes bankrupt you don't go down with him.'

In her own words let her tell how Edmonds International got going. She explained:

'The company is owned by my husband, Graham, and myself and both of us hold class 1 HGV licences. We operate from a small mid-Norfolk village, Ashill. At present we run four 38-tonnes units

IT'S BIZARRE

Under police protection

They gave **Mick Collins**, of Watford, a police escort to drive a wide load through a busy town. He had a police motor-cyclist advertising in front and a police-car advertising behind. There was a hold-up in the town centre. 'Pull over and park by the roadside,' the police advised him, 'we'll have a cup of tea and a bite to eat in the café and wait until they've sorted it out.' Mick's load took up four parking meter spaces, the motor-cycle a fifth and the car a sixth. 'I hope I don't pick up a parking fine,' Mick laughed. 'Don't be stupid,' snapped the policeman, tartly. Mick came out and found a bundle of little plastic packets jammed under his wipers and a meter-maid sauntering away down the street. 'Silly bitch,' fumed the policeman and ripped up the tickets.

and refrigerated trailers, which includes one owner-driver on permanent contract.

'Graham began work as a mechanic before he started driving lorries and I had a banking and commercial background.

'In 1975, a driver friend asked Graham to join him as a partner in a haulage business with each of them operating one truck. We agreed but insisted on finding work first. That was when I got the nickname 'The Chancellor' which I still have. We applied for a contract hauling paper from the docks and got it. Then the friend backed out but we went on. This meant we had to borrow £1,300 from the bank, with which we bought a 1969 Scammel Handyman unit for £850, paid for three-months tax and put a deposit on a flat trailer. And we applied for an 'O' licence.'

That is the way that nearly everybody begins, but there were three important qualifying factors in the Edmondses' case which, in my personal selection of priorities, should be placed in this priority:

1   Philippa had banking and commercial experience.
2   Graham was a fully qualified mechanic.
3   They obtained work before they bought a truck.

So the latter point was clearly because of Philippa's training — why else would they call her 'The Chancellor'?

Even so, the going wasn't easy and it still isn't. Philippa continues:

'Graham started work and I began to look for back-loads — I didn't believe in running back empty even in those days. Later in the year the engine blew.'

A blown engine means time off the road and money for repairs. Time off the road means no earnings and no profits, and all the time the bank loan is running up interest charges and the HP has to be paid. But, of course, Graham was a mechanic...

'We repaired the Scammel but decided that it was time it had to go. We had tidied it up a lot and sprayed it so we managed a very good deal, we sold it for £1,500 in part-exchange for an Atkinson Borderer, which we thought was real luxury stuff.

'We built a home-made sleeper on the back and again resprayed the whole rig which meant that later we were able to sell that too at a profit against a Volvo FB88.

'In the meantime I had started to drive and took my class 1 test and passed. Gradually I did more and more driving. By this time we had tried our hand at tilt work and begun to do odd loads to near Europe. We were working so hard that Caroline, our youngest daughter, was only five weeks old when she took her first Continental trip — she slept on the dash of the Aki when I was driving.

'Then in 1979, four years after we had started, we really lashed out — and it nearly broke us. We brought our first *new* tractor unit, a Bedford TM 3800; the fuel it used was ridiculous and it was never out of the garage. It was under warranty but off the road! After 21 months, when it was nearly out of warranty, we part-exchanged it for a new ERF.

'That was when it was a really hard struggle. Road haulage was going through a terrible time and looking round for new prospects, we decided to try our hand at reefer work — we looked at it from several aspects, no more ropes and sheets, no more tilts to strip — wonderful.'

It is worth an interruption at this point just to stress the fact that by now they were four years and a quarter of a million miles and more down the road and still struggling. And in their case a struggle shared was a struggle halved. There had to be some good luck and it came six months after they bought an old Silverdale Fridge, as Philippa recounts:

'After those short six months learning with the fridge we were offered a contract doing Continental work...'

Success — so the breaks do come for those who keep trying. But behind Philippa's rightfully proud claim 'after only six months' there lies another story; to be offered a contract you will have to have shown yourself to be good, reliable, efficient, conscientious and available — all that guff which isn't guff when it comes to getting and keeping work.

Then when you think you've got it just about made, as fast as luck comes it can fly out of the window again.

'In March, 1981, an Italian decided to drive on the wrong side of the road...

'*BANG!* Upside down, the unit a wreck, the trailer a complete write-off and me in hospital. The unit was only repaired — had to be repaired — because the insurance wouldn't have paid off the finance. We were off the road for eight weeks.'

That meant knocking on the bank manager's door again. 'Thanks to him and mums and dads and perseverance we survived. Five years later we are still waiting for compensation from the other side though liability was never disputed.'

IT'S BIZARRE

All is revealed

When **Mary Callaghan** took over the Welcome Inn at Trafford Park Truckstop, on live entertainment evenings, for variety, she introduced cabaret artists in place of some of the strippers 'the bottom fell out of the market.' Now the girls are back... and full-frontal.

Six Years on

Remember, they're now six years into the saga, still in hock and still borrowing to keep afloat. And remember also that there are two of them with a closer relationship than you will ever achieve with a partner or agent, and both with rather specialised skills.

By this time, of course, they have got the 'white line fever' and diesel in the bloodstream...

Today, eleven years on, the story is different:

'Only through giving reliable and conscientious service have we gradually picked up *good* work, working for producers rather than other transport companies. Companies have recommended us to each other until we now have the four 40-foot, 38-tonnes reefers. Two operate in the United Kingdom mainly on frozen vegetables, the other two run near-Europe mainly with chilled produce.

IT'S BIZARRE

Travelling with the bare necessities

There are desolate stretches on the A38 between Birmingham and Derby especially at three-thirty on a Saturday morning. At that time, in the middle of nowhere, **Richard Dembizky**, a Derby driver, saw a lonely figure walking towards Birmingham. It was a woman and she was stark naked.

'Now we buy second-hand, usually ex-rental, and Graham puts them through the workshop. We re-spray and sign-write them before putting them on the road. We do all our own servicing and breakdowns because garages are too expensive and also not too reliable.'

In that last paragraph there is a wealth of vital information for the prospective go-it-aloner and it can be summed up as self-sufficiency. Without it the chances are that you will be fighting a losing battle. The Edmondses, after eleven years, have established a position in which they can virtually control their own costs or, rather, keep their own costs under control in respect of those vital elements of buying and maintaining vehicles and, above all, keeping them on the road.

Just how much a problem that is can be judged by the fact that many huge, wealthy companies are closing down their fleet maintenance depots and contracting out because of the costs of running such an operation. You will hear a lot of talk that the closures were caused because the workshops became clogged by the amount of 'freebies' going through, like the managing director's wife's car getting its service 'on the firm' and the marketing director's second car being 'customised' while the fleet vehicles stood idle in the yard awaiting attention. Yes, there is an element of truth in that, a garage facility seems to be more tempting than an open till and its misuse less easily detectable (or possibly more easily concealed) than nicking the petty cash. Yet the fact remains that maintenance can be a cripplingly expensive business. And even with a new vehicle, as the Edmonds' Bedford experience fully illustrates.

Naturally, being the sharp character you are, you will immediately have seen the great opportunity opened up for the little man by the big firms moving over to contracting out; it is true that as fast as one door closes, another one opens up. So let us seize opportunity while it is there and take the positive view again. Let us imagine you have your own rig, in perfect nick and running as smoothly and sweetly as a pint of draught Guinness going down after a ten-hour day. You have found a site to operate from and the neighbours have welcomed you with open arms; the local planning officer thinks you are Mr Wonderful and admires your enterprise; you are 'boss' and captain of your own fate, and life is Good with a capital G. Just how good, let Philippa Edmonds tell us:

'Running the trucks is a 24-hour-a-day job for seven days a week. The phone never stops. In our case mostly with orders, for which I'm not complaining. But each ring could, and often does, mean a problem — the load isn't ready, the agent booked the wrong boat, the lorry is delayed and there is no way it can get back in time to pick up the next load it is committed for... if you cannot cope, you lose the job.

IT'S THE WAY YOU TELL'EM

Brain teaser

Two Irishmen applied for jobs driving tippers for Wimpeys and were asked to take a simple reading and writing test. The first one's questionnaire asked: 'Who killed Cock Robin?' The second one's wanted to know what two and two made. The second one asked: 'Hey, Pat, what's two and two?' And Pat snapped: 'Don't mither me, Sean, oi'm on a moider case.'   **Roy Hudson**, *Sale, Cheshire.*

'We don't consider 5.00 a.m. an early start and our drivers don't finish at 2.00 p.m. either. They tend to be at the bottom of the line wherever they go. They may not have to 'hand-ball' much, but the paperwork, the frustration of waiting and then trying to meet booking times and so on is something else... and food doesn't come too regularly either. Canteens range from good to indescribable, and usually they close just as you get there.'

Creature Comforts

That is not just tough talk, it is plain fact. That is the way the business works and if somebody else has been doing the worrying for you, then you should think carefully about it now that you are driving your own outfit and paying the bills. It is a hard life and it can be a miserable one unless you arrange your own comforts. These are not, in fact, luxuries, they are essentials to make life tolerable. The Edmondses know that:

'We are proud of our fleet. All our vehicles, including the owner-driver's one, are in our fleet colours. They are sprayed regularly; the interiors are carpeted throughout and fitted with night-heaters, televisions, radio-cassettes, CBs, cooling fans, extra storage for personal goods and air-horns. Done out like this, the drivers have something to be proud of and they look after them. Each driver has his name on the door and each truck has its own name, each beginning with the name of our village — Ashill Wanderer, Ashill Explorer, Ashill Viking and Ashill Voyager.'

Some transport managers — many, alas, most transport managers if drivers' observations are to be believed — would curl up at the thought of such frivolities. Think how reluctant they have been — and still are, to fit night-heaters, and think how bitterly the unions have opposed sleeper-cabs. Yet all the time company offices become plusher and more ornate with the purpose of improving the working environment. The cab is the drivers' working environment and the Edmonds' philosophy is that they do a better job in a civilised setting. But, of course, both Graham and Philippa Edmonds often climb into their own cabs and do the job they ask and expect others to do, so they know all about it. They know also that a driver's day doesn't run to office hours. That cab is not only a working environment, it is a home as well.

All this is very important to you in your new-found independence with your own truck and new responsibilities; we are actually talking about your standard of living and will it be better or worse than when you were an employee. Or in the cold truth of the 1980s, would you actually be better off on the dole?

By pure chance, through a meeting at Truckfest, I picked on a very enlightened small company to look at in detail. And, as it happens, that wasn't a bad thing to do. The industry could do with some enlightenment and might benefit generally by adopting the Edmonds International viewpoint:

'We have four very conscientious drivers who love their vehicles and wear the firm's jumpers with pride. They are ambassadors for us and we like to think of them as partners. They do their jobs well and we like to look after them.'

Now that you have achieved the impossible dream and are sitting proudly in your cab viewing the rolling road to riches through your own sheet of Triplex glass, your worries are just beginning. 'You are just trying to do your job, and every bugger in the world seems suddenly against you. They go out of their way to make it difficult if not impossible for you,' bemoans **Black Label**, from his Essex hideaway, 'I did everything right and couldn't make it work. Mind you, it isn't always the customer, or the law, or the public who make things bad; I employed some casual drivers and, believe me, there are some right Charlies among 'em, some proper lunatics and idle bastards. I've been on the road for more than twenty years and I've met 'em.'

Well, that is another fact — and we've all met 'em. It is no use pretending that they are not around busily working at getting a bad name for the rest, they are.

Brushing up the image

When it comes to the nitty-gritty of making a living from your truck — costs, machinery, loads, back-loads and time apart — much depends on public relations, public acceptance and goodwill. Put at its plainest, you will never be able to make it work without goodwill. Goodwill is like having a decent and happy home life, without it, life can become a drag. Graham and Philippa Edmonds took goodwill very seriously, coupled with reputation, and they set about gaining it in the most positive manner possible (I did say I would accentuate the positive).

There was a purpose behind naming the four trucks after the village as Philippa explains:

'We have taken great pains not to upset our lovely villagers and most of them are very proud of their Ashill trucks. We are smart and we try to be considerate and make the trucks a part of village life. We loan trailers for fêtes and we allow our yard to be used for various purposes. For instance, this week the St. John's Cadets, eight- and nine-year-olds, are coming to wash a lorry to earn themselves a badge. After that they will be holding a sponsored car-wash at the yard. We have had pupils from the local special school over to see one of the lorries. They were thrilled when the driver showed them over it and let them blow the air-horn.'

There is nothing so special about doing that, except the fact that it *is* done and it makes friends. In effect it is simple good-neighbourliness and not all that much trouble — and everybody concerned benefits from it, kids, neighbours and operators alike. It should not be necessary to mention it at all except that the public image of lorries and road haulage is so bad and if you, as a self-employed owner-driver, are working from the basis of a bad image, you are scoring own-goals from the outset.

Now listen to Philippa Edmonds talk about the *work*:

'Reefer work is very specialised and even within it there are distinct categories. There are chilled and frozen vegetables, meat and fish — boxed, bulk and hanging. So mostly you specialise — if you do vegetables, you need pallets, but you must not have pallets for hanging meat.'

Somebody reading this book will say testily: 'Everybody knows that.' So everybody should, but it doesn't stop people going into the business — not just the reefer business — with only a part of the basic gear necessary. It happens all the time.

The voice of experience has the final word:

'The equipment for reefer work is very expensive. A new unit and fridge will easily set you back £70,000 without tax or insurance, for which special cover is needed. The work needs a special degree of skill and care because so many things can go wrong. The produce is often still in the ground when the haulage is ordered. But that means if you provide a good, reliable service customers come to you.

'From a business point of view, temperature controlled work is a vast and growing industry. Today most people have freezers and expect most produce to be available all year round — and we provide just that.'

IT'S BIZARRE

Hunted

The driver of a private car motoring over Shap on the M6 to Penrith, looked in his mirror and saw a truck chasing him. He put his foot down but he couldn't shake off the pursuer which hung on his tail flashing its headlights and blasting its horn. He went faster, still the truck pursued. For eight miles the crazy chase went on with the truck horn blaring and headlights blazing. The motorist was convinced he had a madman on his boot. Truck driver **Frank Baker**, a St. Helen's, Liverpool, man explained: 'I was only trying to tell him his roof-rack and four cases had fallen off back down the road.'

So pay attention to that, 'reliable service'. Philippa is entitled to her little lecture. I mean, she isn't called 'The Chancellor' for nothing. And people talking good sense do seem, at times, to be preaching just a bit. Yet it is necessary to lay down the law at times and to state the obvious if only because people can be carried away by dreams and the wakening comes too late. There is no point setting yourself up to carry goods in a shrinking industry — and there are plenty of those about. It is only common sense to look for expanding industries where the work is and will be for the foreseeable future.

The lady has one more thing to say as she carries the banner into battle:

'If only the public could be better informed, they wouldn't resent lorries so much. Unfortunately the sheer size of lorries frightens people even though lorries are safer now than they have ever been. And a few drivers, often local trucks on bonus work, give us all a bad name.

Call to Arms

'Events like Truckfest give lorry drivers a status. If you make them proud of their vehicles they will stand tall — they are still "Knights of the Road".'

How's that for a clarion call to arms?

In truth, Philippa is as good an advertisement as you will find for trucks and their safety: if a sylph-like slip of a girl like that can handle a 38-tonner with consummate ease, what can be so terrifying about them?

78

In the end you will go your own way and do what best pleases you. And nobody should stop you. But always bear in mind the three salient points:

1   The rates are too low.
2   The taxes are too high.
3   And it's a tough life on your own.

IT'S BIZARRE

Distilled water

Sal Chester, of Leeds, spotted the overheated car on the hard-shoulder with its bonnet up and steam pouring out. The driver was standing on his bumper peeing into his radiator.

That was to be the end of this chapter, but this is a moving, changing game. It is seldom the same for two days running. A book was published. A dull, dry and boring book you should be thankful you didn't have to read, full of facts, statistics and figures. It was *The Transport of Goods by Road in GB, 1985*, from the Department of Environment and Transport, £8.00.

Out of those dusty figures came some fascinating and enlightening facts which could be of great use to an enterprising person determined to be independent.

The statistics revealed that freight moved by heavy lorries increased by 2½ per cent between 1984 and 1985 and reached a total of 1,400,000,000 tonnes — that is nearly 1½ billion tonnes. So it is a massive market, which we all know already, and it is continuing to grow, which none of us could be sure about with all the fleets being dispersed and drivers laid off.

What was confirmed was the swing to the use of haulage contractors rather than own-account fleets and more of the work was done by 38-tonne vehicles.

The intriguing part of the statistics showed that the number of five-axle 38-tonne vehicles rose from 19,000 in 1984 to 26,000 in 1985. Though this is only 6 per cent of the HGVs on the road they accounted for more than a quarter of the tonnage moved. That is indeed food for thought for anybody set upon going it alone.

And that, as they say, is some business. Business to the extent that, if the Ministry figures are anywhere near correct, each of those five-axled trucks shifted 13,400 tonnes a year. What seems to confirm those figures is that the five-axled trucks were recorded as travelling an average of 50,000 miles a year compared with an average of 23,000 miles for all HGVs.

Figures are figures are figures — but they can't all be liars. The indication is that the market is strongest for the big boys on the road. With a work load like that — even though it is based on averages — you will not starve. And you might even grow moderately well-off.

SOCIALISING

Attitudes change, and sometimes change for the better. And many of you will say: 'Not before time.' Essentially it is part of the general improvement in conditions for drivers — all right, it isn't all that it should be, but things are getting better — like the thought given to drivers' comfort in new truck cabs, and drivers' safety, and even drivers' convenience. A start has got to be made somewhere and it is beginning to show in the social aspects of the trade.

TRUCKFEST
That remarkable event Truckfest showed the way. What it demonstrated most of all was that up to 100,000 trucking folk have sufficient interest, even fascination, in the job to take time out from their own leisure time, travel from all over the country with their families, congregate at Peterborough and, for two days, revel in a festival of trucking and everything associated with it. The beer flows, the bands play — Country and Western — the fun comes thick and fast, like the mud on a couple of occasions (but nobody minded), celebrities perform their strong-arm stunts or chat-show skills; there are old trucks, new trucks, stunt trucks, special trucks, custom trucks with enthusiasts for each category, and the trucking fraternity with its hair down for once shows a smiling collective face to the watching world.

In a word, success.

But what hard-won success. It didn't come easily, nobody leapt from the bath shouting, 'eureka'. Nobody even said: 'What a great idea.' Conversely, they nearly all said: 'Oh, it just won't work. And they were still saying 'it just won't work' right up until 8.30 on cold, snowy Eastertide morning at the Newark and Notts Showground where the 'pilot' event was held. Then suddenly they discovered queues of cars waiting to get into the showground. At that time even the gate people hadn't arrived and the traffic queues were building up.

Boggle-eyed, the doubters muttered under their breath: 'By god, it is working.' And that was heart-surge and palpitation time for Colin Ward. Altogether 30,000 people turned up and Colin Ward's reasoning, intuition and faith had been justified.

It all began with Colin, or rather with his elder brother, Derek, who is a class 1 HGV driver working permanent nights delivering

'Go on, eat it — that's what you get when you ask an Arab driver for an eyeball on CB.'

vegetables to all major markets and a dyed-in-the-diesel truck fanatic. Together they were watching the Eurovision Song Contest on television. It may have been the music, or Katie Boyle, or Terry Wogan, or Buck's Fizz or what-the-hell but brother Derek was more intent on his truck books than listening to 'Le Rois Uni deux pointes... United Kingdom, two points...' when suddenly he burst out: 'You know, there's absolutely nothing for the truck driver in England.'

Now, that is a bit of a show-stopper when the top Yugoslavian rock-band is beating itself into a frenzy in pursuit of pop-glory and Colin was suitably stopped in his tracks. So he too turned his attention to the truck magazines and publications, and his list of events and festivals which, as a show, exhibition and Country and Western concert promoter, he had to hand.

He found to hand Go-kart racing, horse shows, motor-cycle racing shows, steam-engine rallies and rabbit and cage-bird shows but nothing remotely connected with truckers and trucking.

81

So he said, as you would: 'You're absolutely right, Derek.'

Colin is a director of the Spalding-based small company Live Promotions and they had been into shows and concerts with motoring or Country and Western flavour for fifteen years. After that time they thought they could spot a winner when they saw one. Enthusiastically they set about planning a trucking project.

Alas,they found that they were out on their own.Nobody wanted to know and the chant set up like an incantation: 'It just won't work, forget it.'

Colin and his partner, George Slinger, had organised one successful big motoring event for Austin Rover, a giant Summer Spectacular at Donnington Park. So they knew how to put the thing together, if only they could get the support.

Colin recalls: 'We were rejected time and time again by many manufacturers and dealers always with the chant, 'It won't work. Get lost.'

Actually, it was a time of great change in the trucking business, greater change than many of those then powers-that-be appreciated; little did they know that they themselves were in the process of 'getting lost' for ever and a day. The industry was in a state of turmoil and sliding into what a Volvo top executive described to me as 'the most desperate trough the industry has ever experienced'.

The above observation is not as much of a digression from the story as you may think because what happened with Truckfest was all the more remarkable for it.

Opposition crushes some people and galvanises others; Colin Ward and George Slinger were the second type, they pressed on.

Colin Ward explains: 'I thought it was ironic that if a haulage company was buying a new truck a dealer would provide them with a demonstrator. In turn the demonstrator would be given to a company driver to 'test drive' and his comments would often be vital in deciding whether or not to buy. A few people began to sit up when I made this point.

'By this time we were so determined that we went ahead and planned the "pilot" event at Newark and Notts. Then a Mercedes dealership decided to give us trade support and a number of suppliers, including Bandag Tyres, came in. Once you get one, the floodgates open and others rush to join. Over 100 trucks decided to attend, and that in itself was a record...'

IT'S BIZARRE

High speed funeral march

Motoring fast up the motorway, **Gordon Milne**, was surprised to be overtaken by a funeral cortége. And to prove that they get 'em under double-quick nowadays, Mr **J. Lynes** was overtaken by a laden hearse while travelling at speed. (R.I.P. − rushed into paradise pedal to metal?)

So they stood, cold, shivering and stamping their feet in the snow to keep warm and full of doubt on that windswept site that freezing Eastertide morning. Then they looked over the gate, saw the queues — and suddenly it was springtime.

Like spring in Park Lane, spring in Newark and Notts can be wonderful — but it means bloody hard work. Everything begins growing faster than you can cope with it and if you turn your back for a minute, you are up to your knees in weeds.

The Ocean Cory managing director of Bandag Tyres, Antony Palmer, was one of the then new faces in trucking, his company having taken over the Bandag franchise. He liked the idea of a festival and he listened as Colin Ward talked about it. He explains: 'I thought, here's a man who is going to make this work, we'll back it.'

Naturally, Bandag, Mercedes, Volvo, British Leyland — or anybody in this tough old business of trucking — do not do things just for the fun of it or for love. They quite properly expect a return. But that isn't all there is to it by any means: Truckfest means that drivers matter.

The surprise is that the whole Truckfest shooting-match is run from an old, converted pub, The Millstone. It must have been a good pub in its day, there is a lot of atmosphere about the place.

George Slinger, the co-impressario of this annual celebration of automotive high-tech, also has an unlikely background for such an enterprise. He was once the local 'crimper' and he tells with great jocularity that the hairdressing trade in Spalding was so thin that it was a struggle to find the rent, rates and electricity money every quarter. (If you look around carefully, there are a lot of bald-headed men in Spalding. It could be the flat 'ats they all seem to wear.)

So rather than sit around gathering dandruff, he began to promote shows and entertainments.

The transition worked marvellously well for George and Colin. They call the old pub offices 'the dream factory' and work becomes fun to the extent that George enjoys it so much that he is apt to say: 'Christ, it's Saturday,' when he wakens at the weekend and realises that the office is closed.

That, you will agree, would be an unlikely history for a major truck event yet still an encouraging one — where there is the will there is a way. And it led to that first cold Eastertide morning at Newark and Notts and a brilliant business success.

Seen from the other side of the fence — those people waiting in the cars outside the gates at Newark — Truckfest took on another aspect. They had no idea what to expect and they were rather suspicious. As **Dee Rayson** recalls:

'We thought it was sure to be another rip-off. But that first Truckfest was fantastic. That showground is an old airfield and the whole show really took off when they began racing trucks down the runway. But it became clear that it was for the lads and it turned out to be great fun.'

The funny thing about the trucking business is that it seems to have reached its liveliest peak of social activity for drivers during the biggest slump the industry as a whole has ever known. Think about it, you can really only talk of British Leyland in hushed tones, like having a sick relative in the room next door; and Volvo — mighty Volvo, market leaders as they proudly claim — writes in its brochure advising dealers how to set up its trade clubs, the Viking Clubs, 'We are all having a hard time.' And all that ever comes out of Bedfords at Luton is the threat of impending redundancies or closure: the danger is that it could have closed before I finish writing this page, let alone before it is printed. (And, of course, before I read the proofs, it was. And BL trucks was taken over by DAF.)

Yet still the clubs form and blossom — and add to the gaiety of life for drivers.

JOIN THE CLUB

First let us look at the 'professional' clubs, those which are unashamedly commercial and designed to promote their backers' interests and are run by advertising agencies with professional staffs to market products direct to the drivers.

T45 Team Club

The T45 Team Club is an unashamed commercial 'gimmick' or enterprise, whichever term you think fits best — but don't knock it for that. Certainly don't knock it on that account because it is a pretty good set-up which has proved that the idea can be bigger than the commercial motive and bring direct benefit to both sides of the counter.

To some people there is a stigma attached to being 'commercial' and it is hard to see why. If a major company does nothing for its customers, it is bitterly criticised for indifference; when it does do something, the knockers immediately yell 'commercial'. After all, we are all 'commercial' and this is a book for commercial drivers. The drivers I know are double quick to know when there is something in it for themselves and they jump at opportunities.

T45 came about because the Leyland name — rightly or wrongly — had a smell about it and the Leyland image was in tatters. Whose image wouldn't have been in tatters after the political and financial hammering poor old Leyland had taken over the years? So they set about trying to repair the damage the in-fighting had done and instead of spending their money on expensive advertising campaigns and glossy symbols they decided to put the money where it counted most and that, they decided, was where the drivers were.

That was in 1983 and the 'wind of change' I've mentioned was beginning to blow through the corridors of automotive industry

'Well, he might only have said he'd take us to a party at the truckers' club, but I couldn't hear him properly over the noise of the engine and I'm not taking any chances!'

power at gale force; five years earlier, if you had said, 'Spend some money to give the drivers a bit of fun and pleasure,' they would have put you in the car-crusher.

The difference between the Team 45 Club (also Shell Diesel Drivers' Club) and the ordinary private truckers' clubs is that they got in professionals to organise it and gave them the wherewithal to do a good job.

That is no slur on those other excellent clubs. All it indicates is a difference of scale and approach. Long live the private clubs, and may they thrive, and may this book help them. But the hon. secs. will tell you, like Dee Rayson says, they can be run ragged trying to organise events and do a job at the same time.

The truth of the matter is that drivers like clubs and flock to join them. So much so that the club officials can be overwhelmed.

The T45 Team people first of all set about seeking 'hostesses' and they interviewed dozens of girls. Kay McDowall got the job as Number one girl and soon she recruited a glamour assault squad. All the girls had to be something more than just a pretty face (and figures, and legs), they had to be able to entertain and make things tick at club meetings. The girls do not just join in the fun, they make it happen. And they also take a lot of stick while they are getting the party swinging — like Tracy Westwood who found herself on the receiving end of ten litres of lager at the end of the strong-arm beer-lifting contest at Truckfest '86 — she didn't drink it, they poured it over her.

So what is it all about?

This is what: they launched Team 45 Club at the Scottish Motor Show in November 1983, in three years membership has topped 14,000 and is still rising. The fact that they flocked to join shows that there was a need for such a club and a need for such social gatherings.

And with considerable foresight, Leyland, who put up the money, opened the membership to all drivers of all vehicles.

Sometimes the Leyland people refer to the club as an 'after sales service' which maybe is not the happiest of phrases in the context of what the club actually does — there is a touch of the showroom and workshop about it.

Yet it is true. Perhaps it is high time that drivers were given the same after sales service that their trucks receive.

IT'S THE WAY YOU TELL'EM

> ### Party games
> At the fancy dress party she was feathered and plumed and said she had come as a turkey. 'Great,' said the truck driver, 'I've come as sage and onion.'
> **Deerstalker**, *Bodorgan, Anglesey*.

Shell Diesel Drivers' Club

Of the other sponsored clubs, this carries top weight of all. And that weight comes to 53,000 members actively participating in the benefits the club offers.

The Shell club is different from all others, it comes free. In its construction the club is a curious hybrid between a straight commercial promotion and a service to drivers — and it is both of those things at the same time. It could even be that the latter point has overtaken the former in Shell's thinking because of the success the club has met with. There has been a pretty good response from drivers and the promotional benefits have proved worthwhile to them. Shell has been open and honest about its intentions and its aim to sell more diesel. Its application form says:

> When you stop to think how much you spend on diesel every week, it can add up to a staggering amount.

That makes the diesel driver a very important customer. But how many oil companies treat you like one?

Shell will.

Because when you fuel-up with Shell diesel, we'll give you a lot more than just a 'Thank you!'

Absolutely to the point, no messing about, no attempt to conceal the commercial motives; that offer is an inducement, a perk, a 'bribe' even. So what? It may as well go into the drivers' pockets rather than the transport manager's. The other point to consider is that the transport manager as such is a dying species, with big fleets declining and the work being contracted out. To oil companies that is an important thing, with more than 70 per cent of the industry in the hands of 'little men' and owner-drivers, that is where their market lies.

Just thank the good lord that they have eventually realised it and are beginning to look after you as well as they once looked after managers with the authority to buy.

So Shell now give you a wide range of discounts on quality goods, very good offers on a variety of services, holidays, events and entertainment. In effect what they are doing is offering you a tiny share in their immense buying power and, if you use Shell, you would be a fool not to take up the opportunity.

It is a club in the sense that you can only be a member if you are an HGV driver. So its benefits are yours alone.

The newsletter they send out is highly professionally produced with plenty of real information in it. And, naturally, they have a cracking hostess to head-up the operation — Liz Jefferson is very popular and always well spoken of by the lads.

One thing about these clubs is that many — most, even — members of Shell are also members of Team-45 Club and their own local truckers' club; it makes no difference, the more the merrier.

To join, pick up an application form at your garage or write to: Shell Diesel Drivers' Club, 99-101 Pedmore Road, Lye, Stourbridge, DY9 8DA.

IT'S THE WAY YOU TELL'EM

Overloaded

The driver had a brand-new Scania 142 which he drove all day and lavished so much attention on in his spare time, washing, polishing and tuning, that his live-in girl friend said: 'I'm leaving you, I can't stand it any more. You love that truck more than you love me,' Three months later, he missed her. He telephoned: 'There's nothing more I can do with the truck, why don't you come back?' She told him: 'I'd love to, but there's a problem — I'm pregnant.' Gallantly he said: 'In that case, give us a bell when you're tipped.'
Tarmac Junkie, *Basildon*.

The United Kingdom Truckers' Association

When drivers got together to form a club, the idea was entirely different. And drivers' clubs proliferated to the extent that they have now been able to form The United Kingdom Truckers' Association which may prove to be yet another turning point in the trucking scene — early days yet, but we will look at this a little later on.

A1 Truckers' Club

Meanwhile, the A1 Truckers' Club is a typical example of how a club began and grew, and grew — and damned nearly outgrew itself — and became more than a bit 'if-fy' in the process.

It all began to happen in the summer of 1981 when two regular CB breakers decided they would like an 'eyeball' with all the truckers who regularly use the A1 and talk to each other — included in this were the ladies who gave out traffic information over CB and also served up the grub at the roadside caravans.

The breakers were **George Swanson**, **Jack of Diamonds**, and **Gary**, second names are hard to come by in this informal club so he is **Bumble Bee**, and they were joined by **Super Lady**, who is June Crowther; **Lincolnshire Lass**, **Dee Rayson**, who drives a chemical tanker for Tankfreight, Newark; **Marmalade, Freda Sharpley**, who is also a trucker, and **Val**, **Body Warmer**, who used to have a mobile snack-bar on the north side of the A1 just south of Sawtry.

That gives you the feel of the club. They all met at the Royal Oak, in Castlegate, Newark, where the landlord, Jerry Carroll, is an ex-trucker. He quit the road in 1981 just about the time the club was forming.

June, Super Lady, runs the caravan snack bar in the lay-by between Markham Moor and Worksop (a pull-up which can have its moments when the tap-dancing and inpromptu cabaret begin) and she put up a notice asking if anybody was interested in a club.

Came that first 'eyeball' in the Royal Oak and they discovered that about 800 were very interested and they all seemed to be crowding into the bar at once.

Well, maybe it wasn't all 800 but the place was packed to overflowing. And it has been at pretty well every 'eyeball' since. Now the membership is between 1,800 and 2,000 and the problem is to find accommodation big enough to house all who want to attend 'eyeball' meetings.

It is a jam, and some people find it too much of a crush. But that is the penalty of success. Informal as the club is, they found it necessary to elect a committee to cope with the deluge of paperwork that flooded in. And a committee needs a chairman — so who better than Iron Horse, who is Bob Wilson in his trucker's working clothes. Then the problem was that Bob's trucking took him far and wide, as work took most other committee members. They also appointed a secretary, treasurer and a social secretary.

They all worked voluntarily and the club was organised on a strictly non-profit-making basis. The £1.00 membership fee went to pay entertainers and sandwiches for the social evenings and to finance sun-strips which members wanted.

A lot of the original ideas and intentions, alas, fell by the wayside simply because they were too difficult to set up. The idea was to have a designated pub in every major town where members would be particularly welcome and would meet other members there. But that could never be established.

Eventually June Crowther took over as chairperson because she was static, and Pauline Carroll took over as social secretary working from her pub. Yet still the membership grew — and grows — until it became nationwide and international.

Germans, Dutchmen and even Americans have joined. Which makes the problem all the more acute: how do you arrange to get a wandering membership together in one place at one time? The answer is that you don't: all you can do is to arrange 'eyeballs' every alternate Wednesday, with live entertainment once a month, and try to pack them all in when they come.

One good point about the club is that every truck driver, member or not, is invited to the 'eyeballs' if he or she is in the Newark area at the time.

To join apply either at the Royal Oak, Newark, at June's Country Kitchen in the lay-by, or at Captain Morgan's snack-bar near Sawtry.

Dee Rayson has had to opt out of her duties as treasurer and she, poor lass, is embroiled in a bitter fight with authority in her village of Stragglethorpe, Lincolnshire. They designated a nuclear waste dump 200 yards from her back door and she led the protest and stopped the Nirex men moving in in August 1986. There are not many quicker ways of having the value of your property slashed to rock bottom than finding a radiation tip at the bottom of your garden, albeit low-level radiation.

IT'S BIZARRE

Golden Delicious turn-down
There is more than a touch of *C'est la guerre* about Frenchman **Jaques Boeking**'s feeling towards our researcher interviewing him when he says: 'Tonight I have a beautiful blonde sitting at my table. I will ask her to come to France with me — she will say NO!' It's a long, lonely road to Berck-sur-mer.

The A1 Truckers' Club's success serves to prove the point that there is a need for such clubs and that truckers like a good night out with their own sort: the sponsored clubs are great, but the spontaneous clubs created by truckers themselves are a social phenomenom. There are said to be about sixty of them.

There is another point about the A1 Truckers' Club which may not be so favourable to its general ambience, and that is that it failed to do what it originally set out to do. It did not develop in quite the way envisaged and the running of it has gradually slipped out of active truckers' hands. Though when I spoke to them Pauline Carroll and Phil Smith — State Express — the new secretary, were both anxious that more drivers should be recruited to the committee.

The way it has worked out, the club revolves round the pub in Newark, and the Royal Oak isn't the most capacious of places when it comes to holding the 'eyeballs' — it gets too full for anybody's comfort. This tends to put off various members and the Carrolls are fully aware of it.

It is a good pub and ideally situated for the club's purposes, and it comes with a very good line of chat. Newark, of course, is an ancient town and this is the third oldest inn within the boundaries, dating from 1610 which is quite a pedigree.

IT'S THE WAY YOU TELL'EM

A perfect infusion

She slapped my face when I asked her: 'What goes in dry, comes out wet and gives terrific pleasure and satisfaction?' I was talking about a teabag.
Bobcat, *Macclesfield.*.

Drivers do it with the tacho ticking.
Gordon Milne, *Glamis, Forfar.*

The pub is very popular with drivers at all times and they walk across from the lorry park near the castle every night, as well as on the nights when functions are held. This goes back to the point made in our list of cafés, the companionship factor: it is a boon for drivers to be made welcome and meet their own sort in pleasant surroundings and a good atmosphere.

Yet I feel a trifle uneasy about the way the A1 club has developed. In all clubs there is a danger that the club itself becomes more important in the minds of the organisers than the members and the members are seen as a means to an end. In this case the club is good business for the Royal Oak and my trifling uneasiness stems from a suspicion that perhaps there is just a little too much pub and not quite enough club in the way this is being run.

Make no mistake, the Royal Oak and the Carrolls — Pauline principally — are doing a fine job for truckers and providing a unique service. But the question remains, is it essentially any different from the way the sponsored clubs are run, except in a matter of scale?

Don't be put off by this, but just remember that a club is a club, and a pub is a pub — if the two can meet and mix on equally beneficial terms, then that is fine.

It is all rather a pity. Great potential is there, but other truckers are rather derogatory about the A1; they call it the 'sun-strip club' because, they allege, that's all anybody ever gets out of being a member. That is a harsh judgement and a little unfair. Nevertheless it is food for thought for the committee and it shows that to be a proper truckers' club it is essential to have truckers running it for truckers. Certainly a publican's co-operation is a welcome boon, but a club should not be a simple adjunct to the licencee's trade.

There is more to a truckers' club than just a booze-up and a sun-strip; though both of those are vital parts, the latter if only to keep the dazzle out of your eyes the day after the former. Real truckers' clubs are a fraternity in which members do a lot for each other and for many others outside the fraternity. The money that truckers raise for charities would astonish a lot of people.

South West Truckers

Tony Taylor's club is a good example: the club was formed officially in 1982 but it had been running on an unofficial basis before then. It has had 1,500 members on the books since then — they come and go as people move on — and it keeps a steady 400 active members meeting regularly at various events. The monthly news letter (very lively) keeps everybody well informed of activities.

So what do they get up to? In summer they play cricket matches, though they seem to get flogged about a bit when they meet a real cricket team, according to the news letter; they pull trucks, go on trips, hold dances; they have painted the Springfield Home and dug its gardens, raised money for the Heart Foundation and put up a tough fight against authority to get the best possible treatment for a seriously injured driver colleague. They also stop to assist a fellow member broken down by the roadside. One such member, Blue Max, found that so many stopped to help him in his predicament that he couldn't remember all their names. Nevertheless, he was stuck for a full seven hours — but it's nice to have company and feel that the world hasn't forgotten you.

In short, they act like a club should do when the members matter as much as the club itself. There are other advantages too: an impressive list of discounts has been arranged for various goods and services throughout the West Country — it all helps.

But in case you think it is all sunshine, there is a shadow over the committee rooms. Some committee members have been subjected to abusive letters and obscene phone calls about their club activities; the attacks have been so offensive that a couple of good voluntary servants of the club have quit because of them. This is all recorded in the news letter: it's life, it happens — it is not pleasant and it is extraordinary that it should happen in so amicable an assembly. At worst it is annoying, at best it shows the club is alive and effective. But should such an incident be written about at all? Not to write about it would be dishonest and probably do a disservice to a cracking good, progressive organisation. Maybe it reflects the condition of the industry in general, there is one in a hundred whose disgusting behaviour has dragged down the reputations of the rest.

South West Truckers is a very good club and worthwhile.

Southern Truckers

Another club on the up-and-up, this was founded with five members by Pat Noyce in 1982. Now the membership has topped the hundred and Salisbury has a thriving truckers' community working for the local hospital and other charities as well as for members. The sheer social goodwill of the trucking fraternity is shown in these clubs, and it is quite contrary to the concept of truckers presented by the media. Tony Taylor commented: 'The press and other media need no help in degrading our members but are dumb when praise is needed.'

Southern Truckers is practical as well. They have a fund to help drivers who have accidents away from home, the money goes to the wife to help with travelling expenses and to keep the home going. It is not called on often, but it is there as a comforting reassurance should the need arise. So too is the £1,000 accidental death cover.

The whole working basis of this club is to find people who need money and set about raising funds for them; the members bring in suggestions and a spur of the moment event is arranged. It could be a lorry pull, skittles match, dance, disco, even a tramps' ball — so the local hospital children's intensive care unit has benefited, as have other charities and the wife of a driver who was injured in an accident near Birmingham. She was financed to travel daily to Birmingham to see her husband while still keeping the family going at home.

On the basis that one good turn deserves another, the Salisbury Hi-Flex Social Club gives a room free to the club for meetings, knowing that they are working for charity, and also provides a disco at functions. Sounds a nice city, Salisbury.

The secretary is Barry Ascough, 41 Woodside Road, Salisbury, Wiltshire, SP2 9EE, telephone (0722) 20484. And membership is £6.00 a year.

IT'S THE WAY YOU TELL 'EM

Blow by blow

A bar scrounger whispered: 'Can I tap you for a fiver?' And the burly truckers answered: 'Yes, if I can hit you first with a jack-handle for a tenner — cash up-front.'
Jade Warrior, *St Mary's, Southampton.*

A19 Truckers' club

A comparative newcomer on the club scene is the A19 Truckers' Club which secretary Ann Earrey tells me was formed in November, 1985, to 'give drivers somewhere to go if they were in the area'. Whether or not it was an omen, the club's first meeting place, the Wagon and Horses pub, closed down. So the club had to move to the County Arms, in Northallerton, where they meet every second Friday in the month and put on games nights, C & W and so on. A major social event is held every three or four months and those have been well received and successful.

The A19 attracted 50 members immediately and is still growing. It encourages HGV and PSV driver members as well as members from the public at a special rate: £1.50 for drivers, £3.00 the others.

They are in the process of spreading their wings by contacting all other clubs and extending their influence. To join you can write to Ann Earrey at 27, Linden Road, Northallerton, North Yorks., DL6 1HV, or telephone (0609) 5519 — or contact her on Channel 19, **Babycham**, or the chairman, **Coppertop**.

Spitfire Squadron Club

The Spitfire Squadron rides under its club sun-strip with pride. It was formed in pride and has stood proud ever since.

This Potteries club was formed by Harry Kelly on the simple basis that he was 'sick and tired of being treated like an underdog and the way people thought about truckers'.

The persistent drip, drip, drip of malice and criticism of lorry drivers and the haulage business had got to him like it has got to so many HGV drivers. It raises the question yet again of what role the critics play in 'protecting' the environment and the living conditions of the public.

Do they consider that 340,000 truckers, their families, their friends, their associates and employers are not actually a part of the environment? Do they think it a balanced and fair approach to stigmatise a whole section, a massive section, of the community in pursuit of their own particular objectives?

Abuse, calumny and downright slander, those were the factors which motivated Harry, almost in desperation, to collect a group of fellow drivers around him to show that they were 'ordinary, decent and caring human beings'.

It is a tragedy that the HGV men we all meet on the road should even have to think like that: it seems a very funny sort of 'caring' conservation that puts an army of conscientious workers into the category of lepers.

IT'S BIZARRE

The sting

On a trip to Stirling on a warm day, Bradford driver **Colin Roadnight**'s mate pulled into the services for his break and parked with his sun-roof partly open. He returned to his cab to find it had been taken over by a swarm of bees. Then he waited for 29 hours for the pest control officer. He kept a bag of dead bees to prove the story to his doubting boss.

The Spitfire Club got together specifically to do charitable work. They wanted a good, distinctive title and one with local associations. In Kidsgrove is the house where R.J. Mitchell was born, the Mitchell who designed the Spitfire aircraft and thus a man with a good claim to be a saviour of Britain.

But the club did not just appropriate the title. They enquired and discovered that the RAF has registered the title Spitfire Squadron so they applied for permission to use it explaining the purposes of the club.

'Great,' said the RAF, 'we like the idea and wish you luck with it. Providing you don't ever use it for disreputable purposes you are welcome to the name on your trucks. Keep the charity work going and success to you.'

In appreciation the club make an annual donation to the RAFA on top of the thousands they have raised for other charities in the five years they have existed.

That is how the Potteries men set about giving truckers a 'decent image'. And sixty of them still keep it up.

The club evolved out of chaos with the aim, Mr Kelly says: 'To use our spare time in the pursuit of enjoyment while raising money for local charities. So we have fancy-dress dances, tramps' suppers, fun runs, sponsored swims, in fact, any local function that can use our muscle and easy-going charm.'

One such function was to help marshall the **Spastic Games**.

'Our hopes are for a united transport industry with the respect that HGV drivers deserve. In fact, a return to being known as "Knights of the Road".'

Contact Mr H. Kelly, 22 Bennet Street, Middleport, Burslem, Stoke-on-Trent, Staffordshire, ST6 3LS.

Diesel City Truckers Club

Without embarrassment, I trust, you can say that big hearts play a big part in the truckers' clubs scene; what's wrong with having a big heart? Like most other clubs the Diesel City Truckers Club came about because of CB when Terry Hayter and Bill Toms decided they would like an eyeball in 1983. They organised a social get-together for truckers and their families and from that there evolved a 'small but adequate membership' which is committed to charity.

They have a philosophy: 'We take a lot out of life, so we should put a little back into it. And also give the trucking industry a better image while we are at it.'

The idea was to have fun at the same time as doing good for charity. Says chairman E.H. Southwell, Silver Dollar, 'We all work hard as truckers and we play hard as well.'

In the past the charity effort was directed at the cystic fibrosis appeal, but now it is concentrated on the Peterborough Hospital Special Baby Care Unit. 'We don't believe in giving money to big organisations where they can take out as much as 75 per cent for administrative costs,' explains chairman Silver Dollar.

There are sponsored bike rides, bed pushes — in full dress, Dennis Barret in a nappy, the wives in nightdresses and carrying dolls, and such events as a Pool Disco at the city lido. That last event involved some fully-clothed, unexpected swimming.

They are a boisterous, social crowd and all they ask is some dedication to the causes they support.

Super Stud, **Steve Preacher**, is the treasurer, **Mercedes Lady**, Eve Johnson, looks after entertainment, and the Charity Officer is Gringo, Dennis Barret. All enquiries, contact Tricia Southwell, 67 Victory Avenue, Whittlesey, Peterborough, telephone: (0733) 205478.

IT'S BIZARRE

You lose some, you win some...

The funniest thing **J. Benson**, of Lurgan, ever saw on a motorway was, he says: 'Two Bandag blow-outs on one side of a truck.' But **Dougie Vick**, of Cheltenham Spa, says: 'Any tyre problems and Mr John Buffin, of Bandag, Cheltenham, moves heaven and earth for Santa Fe — as for all his customers.'

East Coast Truckers' Club

If you like your clubs a little more flamboyant and with a more vivid, chequered history, look east. Look, for instance, at the cavalcade of trucks in line astern confounding the inhabitants and holidaymakers of Yarmouth on a sunny summer's Sunday afternoon; in convoy they drove through the town and along the prom where the mayor took the salute. This time they were 21-strong, next time they will be over a hundred.

This was the East Coast Truckers' Club '86 in action and showing that it can still do things in a big way when required. In 1981 the club adopted Repton House, a home for handicapped children in Norwich, and this event was their summer treat — a trip to the seaside and the pleasure gardens at Pleasurewood Hills.

The summer treat is in addition to the annual Christmas party, and this one produced some touching tributes like this one:

'A special thanks to you all for giving the handicapped children a smashing day out at Pleasurewood Hills. My eyes filled with tears on numerous occasions when I thought about the fun you gave all the kids, and my handicapped son.'

This is the 'cowboy' club come good — after quite a few bad times. They began as 'cowboys' and completely illegally. They set themselves up to beat the law. They tell you that openly, they're nothing if not honest, these East Coast lads.

Back in 1980 they were all on illegal AM CB and life with an illegal CB was becoming 'dodgy', secretary Bob Morriss explains, because the police were confiscating every set they discovered. The breakers on the network formed a CB club and started a fund to replace any member's set which was impounded. The idea was tremendously popular and 400 members joined instantaneously.

Forbidden fruit is always the sweeter, and when CB was made legal on FM arguments broke out in the club whether to go legal and use the FM channels or stay defiantly on the old system. When they decided to switch to FM many members left and the club strength slumped to about 60 — now it is going up again.

By this time the social side of the club had developed with discos, dances and barbecues, and a friendship was struck up with the South West Truckers' Club with an 'eyeball' arranged in Cheddar Gorge.

I did say they were honest. For the Cheddar Weekend, they left in a convoy of private cars. About 15 miles out of Norwich, in their eagerness to get to Somerset, three or four cars ran into the back of each other. 'Truckers should know better,' the secretary wryly comments.

They arrived at Cheddar with a few bent cars and red faces, but the night out in Bristol which followed was a rip-roaring and memorable success.

IT'S BIZARRE

Mobile home 1

Driver John McMallum of Ashford, Kent, has made trips to Bournemouth and Hull without harming a bird's nest with two eggs in it found under the tilt cab of his truck.

Other troubles followed. Too many non-HGV-driving members had been allowed in. Originally it was a condition of membership that you hold a current HGV licence and be vetted by the committee. But that rule had lapsed. Then it was suggested that wives should have a vote in the club's affairs. Bob Morriss says: 'Most of the clubs today wouldn't be around if it wasn't for the wives.' Yet, at that suggestion, more members left.

The crunch had come, and on the spot, they decided to close the club down. On the same spot, in the same room, at the same time they decided to begin the East Coast Truckers '86 Club.

Out of the ashes, phoenix-like, the new club has arisen. The monthly meeting place has been changed and slowly the club is building its strength and membership.

It is a salutary but encouraging tale. It does prove a point: when a truckers' club is run by and for truckers, it works; when outsiders become too involved, the trouble starts.

Somehow good seems to come out of troubles and in the middle of all its vicissitudes the club became involved with a really brilliant idea which won them a lot of publicity and friends, though that at the time was not sought. The charity Age Concern, in Norwich, decided it would be a good idea if lonely pensioners were equipped with CB radio to allow them to keep in contact with the outside world. At the first suggestion East Coast Truckers donated half a dozen sets and in no time at all a pensioners' network was running and in constant touch with truckers passing through the area. **Able Mable** went on the BBC radio to describe her friendships with truckers.

Now, in north Norfolk, there are a great number of old folk and disabled people safe in the knowledge that they have a direct contact with the outside world, which makes it difficult for muggers and con-men to get at them — and if illness strikes, they don't have to wait until a neighbour misses them.

Contact Bob Morriss, 121 Desmond Drive, Norwich, Norfolk, telephone (0836) 610515.

West Midlands Truckers' Club

This also has a strong CB connection that is developing. Stemming from about the same time, 1979, as East Coast Truckers, and formed for much the same reasons, it developed along slightly different, possibly more pragmatic, lines. 'Not many firms in the Midlands have a social club of any kind,' secretary Brian Maydew explained, 'but after attending one or two functions at those which do, a group of truckers decided to have one of their own.'

The proposal was to 'provide a social outlet for the trucker and his family, and give general information on the industry' and the first meeting was an instant success. There were calls for a second — and the club was on its way with dances, discos, beer and skittles, treasure hunts and Christmas parties.

Membership has run around the 100 figure and has been recruited usually by word of mouth. This was about the right number to be accommodated in the old headquarters in 'The Vic', Halesowen road, Warley; but clubs in pubs are a problem — like the A1 mentioned first in this section of the book — and in 1986 the club moved its headquarters to the Birchley Social Club, which is opposite the BRS lorry park at junction 2 on the M5. With no disrespect to 'The Vic' pub, the new place offers a lot more facilites for members and allows for expansion.

Naturally, everybody looks for something different from a club, what suits one doesn't suit another. In East Coast Truckers when anything like lectures or discussions were suggested, the response of some members was: 'Hell, no. I want to get away from work. I want to forget it and I don't want to talk shop.'

In the West Midlands they asked the Freight Transport and Road Haulage associations to talk at meetings, together with the Department of Transport, local police and truck manufacturers' representatives. They were all very popular.

IT'S THE WAY YOU TELL 'EM

Blow up

The driver was fiddling his air-line to fix a tyre when the stroppy policeman asked: 'Have you got a foot-pump?' Sympathetically the driver enquired: 'Why, have you got flat feet?'

R. Sudale, *Louth, Lincolnshire.*

Also popular was the 'Driver of the Year' title competition. This was no walk-over. Held at the West Midlands Training Group grounds, at Dudley, Henry Clark, a director of the training group, set the tests and they were very exacting: reversing an artic, to an L-shaped position and stopping dead on the mark; driving a double-decker bus through an intricate series of cones and then reversing it back to where it began sounds easier to do than it is; there was also a motor-cycle test and some members had never ridden a bike — exit Exador biting the dust cowboy-style.

The club succeeds in generating public interest. It has been televised on Central TV's 'Newshound' programme, broadcast on West Midlands Radio, and made a lot of headlines in the local paper with its driving contest and children's Christmas parties — which was part of the original idea.

Now it is coming to national prominence through CB — at long last somebody is getting CB organised as a predominantly useful driving and safety aid. A National Monitoring Control Steering Committee was set up in 1986 and club secretary Brian Maydew became a member, he became chairman in fact.

The Committee had a fair amount of elbow with representatives of the Central Office of Information. Department of Transport, ROSPA, the RHA and the Radio Investigation Service in attendance.

Clearly, CB is a powerful system of monitoring road conditions; I have already pointed it out as an HGV driver's 'secret weapon', a powerful tool for his own advantage and protection. It has taken a long time for 'them' — the powers that be — to realise its potential for good.

Because of the limited range of CB radio, the idea was to set up a series of monitoring and relay points so the CB networks could be fully informed about traffic conditions over a very wide area and forewarn drivers of conditions way up the road and out of their immediate range. The advantages of this are self-evident, it could save hours of untold aggravation, and it could keep the traffic moving.

There was a problem however. CB operators like to remain anonymous and don't care to reveal their identities — after all, that is part of the fun. You need a breaker to know a breaker and to be able to talk to one. Yet even for a top CB man like Brian it took a fortnight of persuasion and wheedling to get six of the drivers' 'secret army' to 'come out of the closet' and say who they were and that they would join the scheme. It was rather like a Midlands version of ''allo, 'allo' with the radio under Grandma's bed and Brian saying 'I shall say this only once.'

One of the original intentions for the club had been to find a way of 'voicing the opinions of truckers'. So in that objective they have been remarkably successful. They now have a loud and strong voice and, more importantly, a voice which is being heard in the highest and most influential quarters.

To join costs £6.00 for the first year and £5.00 thereafter;

membership includes a £1,000 death or disablement insurance cover, and accident cover of £10.00 a week after the first week of injury for a limited period. There is also a free half-hour with the club's solicitor regarding traffic offences should you fall foul of the law.

Contact Brian Maydew, 3 Kennford Close, Rowley Regis, Warley, West Midlands, B65 9SF telephone (021) 559.2380.

IT'S THE WAY YOU TELL'EM

> **Shaky evidence**
> 'I'll book you for your speedo not working,' the Smoky told the trucker driving a clapped-out old rig. 'Don't need it,' responded the driver, 'At 30 m.p.h. the exhaust rattles, at 40 m.p.h. the door rattles and at 50 m.p.h. I rattle.'

South Coast Truckers' Club

It came on the scene on 30 October 1983. It is nice to know the exact date, they could get a horoscope cast for the club. It was conceived in a pub — where else? This was when Victor Burgess, Chris Coleman and Tony Ellis met in the Rodmel, in Eastbourne, and had the 'brainstorm' of forming a club for all truckers in the area. They formed a committee and established a pecking order: Victor became president, Chris chairman and Tony charity worker and fund raiser — it's easy to see who got the mucky end of the stick in that deal.

Yet it must have been a good set-up because the same three people are still in office though the committee has expanded to thirteen members. Now, as well as a vice-president, Les Cromeeke, they have a sports secretary, Steve Funnel, darts secretary, Steve North, a social secretary, Terry — Big-T, as he is known all around the South — and a news editor, Diane Williams. Apart from the officers they also have about 130 members.

They are an active and progressive club strong in the charity field and working in the community in general. Secretary Victor Smith says: 'In 1986, more than any other year, we got the club name spread around. And word of what we do for those less fortunate than ourselves has spread faster than fire.'

Attending local fêtes and taking part in the entertainment has brought the club to public attention, and taking a stand at the Southern Festival of Transport did them a power of good.

It is all in the game, to get a better image you have got to show yourself in a good light.

Charities which have benefited from club efforts have been the local District and General Hospital which received a contribution for a foetal heart monitor, the Horder Centre for Arthritic Sufferers and, latterly, the Grove Park Mentally and Physically Handicapped Centre, at Crowborough, which received £400 for special bicycles and equipment.

The charities to be supported are selected at the annual general meeting when any charity dear to a member's heart is put into a hat, and the one drawn out wins the year's effort. That way everybody has an interest.

Though to read some newspapers you would not believe it, we do live in an intensely charitable society. Bob Geldof and Band Aid, and the huge disaster funds apart, the tiddler charities gain considerable support; there seems to be an urge in the average British character to fork out when needs be, and to volunteer assistance when required. Hundreds of thousands of people — with Ian Botham just one of the multitude — go around raising money for good and worthy causes. It is good to know that British truckers are voluntarily at the forefront of this, as is illustrated by the very short account of truckers' clubs activities.

Scottish Truckers' Club

It is hard work and time-consuming to run a truckers' club, and it is tough on those who spend so much time up the road and away from home. But there is a lot of satisfaction in it particularly when the club becomes effective, useful and recognised as the *Scottish Truckers' Club* is north of the border.

On 13 June 1981, 21 drivers met at the Bruce Inn, Stirling, brought together by a mutual interest on CB, and from the meeting the Scottish Truckers' Club was formed. The rules were strict, everybody had to hold a current HGV licence and the licences were checked. And those who joined were required to attend meetings.

Whether it is the Scottish character, or maybe the clannish history, but Scottish Truckers seems to have had a more solid basis and practical purpose from the outset. And several founder members are still active on the club committee — like Jim Cairns who has been secretary, chairman and secretary again. The unique problem the club faced caused by its own strength was that it grew too big. At one time there were 575 members.

For an entirely voluntary organisation staffed by part-timers such a membership is a severe strain on club resources from many aspects: it is more difficult still to keep in contact with them all, a mailing list of nearly 600 takes some handling; and distance presents problems for attendances the more widespread the club membership becomes.

To be able to work properly the club had to do two things, reduce its numbers and find bigger premises, which it did by moving to the United Glass Social Club, Bridge of Allan. The club goes in for all the various activities other clubs indulge in: discos, dances, competitions, they run the club Driver of the Year contest every May, charity work — they pulled a 40-foot artic seven miles in an hour and a quarter through the centre of Stirling in aid of charity — outings, a coachload of them travelled to the Truck Grand Prix at Silverstone — a fantastic weekend! But they do other things as well and they are good at establishing relationships.

In several ways the Scottish Truckers' experience is revealing and significant: to every club treasurer size seems to be a marvellous thing because it brings in the subscriptions, yet it may be a drawback because of the administrative problems it creates; if part of a club's functions are social, then the membership must live close enough to each other to be able to meet easily in order to be social because distance is a killer socially. Which seems to suggest that truckers' clubs are best as small, compact, localised establishments.

Where Scottish Truckers have scored in a big way and possibly shown the way to others is in the relationships they have cultivated with the authorities: with police forces and chief constables, the traffic commissioners, Department of Transport and everybody who has a finger in the roads and traffic pie.

Where they have scored doubly is that they have managed to win the respect and co-operation of all those authorities. That, quite simply, is *the way ahead*.

Secretary Jim Cairns says: 'Conditions are different up here north of the border. We are running on single track roads much of the time, and narrow roads.' That is true, the length of motorway and dualcarriageway in Scotland is not very great when compared with England.

IT'S BIZARRE

Watch the pence...
...and in this case watch the pounds fly out of the window. When **Fred Flowers**, of Staines, went to collect a stand at the Boat Show in London, he couldn't get in. So he went to see the fitters and call the owner on a reversed charge call. For his trouble he got an ears-bend. 'Don't reverse the charges, it costs 36p,' he was severly admonished. When he returned to his truck, it had been towed away — it cost £36 to get it out of the pound.

With one exception, all the police forces of Scotland have sent representatives to club meeting, to state their own cases and listen to the drivers' problems. The one exception is the Borders and Lothian force which felt that visiting a club in another police area was outside their remit. The local chief constable said he had no objections to such a visit, but Borders and Lothian preferred to stand on protocol, which is their prerogative.

Yet every other force, and in Scotland they are very big forces covering a great deal of territory, was happy to attend. As a result every proper and legitimate complaint raised by drivers at the meetings was duly rectified and put in order in a matter of days or weeks, depending on the complexity of the problem.

'We have great respect for the police and we find them very helpful. We have a very good relationship with them,' Jim Cairns emphasises.

101

Similarly, the relationship with the Department of Transport couldn't be better. Jim Watt, one of the traffic bosses based in Edinburgh, travelled to Stirling to explain personally to a club meeting the changes in tacho rules coming into force on 29 September 1986. And obviously to answer drivers' questions on the spot. Accurate information straight from the horse's mouth — doesn't that make you wonder if they don't do things better in Scotland?

Here is a special note which throws a different light on another section of this book. In the police chapter Dumfries comes out as the worst town in Britain for relationships between police and drivers. It is castigated by drivers who use the A74 and Dumfries and Galloway police are coloured deepest black. But not so with Scottish Truckers' Club members.

There were problems once. In particular regarding the big weighbridge and the fact that the A74 as a major trunk road carrying the volume of traffic it does is, by any standards, a total disgrace. The club telephoned and then met the chief constable, and the problems were ironed out. Now Scottish Truckers' Club members have no difficulties and suffer no 'harassment' in the area. This is not to say that others don't, they would not have marked the area's cards so strongly and unanimously if they didn't. But it does suggest that the problem could be a question of attitudes and approaches on either side and that a little give and take and understanding might be effective.

Another problem vanished after it was raised with the Glasgow police. Drivers had been plagued on the few miles of motorway they were privileged to use in Scotland by 'middle lane crawlers' — slow drivers sitting in the middle motorway lane and preventing HGVs from overtaking. The club raised the question with Glasgow police and virtually overnight the problem disappeared. Now that motorway leading into Glasgow must be the only place in Britain where the 'crawlers' have been put in their proper place, the slow lane.

Of all the clubs, the Scottish is perhaps the one which is furthest along the way to developing and realising its full potential. Now it is expanding again on the strength of its greater capacity at its new HQ. Contact Jim Cairns, **Steel Trooper**, at 3 Corton Crescent, Bridge of Allan, FK9 4DD. Tel: 0786 833775.

IT'S BIZARRE

If you want to know the way...

In summer, 1985, **Driver**, from **Melksham**, was following a saloon down the M4 and was surprised when the brake lights came on. The car stopped and brought traffic to a standstill. An elegant woman got out, ran back down the motorway and asked him sweetly: 'Tell me, am I on the right road for Cheltenham?'

The T-100 Club

This was formed from quite different motives than most other clubs and is unique in not being CB-based, though most members do have CB in the cab.

Back in 1983 the founding members decided that they should 'bring truckers and their families together in a bond of social friendship'. And furthermore: 'Whereby the whole of the truckers' families could participate in some of the activities of the trucker and gain a greater understanding and interest in the role of their loved ones'.

Now that is very lyrical. They are all Welshmen so it would be, wouldn't it? Yet the sentiment reflects what is felt by a great many truckers who haven't quite got the gift of the gab particularly when they also say: 'The club was also greatly concerned in trying to bring back the comradeship among drivers which seems to have gone since the introduction of high-speed motorways, high-speed trucks and bosses demanding ever greater mileages.'

Don't scoff, it is a serious problem and well expressed by the T-100 Club members. You cannot go belting pedal-to-metal up the motorway on a knife-edge on the tacho and stop to play the Good Samaritan to a mate broken down on the hard shoulder. It is almost as much as you can do to give him a 'hard Cheddar, chum,' on the CB.

The South Wales club put their altruism into practical form and created the splendidly named 'Emergency and Compassionate Get You Home Service' which works for members who run into trouble. It was soon called into service: a member fell ill and went into hospital away from home. The system is that in such a case they check if the person can be moved in a few days and if so they collect and bring him home free of charge; if he cannot be moved, they take his family to see him.

Conversely, in cases of illness, they look after families when members are away up the road. It is a very practical, helpful system and works well.

Like most clubs they have suffered a drop in membership because of the recession in the industry. And there is always a recession when it comes to people to cope with the nitty-gritty of running the club and organising events, though all the social functions are eagerly awaited and attract a big turn-out. That is the common complaint of all clubs, they have a lot of 'We're only here for the beer' members who come good on party nights.

It all sounds pretty parochial, and so it is. But why not? All the best clubs are parochial, that is part of the pleasure of them.

T-100 however does broaden its horizons. Full membership is restricted to HGV licence-holders only, but they allow 25 associate members who drive for a living but don't hold HGV qualifications. And a rule of the club is to help private motorists in trouble as well as commercials as a way to improve the image of the job.

Contact Llewellyn Simmonds, (0222)564171.

103

Boston and County Truckers Club

Last in our survey but way up among the leaders for activities and ideas. They are an active and innovative organisation, and they get about. The emphasis is on socialising, fun and enjoyment, which, it could be argued, is why you join a club.

So their pursuit of pleasure has taken them to Sweden and Denmark: a couple of nights on the boat where you don't have to worry what the hell you do because there is somebody else upstairs driving, and a couple of nights in a hotel where you can only blame yourself if you fall over because it isn't rocking and rolling about — though it may look as if it is through your own bleary eyes.

And they go to truck-racing at Donnington Park and Silverstone, and to Truckfest, travelling by coach. A couple of hours in the charabanc when you don't have to worry what the hell you get up to because there's somebody else with his feet on the pedals and his lips pursed for the breathalyser. Good sense makes for a good time with no recriminations.

Coupled with the fun come the good ideas for promoting the industry and the social role of the truck driver in another sense. And they have come up with one really striking good idea: working with the police and the Road Safety Officer they have arranged to park a complete rig in a school playground where the kids can get at it.

IT'S BIZARRE

What held you up, driver?

David Lowndes, of Cumnock, observed a truck which had toppled over between junctions 4 and 5 on the M5. The motorway contractors arrived before it could be moved, bollarded off the area and it lay there on its side for three weeks until the roadworks were finished.

The children will see the road from a driver's point of view, they will be shown all the blind spots and problems from the cab; they will be told all about engine noise and the 'silent ghost' effect of moving trailers. A lot of accidents come about because children think that danger is past when the engine noise has passed by, they forget the trailer at the back. That , I suggest, is a cracking good idea.

Every kid in the Boston schools which take part in the scheme will, after first-hand, touching and climbing-over knowledge of a rig, know more about trucks and safety than a dozen dry classroom lectures could ever impart. Congratulations to Boston and County Truckers.

The club was formed in 1981. In 1983 there was an organisational shake-up and the new committee was elected — and has been re-elected ever since. The more you look at the clubs, the more they seem like Football League clubs, the management is subject to change at short notice. It doesn't matter — it is all good, clean internecine warfare and much the healthier for it.

Boston has sports days, dances, discos and suchlike to fill in the duller moments between their globe-trotting activities. Contact Christine Taylor, at Chapel Hollow, Ralph Lane, Frampton West, Boston, Tel: (0205) 722605, or chairman Geoff Burch, 202 Carlton Road, Boston, Tel: (0205) 67883.

Club member **AT** tells the following story, which is a terrible slander on all truckers' club members: the trucker returned from a long Continental trip and his wife told him: 'Darling — I'm in the club now.' And the driver said: 'Hell, when I told you to contact the social secretary, I didn't expect you to let him get as social as that.'

Affiliated clubs and their secretaries
Ted Pratt BOSTON AND COUNTY TRUCKERS 13 Ingelow Road, Boston, Lincolnshire

Ron Wilkins CV & RT CLUB 25 Hoser Avenue, Baring Road, Lee, London SE12 9EA

Glyn Richards FOUR RIVERS CLUB 1 Woodfield Terrace, Hopkinstown, Ammanford, Dyfed, South Wales

Colin and Naomi McKay SOUTH EAST COAST OWNER DRIVERS 49 Cobdown Close, Ditton, Maidstone, Kent ME20 6SZ

Kenneth Reeves THAMES VALLEY TRUCKERS 9 Cornish Close, Basingstoke, Hampshire RG22 6SO

Phil Cornelius TRUCKERS 100 CLUB 1 Rowan Close, Pencoed, Nr Bridgend, South Glamorgan

IT'S BIZARRE

The spy ON the cab
The *Daily Telegraph* reported:
A 50,000—strong network of 'informers' is being set up by the Greater London Council to try to make police enforce its weekend and night ban on heavy lorries on most roads. The GLC says: 'Vigilantes will keep their eyes and ears open for lorry operators breaking the ban.' The informers have been given a '24-hour hotline number' to telephone to report suspected offenders.
The 'vigilantes' were designed to operate *after* the GLC was abolished — **the memory of 'Red Ken' and his cronies lives on.**

Truckers International
It is about 100 strong in Britain and therefore not even a mouse-squeak in a thunderstorm, but the idea is there as a voice for the truckers' side of the industry. And it is an enormous organisation on the Continent. The association does not want to be political, militant or even partisan; all it wants is to be there when the powers-that-be

in Whitehall or wherever and particularly Brussels are laying down the laws which govern a trucker's life. It wants a voice — the voice of the people who actually drive the damned things and live by them — from the very beginning when the rules are being thought up. The idea is to make the rules workable by consultation and discussion from cats'-eye level before they come into force rather than have them knocked into sense and shape by protest after they have become law.

The transport unions will protest loudly that truckers already have a voice and a presence in *them*...

Not many drivers will believe that. Very few drivers, in fact, will give it any credence at all. Unions and drivers don't seem to get along too well and many who are in unions protest that they are there only by the compulsion of the closed shop — they have to be in otherwise they couldn't work where they do or pick up loads. The most common thing a questioner is told is that the Transport and General Workers Union is misnamed, or rather misleadingly named. 'It's all right if you're a docker. But it's buggerall use for anybody on the road.' The speaker has to remain anonymous because he works out of a closed shop on a docks and is fearful for his livelihood. 'You're not free to speak your mind no matter what they say. If they knew I was saying any of this, I would be black-listed the day after it was printed. They have done damn all for drivers. They were going to contest the tachograph and they did nothing. They've persistently fought against sleeper-cabs when the people who need them desperately want them. The union people are all-mouth-and-trouser-men, you just listen to their prattle, then go away and do the opposite. Look at the miners' strike. The union was blurting out, 'Don't cross picket lines,' and what happened there was that there were so many lorries driving through the picket lines that the pickets couldn't cross the road. I listen to these people ranting away and I know that they're not in the same business as me.'

IT'S THE WAY YOU TELL 'EM

Knit one, pearl one

The Jam Sandwich flagged down a woman driver travelling at 75 m.p.h. and knitting as she drove. The policeman lowered his window and ordered: 'Pull over.' She looked surprised and replied: 'No, socks.'
Chris Cesana, *Ramsgate, Kent.*

Nice when you stop

Is a woodpecker without a beak a headbanger?
Shy Man, *Friockeim, Montrose.*

The United Road Transport Union is an all-driver union, but what is its real strength? It claims a membership of more than 23,000, which is certainly true. But what does that mean? It means that it represents at most 7 per cent of men on the road. When you think of that as seven drivers out of every hundred, it doesn't seem a lot, and it hardly constitutes a power in the land.

Where the clubs are potentially important and the United Kingdom Truckers Association, formed from the clubs, is highly significant is that, from this social side of trucking, an all-trucker, all man-on-the-road organisation (the loosest of organisations, it must be admitted) has emerged that will carry more clout than the combined unions and will be able to speak for drivers with a driver's voice. And more importantly still, it will be able to speak on every aspect of driving as seen through the windscreen without the issues being clouded or obscured by politics, party allegiances, or TUC in-fighting.

That, I must stress, is the *possibility*, and only the possibility; these things have first to evolve, then grow, and they suffer acute growing pains.

Truckers International has Swedish origins — funny how much in the trucking world stems from Scandinavia, they're all truck-mad (which probably accounts for the fact that they have the highest suicide rate in the western world). It was formed as the Cowboy Club, and it is still best known internationally as that. It took off superbly in Sweden and collected 10,000 members in a rush which enabled them to set up a couple of 'buying' companies, owned by the club, to sell both spares and diesel well below standard garage prices.

Then it spread all over the Continent until it accumulated more than 35,000 members. The founding idea, which attracted truckers in all countries, was to get a 'voice' for the trucker and let it be heard where it matters. Then they got into the business of fixing discounts at truck-stops and garages, so it served a useful as well as social purpose.

If you run Continental, it may be useful to you to have the Truckers International contacts:

GREAT BRITAIN Alan Smith, 83 Mayfield Rd, Bury St. Edmunds IP33 2 NT Suffolk Tel:(0944) 284 61701

DENMARK: Postbox 14 7490 Aulum. Tel: 010 45 7 — 47 36 35

FINLAND: Allan Linden Pl 18 PB 06151 Borgå Tel: 010 358 15-144866

GERMANY Karl Heinz Tachlinski Friedrichstrasse 19 2000 Hamburg 4 Tel: 010 49 40-3194715

HOLLAND and BELGIUM Henk Vegter Anjer 41 Postbox 120 2678 P.C. de Lier Tel:010 31 50 772127

NORWAY Bernt K.R. Melvold, TIA Box 1102 Flattum — 3501 Hønefoss Tel: 010 47 7-20 734

SWEDEN TIA Box 2000 590 21 Väderstad Tel: 010 46 142 — 712 85

SWITZERLAND and AUSTRIA TIA Andy Oeggerli Koppigenstrasse 8 3427 Ulzenstorf Tel: 010 41 65-45456

United Kingdom Truckers Association

After the clubs comes the United Kingdom Truckers Association which is a combination of many of the clubs. At the time of writing it is a very new idea but one full of potential; that potential seems to have been recognised and the newborn infant is quickly getting some squawk into its lungs — for the sake of drivers, let's hope it doesn't suffer a cot death.

For a subscription of £25 each club can become a member of the association, which makes every member of the club an associate; there are no individual members, to become part of the association a driver must join an individual club — all it will cost him is his subscription to his own club. At one time there was some misunderstanding about that.

Yet again, it is all about a *voice*. The pressing urgency, the crying need for somebody to talk for truckers on the road has once again surfaced spontaneously.

Founder members say it is non-political, non-union and, by inference, non-aligned. I quibble about the words. What the organisers really mean is non-*party*-political, because any organisation like this is political by its nature since it is 'acting or proceeding from motives of policy', (Chambers's *Dictionary*). It is a union but not a trade union in the legal sense. It is aligned to drivers' interests but not in the way that sponsored clubs are aligned to trade interests. The exact basis of the association's purpose should be made crystal clear because it is very apparent that many drivers have a dread of being unionised, politicised or ripped-off.

Judge the potential power of such an association by the amazing growth of clubs in the 1980s. The clubs have drawn a spontaneous membership of well over 50,000 which has come about by 'the lads' getting together to share their mutual interests. The established trade unions have failed lamentably to attract them despite vigorous recruiting campaigns.

A trucker's 'voice' is as much in his hip-pocket as in his throat, and money talks. That is where the association could become a power on the highways and byways of the land. An army of 50,000-plus truckers running around buying diesel, spares, meals, overnight accommodation, clothing, and all the extraneous clobber which goes with the job, could be a bit more than a whisper — it could be a full-bellied shout.

So the cry will arise: 'What about the unions? Isn't this what the unions are for? Why aren't the unions doing it?' At the same time the unions will protest: 'This is what we are for. If they would only join us we could do all this for them.'

But, alas, no.

Drivers are disenchanted with unions. To the average driver, going about his job on the roads of Britain, the unions are just another bloody restriction, another authority imposing its will on him, and another hidden tax on his earnings. And if that is the wrong view of unions, then the unions have only themselves to blame.

It is not, as the politically motivated so often claim, that they are not getting their message across. It is quite simply that they are not doing the job for drivers. And if they don't like that appraisal of their value, they should take a good look at their membership lists — and then at themselves.

For the unions' dream of 'organised labour' you first need labour in an organisation; if you get labour *en masse* you can 'organise' but it is a different matter to 'organise' a scattered, wandering rabble of highly independent-minded mavericks. If you 'close' ten big shops you need ten doorkeepers to keep them tight shut; if you try to close 50,000 little shops you are going to need 50,000 doorkeepers with another 50,000 on top to keep an eye on the back doors.

And the trouble is that the doorkeepers tend to be more 'political' animals than transport people.

Associations have worked wonderfully well in Sweden and Norway but let me stress that conditions there are entirely different in most aspects. In the first place there are not as many trucks, dealers, factors, filling stations or ancilliaries, it is a different trade in many ways. Yet the combined purchasing power of Swedish and Norwegian truckers banded together in associations has got them better prices, deals and conditions. And all that *outside* the Scandinavian trade unions. All officers of those associations by rule have to be working truckers (there is one exception, but that man is in the trucking business anyway though he doesn't drive).

Working drivers have to drive and frequently go away, so in order to handle day-to-day business and trading the Swedish association set up two limited companies which are wholly under the control of the association. In Sweden it works remarkably well, though it might not be so easy here because company law may be different — and trading conditions, as I pointed out, are not the same. It is, of course, worth a look-see.

There is, however, one crucial factor which could turn the UK idea into a practical working entity, and that is communications. All business nowadays depends upon communications, it is the spectacular growth industry of the era and big business spends billions upon billions on its communication networks.

By happy accident, and perhaps unhappy precedent, truckers have to hand a sophisticated, highly developed and intensely private communications system which has grown over the years. It has evolved over the years because society in general — and big business as well — decided to ostracise the trucker and keep him from under its feet. Like banning him from Little Chefs and Happy Eaters, and all that. So the trucker is obliged to live in his own world, among his own sort and with his own 'grapevine' which runs from flashing headlights and CB to shop-talk in the caffs and trucks-stops up and down the length and breadth of the country.

That grapevine could be an invaluable asset to an association and it could be instantly activated to the trucker's benefit. You could disseminate information throughout the trucking trade almost in a flash — the value would be, in fact, almost incalculable.   For a moment, forget the domestic scene and think about an existing situation where Brits are thrown together by circumstances and forced to co-operate to survive, let alone succeed — and that is the famous Middle East run where the 'grapevine' works almost to perfection, crude and clumsy as it may be. Even if the message is only something like 'There's a worried-looking bird waiting for you at the International, Belgrade. I'd go back the other way, if I were you,' it nearly always gets through. And a lot of other important messages and information get through as well.

I said 'forced to co-operate' and that is misleading. There is no force or obligation to co-operate, it is a purely voluntary thing but 99 per cent of the people on the run join in. So the Middle East run serves to show also that co-operation is possible, and welcome, providing the opportunity is there.

The idea of a truckers' association was proposed by Tony Taylor, of South West Truckers, and its strength and appeal was clearly illustrated when delegates from six other clubs turned up at the initial meeting. A steering committee was set up with Tony elected chairman and Brian Maydew, of West Midlands, secretary.

IT'S THE WAY YOU TELL'EM

Each way bet

Three Irish gentlemen stopped in a remote village in the heart of rural Wales and asked where the racecourse was. They said: 'We're going to the Cheltenham Gold Cup. We came off the ferry at Holyhead and we've followed the HR, for Horse Racing, signs.' The old Welsh man told them: 'If you stay 'ere till summer, you might see some pony trekking — that's HR for holiday route.'
Jemmets Idiot, *Middleton, Lancashire.*

At that meeting a representative of Shell Diesel Drivers also attended. Later the Routiers Club joined the association.

It's early days (it's always early days in the trucking world) and a lot of little local difficulties have to be ironed out. But the basis is there for a progressive and powerful organisation with the motivation to do what it says it will do: be non-political, represent truckers' interests, needs and views to the Department of Transport, the police, county and local councils, vehicle manufacturers and the media. It could evolve into an organisation like the British Medical Association, or the Law Society, and who can say that those bodies don't represent their members' interests to their benefit?

The answer is very straighforward: if you want to be regarded and treated as professionals, act like professionals. Naturally, that means you personally behaving professionally at all times, but it will be more effective if more of you do it all together. And talk about it in a strong, united voice.

If the authorites consider that the CB networks are a viable proposition by which to spread the word, drivers would be fools not to take note and turn their own 'tools' to their own advantage. With CB all the old problems of contact with drivers who are constantly 'up the road' that have plagued clubs and unions for years are overcome; you don't have to make time or give up your relaxation in order to stay in touch, time is there at the flick of a switch just waiting to be used productively.

To give a bit of power to the association's elbow all you need do is get in touch with Brian Maydew at the same address as for West Midlands truckers. Here it is once again: Brian Maydew, 3 Kennford Close, Rowley Regis, Warley, West Midlands, B65 9SF telephone: (021) 559.2380.

IT'S BIZARRE

Come now, not quite in the spirit of things
In a dutiful reflex action, Roy Hudson, of Sale, eased his foot on the pedal when he read the exhortation on the back of the truck ahead: 'Save gas'. Then he put it down again when in the dust underneath he saw written: 'Fart in a bottle'.

Routiers Drivers Club

There is, and the fact cannot be avoided even by those who would like to dodge it, one supreme organisation in the truckers' club scene. And that is the Routiers Drivers Club. Its very success has spawned detractors and its style has bred critics, but when the complaints are examined in detail they tend to boil down to a resentment — for inexplicable reasons — and a jealousy — for understandable reasons — of the extent by which it has succeeded in bettering the professional drivers' lot.

For the general public and authorities as well as truckers, Routiers has become synonymous with 'class' in the sense of prestige: for services to drivers, for protection, representation, for quality and that all important 'voice' Routiers cannot be bettered.

If the rest are trying to be better than Routiers, that is to the great benefit of the driving fraternity, but they have a long road to travel.

Routiers is international and worldwide and musters about 1,000,000 members. Size can be a drawback, a million of anything takes a lot of organising and administering. Naturally, that is one of the complaints levelled at the set-up: too big, they say. But size also gives weight and a lot of pull, so what you lose in the alleged impersonality of the organisation, you gain in its universal presence.

Routiers in Britain is 4,000 strong and growing steadily. It isn't sensational but it now has something more than a foothold. To judge by performance in other countries, this is just the beginning.

It is celebrating its fiftieth anniversary and it all began as a 'good food guide' when two French journalists noticed that wherever they saw a clutch of trucks pulled up, there were the best cafés in France. French truckers like their food rather more than British truckers do and, offered a choice of pleasurable indulgences, the Frenchman would opt for a gourmet meal in preference to anything else — French women have learned to be very patient, and anyway they've all got headaches from sweating over hot stoves all day.

From the food guide there sprang the Routiers Drivers Club which has developed into a very powerful sort of trade union organisation in France where it pulls a great deal of weight and is certainly more effective on drivers' behalf than our own unions.

In turn there evolved the Union Internationale des Chauffeurs Routiers — the International Association of Professional Drivers — which has its headquarters (secretariat) at Martigny, Switzerland. This organisation carries a lot of clout with the authorities and the police. It issues a passport for members which is recognised by the police and requests the police's 'kind consideration to the bearer' in case of accident.

The secretariat is available at all times for the assistance of drivers in trouble.

The presidency of the club is at present in West Germany, at Munich; a quick glance at where the club has established itself gives an idea of its scope: Austria, Belgium, Canada, Ciskei, England, Finland, France, Germany, Holland, Ireland, Namibia, Norway, South Africa, Sweden and Switzerland — and I almost missed out Bophutatswana, but I don't suppose that many of you will be looking for back-loads from there.

Those are by no means all the countries where Routiers operates, they are just the ones who were strong enough to send teams to compete in the Routiers International Truck Driving Championships, at Breda, Holland, in 1986. The thing to note about them is that there are not many, if any, truckers' organisations which could pull contestants from so far and wide throughout the world. And that makes Routiers a potent force in world trucking.

IT'S BIZARRE

splashing out

Knowing well the feeling of acute frustration, Driver from Bolton laughed when he shouldn't have done. On Southampton Docks, a Scotsman, livid after being senselessly mucked about for two hours, climbed into his cab, furiously slammed into gear, backed into a fork-lift truck and shoved it off the quay into the dock.

The question which you should ask is: what's in it for me apart from a few posh badges? The best thing to do is to let them answer for themselves. This is what they claim:

BENEFITS OF MEMBERSHIP

FREE – **Your interests represented:**
You describe yourselves as the worst treated professional group in the country. We have decided to respond to your urgent calls to act as your voice. We are already talking on your behalf to politicians, planners, the police, government departments, customs, British trade unions, vehicle manufacturers, caterers, oil companies and the general public.

FREE – **Routiers Magazine:**
You will receive with your membership regular news letters containing news and views, hints and advice written specially for the professional driver. Special points of interest and articles on specific developments affecting the driver form a major feature as does a section especially provided for you to air your views. Also, at regular intervals, we provide special offers at very good prices only to you as a member.

FREE – **Membership of the Union Internationale des Chauffeurs Routiers (UICR):**
Better known as Les Routiers, the UICR has a membership throughout the world of over 1.8 million. It is the major internationally recognised organisation for long distance drivers and offers essential assistance and advice for drivers when driving on the Continent. Apart from other benefits, as a member of the UICR you can call on the network of legal advisers established throughout Europe. These lawyers are specialists in transport.

FREE – **Routiers International Handbook:**
This is an invaluable guide to all member organisations affiliated to Routiers. Through this network of organisations you can obtain help in the emergencies that can arise once you are out on the road.

FREE – **Associate Membership for your wife (or husband):**
While you are away on a long journey we can provide a valuable link and two-way channel of communication between yourself and your family. (This is for cases of accident or emergency.) Your wife also receives a special car sticker so that she can easily recognise other member families or be recognised herself by fellow members if she runs into trouble.

DISCOUNT – **at Routiers Truckstops:**
All Members qualify for a 5% discount (more on selected items) on products available at the Routiers Truckstop. Just

show your membership card and you can select from a wide range of merchandise from emergency replacements for your truck to items for yourself and family. There is available a stock of items produced exclusively for and sold only to members. These are also available by mail order.

DISCOUNT – Legal Defence Insurance:
To protect your livelihood, we have organised special cover for members to protect both your licence and bank balance. The cover provided represents the best value for money available on the market today. We have also made arrangements with a firm of specialist transport lawyers to act for you under this scheme.

By common consent those claims are pretty valid, and other truckers' clubs are striving to obtain the DAS insurance cover.

Horizons are widening all the time and Continental runs are a commonplace for many drivers. Even if you don't go abroad much at the moment, there is no telling when you might be asked to go. The rules are different abroad and the DAS cover does give you a cushion to fall back on if something goes wrong. And if you are 'going Middle East' then you really do need cover, otherwise you can rot in a very unwholesome jail for a long time unless you can poppy-up immediately.

I have quoted the experience of Philippa Edmonds when she was accused of crossing a red light, and subsequently found not guilty only to find herself £700 out of pocket.

The DAS legal expenses insurance would have taken care of that; this is what they say their cover is:

Summary of cover
The legal expenses cover include fees and expenses of solicitors, barristers, expert witnesses, court costs and your opponent's costs if awarded against you in a civil case, arising out of incidents occurring during the period of insurance stated on the Certificate issued to the member.

The cover provides legal expenses incurred in:

1) Defending or pleading in mitigation in respect of a prosecution of the member for a road traffic offence excluding UK speeding unless additional premium paid.
2) Appealing against conviction or sentence resulting from such a prosecution.
3) Pursuing claims against negligent third parties in respect of personal injuries and damage to personal effects arising from a motor accident.
4) Appealing/defending an appeal against judgement under (3).

It isn't my job to sell insurance, god forbid. But a lot of drivers and club members think this is a good scheme — so I bring it to your notice.

The British end of Routiers has joined with the UK Truckers Association in moving towards the organised 'truckers' voice' but it is a bit dubious about how the association will grow. If it does take off it will be the foundation of, at last, a real and convincing power base for the men behind the wheels.

This is what it costs to join Routiers: The membership year runs from May 1st to April 30th. The subscription for new members is: May £25, June £23, July £21, Aug £19, Sept £17, Oct £15, Nov £14, Dec £12, Jan £10. Members joining in February, March, April pay £25 which includes their next year's renewal.

For a couple of years past Routiers in Britain have been moving into the area of their founding expertise in recommending truck-stops; there are plenty of first-rate cafés carrying the Routiers badge already, but a distinction should be made between the car and truck recommendations — only on price, not quality.

For the purposes of this book I am sticking to the firm rule of the 'Top of the Café Pops Chart' that cafés and truckstops are listed only by drivers' recommendations: all the Routiers truckstops are in our list, and all come pretty high. No doubt they will rise up the list as they become more firmly established, but as a quick cross-reference they are: Checkley Rest and Station, Truckers Godmanchester, Whitchurch and Findern — formerly Atkins Café, near Derby.

Naturally they want to sell their club; what else would you expect? They do, however, seem to be of like mind to most of the drivers who have contributed to this book. This is how they advertise themselves:

IF ALL OF YOU STOPPED YOUR TRUCKS TODAY, THIS COUNTRY WOULD GRIND TO A HALT TOMORROW!

AND STILL YOU ARE THE WORST TREATED PROFESSIONAL GROUP IN THE COUNTRY

DO YOU WANT TO PUT THINGS RIGHT?

JOIN THE ROUTIERS DRIVERS CLUB!

Whatever you decide to do, it is liable to cost you money: it will cost you if you join, it might cost you more if you don't. It all depends on your personal attitude and the values you place on these things. You could be like the geezer I saw in The Rose Café at Chelmsford, he raised hell about paying £1.60 for his food, then promptly lost £15 in the one-armed bandit. He certainly wasn't a Frenchman!

Truck racing

Truck racing has rather the same effect on people as greyhound coursing: either you are addicted or you want to get it banned.

Some manufacturers are 'implacably opposed' to it, as are some editors of trade magazines. Their argument is that trucks are not meant to be raced, it is the last thing in the world they were designed for, the 'sport' presents them in entirely the wrong light to the public, and the whole business is a distortion of the industry and can only do harm.

All of that is self-evidently arguable and the views of those opposed to truck racing can easily be understood and appreciated. They are not spoil-sports being bloody-minded for the sake of being bloody-minded.

Those in favour of the sport argue that it does no harm at all and serves only to enhance the public image of trucks: 'If a truck is seen by the public to be safe enough to race round a track, then they will realise that it is doubly safe on the road,' argues one proponent. To support that argument he says that private cars were never intended to take the thrashing they get in rallying, nor were they ever intended to be driven like that.

Take your choice of the arguments.

An average of 55,000 to 60,000 of you take the second choice and regularly attend the grand prix truck races. It has become the second-best attended motor sport in the country — second only to formula one racing. Perhaps the most important function of truck racing is that it has become an enormous social event for the trucking fraternity; there are three big get-togethers in the year, and soon there will be four. And the international circuit is rapidly expanding.

There is intrigue and mystery in truck racing which no doubt adds to its appeal. Some manufacturers, while publicly denouncing the sport and refusing to be associated with it, are covertly — secretly — quite deeply involved and are providing special engines and equipment for their mark of vehicles competing on the track: they hate the idea of competitive racing, but they can't stop an owner racing if he wants to, and they cannot bear the idea of losing

IT'S THE WAY YOU TELL'EM

Out of order

What do you get when you use an emergency telephone in a cloudburst? Wringing wet.

Kevin Bannister, *Northfleet, Kent.*

Uplifting

An Otis Elevators' truck carried the warning: 'Don't accept lifts from strange men.'

T. Beetham, *Bebington, Cheshire.*

TRUCK Grand Prix

'It's only Guinness — but then this isn't as posh as Formula One.'

because some other manufacturer has helped the opposition.

The sport is controlled internationally by the European Truck Racing Association, which organises the championships along the lines of formula one racing. In Britain, the British Truck Racing Organisation was set up to administer the sport and to ensure that it was properly and safely run. The committee of the organisation comprises representatives of sponsors, manufacturers and truck racers: Andrew Marriot, a promotions man, is chairman, Chris Tucker, a truck racer who runs a truck company in Kent, is treasurer, and Robin Dickeson, chief PR for British Leyland Trucks is a committee member. They keep a tight grip on the development of the sport, which, of course, is very necessary.

The fact, which cannot be escaped, is that the sport is now producing its own experts and, in a sense, professionals — just like rallying has done. As in any sport, those who are really good will rise to the top, and others not so good will pay to watch them perform.

In Britain the season has comprised two big international events and a third smaller national event. The internationals are:—

117

The LUCAS C.A.V. SUPERPRIX
At Brands Hatch, in April (in 1987 this will be the weekend of April 10-11).

The MULTIPART BRITSH TRUCK GRAND PRIX
Silverstone, in August (in 1987 this will be the weekend of August 15−16).

The 'national' event is:-

The KLAUSHALLER TRUCK GRAND NATIONALS
Donnington, in June (no date yet fixed at the time of writing). For those who might be worried by the sponsors, Klaushaller is a non-alcoholic beer.

Brands Hatch Racing will launch a fourth event in October 1987 at Alton Park. This one will also be more of a national than international meeting. And in November 1987 the British Truck Racing Organisation runs a TRUCK TEST, at Goodwood, to assess the previous season's results and seek improvements for the following year. This is a competitive meeting but a big social event as well.

Internationally the sport is expanding and the 1987 calendar now is:

Britain Brands Hatch, April 11 and 12.

Hungary Hungaroring circuit, Budapest, May 16 and 17.

Austria Ostereichring, May 23 and 24.

France Paul Ricard Circuit, near Marseilles, June 6 and 7.

Germany Nurnburgring, July 18 and 19.

Britain Silverstone August 15 and 16.

Sweden Mantorp Park, August 29 and 30.

Denmark Jyllandsringen, near Silkeborg, September 5 and 6.

Belgium Zolder circuit, October 3 and 4.

Those are the circuits where the international championship will be fought. Other races arranged are in Spain and Portugal, but those won't count in the points. Finland and Italy have also asked to organise races under E.T.R.A. rules — so the spread continues.

As to popularity, the Nurnburgring broke a number of records for attendance with a crowd reported to be 110,000, and Donnington broke records with its meet, so much so that local police arrangements were overwhelmed and the M1 became a car park.

There is one peculiar point of interest about the Donnington meeting which I am sure you will forgive me mentioning: for the first time at any official motor-racing event, the RAC approved the use of retread tyres for racing. Mel Bacon fitted them to his Leyland Roadtrain. They were... I'll give you one guess, and in case you are having difficulty it begins with B.

IT'S THE WAY YOU TELL'EM

Red flag jokes
These jokes were about when you needed a man to walk in front of the motor with a red flag. They must be good, they've lasted.

The cruellest cut
The man took his car into a Jewish garage to be Simonized — they cut two inches off his exhaust pipe.
Anon, *Bolton, Lanashire.*

Jungle stories
Why do elephants have four feet? They'd look silly with only four inches.
R. Walshman, *Eccleston.*

Past tense
What do you call an Irishman with a shovel on his head? Doug.
Mervyn Thomas, *Cardiff.*

Dead funny
The vegetarian died and there was a good turnip at his funeral.
William McWatt, *Denny, Stirlingshire.*

THE DOCKS DOSSIER

Let us let some sweetness and light into this narrative and allow charity to prevail. We will go to Ross-on-Wye first for Mr **N. Powell**'s charity, then second it with the kindly disposition of Mr. **T. Beetham**, of Bebbington, the Wirral.

Mr **Powell** says: 'All the docks are good, especially Liverpool and Teignmouth, we've got rid of the bad ones.' This is a view fully endorsed by Mr **Beetham** who says: 'All docks have really improved over the past ten years.'

Others, alas, are not so well disposed to either the docks or customs. A great number of people said that there were no good docks, only bad ones. And some, like Mr **G. Stockton**, of Middleton, were emphatic about it: 'All docks are bad because the dockers are bone idle.'

He also had a viewpoint on customs — but not the one we were seeking: 'A good custom,' he said, 'is the Eskimo one when they lend you their wives when you are visiting.' And he added: 'All the others are bad because they don't.'

In the same vein, Mr **W. King** of Liverpool recommended 'fresh baths' as a good custom. What he meant by 'fresh' I don't quite understand, unless he was advising against bathing in stagnant water.

So opinions on the state of the docks and customs are varied — remarkably so, and it may come as a surprise to many of you. It will certainly come as a surprise, pleasant or unpleasant, to some dock boards and companies, and some dockers.

To get a docks and customs rating it is best to award a black ball, thus ●, for every criticism (or worse) registered, and a star, thus ★, for every compliment. Wherever comments have been made they are attributed to the driver by his initials. Those who wish to remain anonymous are attributed as AN.

This assessment of the docks is in itself really quite a remarkable social document and one which shows extremes of attitudes. Mr **Powell** and Mr **Beetham**, for instance, have diametrically opposed views from **SC**, of Macclesfield, and **RPF**, of Cleethorpes, and no doubt there is justification for both standpoints. In contradiction of Mr **Powell**'s and Mr **Beetham**'s opinions, **SC** says: 'There are no good docks, we hate all dockers.' And **RPF** says: 'All dockers are all lazy bastards.'

'Switch off your engine mate, the lads are on break.'

Conflict!

There you have two sections of the traditional 'working classes' of the kingdom busily slagging off each other — no doubt the dockers respond in similar terms to drivers. And, of course, it will be confusing to the public who will see them as allied trades and governed by the same trades union affiliation, namely, the Transport and General Workers Union.

Nowadays, that isn't necessarily the case. But the T & GWU is still the dominant union in the industry and has strongish representations on the docks and on the roads.

Where is the 'solidarity' which union leaders vaunt and demand so often?

The answer is that there isn't a lot of it about. Drivers *en masse* are alienated from the Transport Union. And more than that they are bitterly critical of union officials at shop-floor level and militants at the loading points.

This comes out all too clearly in the responses to the questions we asked about the docks; the resentment engendered among drivers at the notorious newsworthy militant hot-spots almost burns through the paper it is written on.

The complaint, apparently fully justified, is that militancy hits the fellow worker and trade unionist harder than it ever hits the bosses — see the comments from drivers about the headline making trouble-spots which are all too often in the news; it ought to be cause for grave concern in Transport House.

Look at the black marks recorded against the Boys from the Black Stuff in particular. Then consider that these are not officials, employers or even High Tories talking: these are fellow workers, the lads on the road — when they can get there.

On the other hand, there was a frequent assertion in the answers that 'all privately owned docks are best'. For the record, not a single respondent made a favourable comment about the registered docks in general.

Naturally, it isn't all black. Quite the opposite; a surprising number of docks and customs come up covered in bouquets of roses. The lesson which becomes apparent from the survey is: go to the right place at the right time and it can be easy. But some docks are so overworked, overcrowded and short of staff that it can be absolute purgatory.

In this exercise we will list all the docks you mentioned in alphabetical order with black blobs, white stars and comments as accorded — at least you might be able to discover when you are likely to get home, or whether you should take a good book with you:

ABERDEEN (●) Comment: 'Very busy,' **YB**

AVONMOUTH (★ ★ ★ ★ ★ ★ ★ ★) Comments: 'Quick and easy,' **GS**; 'Gets the job done,' **AH**; 'Organised,' **MH**; 'In and out on time,' **RAH**; 'Good and efficient,' **GW**; 'Very helpful,' **RH**. (●) Comment: 'Slow,' **AA**.

BARRY (★, ●)

BERWICK (★) Comment: 'Always empty,' **KR**

BIRKENHEAD (● ●)

BOSTON (★ ★ ★ ★ ★ ★) Comments: 'Fairly quick,' **RR**; 'Quick.' **TS**; (● ●) Comment: 'Dockers' attitudes,' **DY**.

BRISTOL (★ ★) Comment: 'Good facilites,' **JM**. (● ● ●) Comments: 'Slow,' **TR**; 'Lazy workers,' **SB**; 'Very slow,' **MJT**.

CARDIFF (★ ★, ● ● ● ● ● ● ●) Comments: 'Too long delays,' **DLJ**; 'Short of work-force,' **MT**; 'Not bothered,' **GB**; 'All day to get loaded,' **CB**; 'Job to get loaded if it is raining,' **DP**.

CHATHAM (★ ★ ★, ● ● ●) Comment: 'Long waits,' **GL**.

COLCHESTER (★, ●) Comment: 'Long waits, no facilities, no help,' **JHK**.

DAGENHAM (★)

DEPTFORD (●) Comment: 'Kept waiting,' **CS**

DOVER (★ ★ ★ ★ ★ ★ ★ ★ ★ ★ ★ ★ ★ ★ ★ ★ ★ ★ ★) Comment: 'Customs helpful,' **TJSG**; 'Good customs,' **TR**; 'Good for café, shower, TV, telephone,' **GC**; 'Computerised,' **IW**; 'Dover West best,' **DS**. (● ●) Comments: 'Too big,' **PS**; 'Too much delay,' **BM**; '24-hours to clear one T-form,' **MC**; 'Can't find your way out,' **NBW**; 'Bad customs clearance,' **ANY**; 'Too busy, very slow clearance, too many trucks come in,' **JdK**; 'Very bad clearance, anything up to 18-hours to clear three entries,' **RBM**; 'Lack of facilities for HGV traffic, not enough customs to cope,' **BB**; 'Everything wrong with customs,' **RH**; 'Far too much delay,' **DJL**; 'Customs don't care if you miss your ferry and will keep you hanging about for ever,' **RR**; 'Stuck 24-hours waiting to clear,' **IE**; 'You cannot depend on them — one entry will take 6 hours, then four entries will take only two hours,' **RB**; 'Work too slow before Christmas and Bank Holidays,' **RS** (Germany); 'Not enough staff,' **LM**; 'Too slow by far,' **FSL**; 'Too busy for staff available,' **RJW**; 'Life is too short to waste at Dover,' **PE** 'Waited up to a week,' **CF**; 'A day to clear,' **HL** (Holland); 'Very slow,' **JD** (France); 'Too slow,' **MV** (Turkey); 'Wait for hours,' **SM**; 'Sometimes takes two days to clear,' **MM**; 'Not clean,' **EL** (Holland); 'Very slow and lacking facilities,' **AN**; 'Lots of hold-ups,' **PN**; 'West Dock officials very ignorant people, truckers are treated like dirt,' **GM**; 'Utterly hopeless,' **AM**; 'Seven hours to clear one load,' **AN**; 'Slow, too slow,' **DW** and **PL**; 'Keep you as long as they can,' **SH**; 'Bad tempered,' **SC**; 'Keep you hanging around,' **GMW**; 'Customs too lazy,' **F** (Holland); 'Especially bad,' **D**; 'Days to clear,' **BM**; 'Average of 12 hours to clear,' **PB**; 'There for hours on end,' **SG**; 'Very impersonal due to volume,' **DV**; 'Dockers living in the past,' **TV**

DUNDEE (●) Comment: 'Dockers very slow,' **IN**.

ELLESMERE PORT (●) 'Too small for number of containers stored,' **AN**.

ERITH (★) 'Quick,' **GL**. (●) 'Militant,' **DV**.

FELIXSTOWE (★ ★) Comments: 'Helpful to me, new at game,' **RM**; 'Access good and fast,' **MH**; 'Speedy,' **W**; 'In and out,' 20 minutes,' **FEW**; 'Good customs,' **ANW**; 'Private dockers you can talk to,' **JA**; 'Good overnight parking,' **RL**; 'Quick clearance,' **JdK, RBM, DW**; 'Well signposted,' **MC**; 'Well organised,' **AN**; 'Quick,' **PK, MB** (Turkey), **RH, SW**, 'Quick turnaround,' **AN**; 'Quick and efficient,' **MB, PL**; 'Dockers are good and will help you,' **BC**; 'For amount of traffic handled, waiting is very limited,' **DP**; 'Never kept waiting,' **C**; 'No militants,' **PD**; 'Fast and efficient,' **GM**; 'Fast,' **TB**; 'Fairly efficient,' **C**; 'Good unions,' **AN**; 'They are not scared to work,' **LM**; 'Helpful,' **CH**; 'Easy tipping and loading,' **RR**; 'Quick, with good road access,' **SM**; 'Easy access, reasonable people,' **PK**; 'Modern and fairly quick, modern dock geared to speed,' **BM, PB**; (● ●) Comments: 'Too long waits,' **NH**; 'Loading ships have priority over lorries,' **DW**; ''72 and 77 parks are slow and unhelpful,' **TC**; 'No washing facilities,' **AvD**; 'Not enough facilities for clearing lorries,' **RB**; 'Slow, too slow, very slow,' **JA, GS, SL, AJS**; 'Too much union,' **DR**, 'Too much queue jumping,' **DY, CM**; 'Bone idle, unhelpful and overpaid,' **KC**; 'Inconsistent service,' **SM**; 'Too many bosses,' **PR**; 'Too many strikes and laziness,' **AM**; 'Too much traffic,' **DC**.

FISHGUARD (●) Comment: 'Too slow,' **CP**.

FLEETWOOD (★ ★ ★ ★) Commens: 'Quick,' **C**; 'Hard working, friendly; early start, early finish,' **DV**.

FOLKESTONE (★ ★ ★ ★ ★ ★) Comments: 'Just right size,' **PS**; 'Good customs service,' **JKT**; 'Good for customs,' **RS** (Germany); 'Very quick,' **FJB** (France) (● ●)

GARSTON (●) 'Useless dockers,' **KC**.

GLASGOW (★ ★, ● ● ●) Comments: 'Bad customs,' **GRS**; 'Militant, restrictive practices,' **DV**.

GLASSON – private (★)

GOOLE (★ ★ ★ ★ ★ ★ ★ ★ ★ ★ ★ ★ ★ ★ ★ ★) Comments: 'Fastest tip in the country,' **HEJ**; 'Get you tipped as fast as possible,' **AN**; 'Quick tip,' **SD**; 'Quick turnaround,' **KT**; 'Helpful gang,' **IB**; 'Quick,' **RF**; 'Efficient,' **PT**; 'Good loading,' **DA**; 'Quickest,' **JS**; 'Dockers load vehicles, not drivers,' **AN**; 'Helpful and quick,' **CD**; 'Helpful,' **DS**; 'Quick and on the ball,' **GM**; 'Hard working, friendly with early start and early finish,' **DV**. (●) 'Approach to docks all one-way streets,' **KR**.

GRANGEMOUTH (★ ★ ★ ★ ★ ★) Comments: 'No problems,' **JM**; 'Very helpful,' **AS**; 'Quick and efficient,' **KD**; 'They take the rope sheets off for you,' **PF** (●) Comment: 'Very strong union,' **RJW**.

GREAT YARMOUTH (★ ★ ★ ★) Comments: 'No hassle, quick tip,' **YB**; 'Well planned out,' **NBW**.

GRIMSBY (★ ★ ★ ★ ★ ★) Comment: 'Quick load,' **HE**.

HARTLEPOOL (●) Comment: 'Too many breaks,' **AM**.

HARWICH (★ ★ ★ ★ ★ ★ ★ ★ ★ ★) Comments: 'The best, but a bit scruffy,'**CS**; 'Fast with friendly people,' **BW**; 'Fast clearing and special facilities for drivers,' **RB**; 'Very organised,' KC; 'Pleased to serve you,' **DB**; 'No problems,' AN (● ● ● ● ● ● ● ●) Comments: '12-hours to clear paper,' **HE**; 'Keep you waiting,' **JB**; 'Slow loading,' **AH**; 'Too slow,' **JBD**.

HEYSHAM (★ ★ ★ ★, ●) Comment: 'Slow because you have to handle it yourself,' SM.

HOLYHEAD (●) Comment: 'Very slow, strip everything out and leave you to put it all back,' **SP**.

HULL (★ ★) Comments: 'Good customs,' **AM**; 'Quick clearance,' **DY**; 'You get tipped quickly,' **AN**; 'Quick, quick, quick loading,' **JS, FT, IF**; 'Very modern equipment,' **RJW**; 'Civilised,' **TB**; 'More organised than most,' **EN**; 'Best nights out are Tuesday, Wednesday and Thursday, Monday and Friday not so good,' **AN**; 'Unloading good,' **DJR**; 'Willing to work and will help you,' **IB**; 'Good organisation,' **DD**; 'Good tipping,' **JFB**; 'Fast unloading — brilliant,' **FH** (● ●) Comments: 'Slow,' **MH**; 'Will not work when raining,' 'Bad Customs,' **JB**; 'Customs keep you waiting all day,' RD; 'Too many tea-breaks,' **CS** 'Dockers not interested,' **SWP, SD**; 'Always on strike,' **SM**; 'Long waits, poor facilities, no help,' **JHK**; 'Lazy,' **PT**; 'Restrictive practices,' AWP; 'Long delays,' **DR**; 'Just terrible,' **LM**,; 'Slow tipping,' **RG**; 'Long waits,' **SM**; 'Too busy to attend to you,' **GN**; 'Bad equipment, out of date, constantly breaks down,' **BM**.

IMMINGHAM (★ ★ ★ ★ ★ ★ ★ ★ ★ ★) Comments: 'Quick,' **NH**; 'EXXTOR, we own them,' **RD**; 'Good docks and customs,' **AN**; 'Rapid loading,' **RS**; 'No wasted time,' **RS**; 'Fast and efficient,' **MM**; 'Helpful,' **DA**; 'Dockers are helpful,' **PLM**. (● ● ● ●) Comments: 'Too many tea breaks,' **FEW**; 'Very slow,' **HE**.

IPSWICH (★ ★ ★ ★ ★ ★ ★) Comments: 'Quick clearance,' **JdK**; 'Good facilities and good canteen,' **AN**. (● ● ● ● ● ●) Comments: '8-hours waiting for delivery and C.M.R. notes,' **RD**; 'Bone idle,'**MN**; 'Slow, too much waiting about,' **RAH**; 'No room for larger tankers.' **PK**.

KINGS LYNN (★ ★ ★ ★ ★ ★ ★ ★) Comments: 'Good loading points,' **IW**; 'Quick,' **JS**; 'Better turnaround,' **AN**; 'Good loading and unloading facilities,' **F**. (● ●) Comment: 'Waiting,' **RH**.

LEITH (★) Comment; 'No bother loading,' **DT** (●).

LIVERPOOL (★ ★) Comments: 'Friendly,' **TH**; 'Pretty quick,' **JB**; Quick turnaround, good customs,' **TR**; 'Improving,' **CS** 'Getting better, good customs, **MM**; 'It had died, so you don't wait any more,' **SWP** 'Fast,' **FSL**; Easy in and out,' **TR**; 'No wasted time in and out,' **RS**; 'Average,' **GH**; 'All but two closed down' AN; 'No problems,' JM; (● ●) Comments: 'Always wait,' **C**; 'Very slow, don't seem to want to work,' **JK**; 'Not interested, idle sods,' **TB**; 'Keep you waiting,' **IM**; 'Time problems,' **JB**; 'Lazy moaning sods,' **JJW**; 'Lazy' **JM**; 'Do not want to work,' **BM, DR, AS**; 'Do not like work,' **DD**; 'Ignorant dockers, not interested,' **JA**; 'Keep you waiting,' **MM, CF, AB**; 'Long waits,' **SM, PLM**; 'Always on breaks,' **GT**; 'Rubbish,' **AN**; 'Lazy bastards,' **NA**;'Waited four days,' **JW**; 'Once waited two days,' **KT**; 'Unprintable what I think,' **DLL**; 'Uncivilised,' **TB**; 'Uncivil,' **PR**; 'Not organised,' **EN**; 'Slow, and too slow,' **JC, MT, PK, RA, KD, JO, DAS**; 'Long waits, poor facilities, no help,' **JHK**; 'You can't get a Scouser to work,' **AN**; 'Very bad and too slow,' **JS**; 'Don't care,' **DJR**; 'Bad unions,' **CA, JL**; 'Unfriendly and idle,' **JH**;'Lazy,' **JJ**; 'Lazy sods,' **DW**; 'Nobody wants to know about work,' **TM**; 'Bone idle,' **DN**; 'Lazy gitts,' **MD**; 'Too slow, lazy' **CB**; 'Hold-ups due to bad organisation and shift changing,' **DG**; 'Attitude is most non-helpful,' **DD**; 'They don't want to know,' **WM**; 'Frightened of work,' **RH**; 'Too much delay,' **GS**; 'Won't give you a hand,' **PF**; 'Can't get a load on and will not clear you,' **D**; 'Dockers are idle,' **DL**; 'Liverpool, what's left of it — dockers and hard work are total strangers,' **GW**.

LONDON (★ ★ ★ ★ ★) Comments: 'Always efficient,' **IM**; 'You are given a number in the rank,' **WM**. (●●●●●●●●●●●●●●●●●●●●●●●●●●●●●●●●) 'Too many tea and other breaks, **AM, AH**; 'Too much waiting,' **MB**; 'Three hours wait,' **TB**; 'Too lazy,' **BB**; 'Do not want too work,' **BM**; 'No facilities,' **DB**; 'Don't want any work,' **SB**; 'Bad, what's left of it,' **SS**; 'Unfriendly and idle,' **JH**; 'Too slow,' **JBD**; 'Too busy,' **GW**; 'Dockers are idle,' **DL**.

LOWESTOFT (★ ★ ★ ★) Comments: 'Never kept waiting,' **C**; 'Good because it is privately owned,' **T**.

MARGATE (★) Comment: 'They are very fast,' **MM**.

MIDDLESBOROUGH (★ ★ ★) Comments: 'Quick,' **AA**; 'Men willing to work and help you,' **IB**; (● ● ● ● ● ●) Comments: 'Slow tip,' **RF**; 'Bad organisation,' **DG**.

MANCHESTER INTERNATIONAL FREIGHT TERMINAL (★ ★ ★ ★ ★ ★ ★ ★ ★) Comment: 'Civil.' **PR**. (●) Comment: 'Paperwork continually mislaid,' **SM**.

MISTLEY (★ ★ ★) Comments: 'Quick and efficient,' **JB**; 'Good and helpful,' **JO**.

MONTROSE (★ ★ ★) Comment: 'Good workers,' **JM**. (●●) 'Too much in so little space,' **GM**.

MOSTON, North Wales (●)

NEWCASTLE (★)

IT'S THE WAY YOU TELL'EM

Golden silence
'Did you know your wife had fallen out of the car down the road?' The policeman asked the driver. 'Thank God,' said the driver with a sigh of relief, 'I thought I'd gone deaf.'
Alan Marsh, *Dinas Powis*.

NEWHAVEN (★) Comment: 'No such thing as good customs due to Government cuts, staff shortages and always working to rule — but, if anything, this one is best,' **AN**. (●●) 'Lazy,' **MW**.

NEWPORT (★ ★ ★ ★ ★ ★ ★ ★ ★ ★) Comments: 'Good because I know the lads,' **FG**; 'Dealt with efficiently,' **TB**; 'Very quick at loading,' **AN**; 'Fast load and unload,' **DB**; 'Good loading points,' **IW**; 'Quick,' **GB**; 'Well organised,' **RA**; 'Quick and helpful staff,' **AH**; 'Quick,' **AB**; 'Fast turnaround,' **AM**. (●●) Comment: 'Slow and too much waiting,' **TR, MH**.

NEWRY (★)

NORTHFLEET (★) Comment: 'Small and helpful' **DD**.

PENZANCE (★) Comment: 'Very quick and friendly,' **DJ**.

PLYMOUTH (★ ★ ★)

POOLE (★ ★ ★ ★ ★ ★ ★ ★ ★ ★ ★) Comments: 'Small and friendly, good customs,' **IE**; 'Not too busy,' **DM**; 'Just trucks, no cars,' **AN**; 'Small,' **GMW**.

PORTSMOUTH (★ ★ ★ ★ ★ ★ ★ ★ ★ ★ ★) Comments: 'Non-union,' **DR**; 'Helpful and friendly,' **JH**; 'Very decent and understanding,' **DV**.

PRESTON (★) Comment: 'No hanging around, all facilities,' **GS**.

PURFLEET DEEP WATER (★ ★ ★) Comments: 'In and out fairly quickly,' **CS**; 'No union bother,' **DLL**; 'Quick loading,' **DU**. (● ●) Comment: 'Long waits,' **DL**.

RAMSGATE (★ ★ ★ ★ ★ ★ ★) Comments: 'Good customs,' **DY, RJW**; 'Organised and helpful,' **KC**; 'Quick clearance,' **HL** (Holland); 'Usually no hassle,' **AM**; 'Another very decent and understanding crowd,' **DV**. (●) Comment: 'Bad customs,' **AD**.

ROCHESTER (★ ★) Comment: 'Quick,' **GL**. (●)

RUNCORN (★ ★) Comments: 'Fast and efficient — and they know me,'**GW**; 'Fairly quick,' **CC**. (●)

SEAFORTH (★)

SHARPNESS (★ ★)

SHEERNESS (★ ★ ★ ★ ★ ★ ★ ★) Comments: 'Loading from 7 a.m. until 9 p.m., good customs,' **DJL**; 'No waiting,' **RH**; 'Friendly, helpful and a good canteen,' 'Easy to find,' **JJW**; (● ● ● ●) 'Always held up,' **DT**; 'Keep you as long as possible,' **SN**; 'Roads rough, people rude,' **MB**.

SHOREHAM (●)

SOUTHAMPTON (★ ★) Comments: 'Good because dockers are worried about their jobs,' **DW**; 'Pretty quick,' **JH**; 'Quick turnaround,' **AJ, SB**; 'Quick turnaround, good customs,' **TR**; 'No queue jumping,' **DY**; '4-hours service,' **SM**; 'No queue jumpers allowed,' **CM**; 'Quick,' **SL, RK**; 'Easy clearing,' **DW** (● ● ● ● ● ● ● ● ● ● ● ● ● ● ●) Comments: 'Too unionised,' **SJF**; 'Too militant,' **DR**; 'Too many officials,' **IF**; 'Bad organisation,' **DG**; 'Unhelpful and awkward,' **CH**; 'Do not like work,' **DD**; 'Shit-hole,' **JL**.

STRABANE (★) Comment: 'Good customs,' **AN**.

STRANRAER (★ ★) Comments: 'Fast turnaround,' **IH**; 'Very quick,' **ML**. (●) Comment: 'It's a dump,' **CP**.

SWANSEA (★ ★ ★ ★) Comments: 'Not kept waiting,' **CS**; 'Quick,' **NW**.

TEIGNMOUTH (★ ★ ★) Comments: 'Quick loading,' **JK**; :Very quick and helpful,' **CS**.

TILBURY (★ ★) Comments: 'Quick off,' **KG**; 'Number 38 shed is very good,' **TL**; 'Containers well handled,' **AN**; 'Good turnaround,' **IW**; 'Good, but too many ships use it,' **SB**; 'Quick,' **IF**; 'Tip in half-an-hour,' **SM**; 'Never had any problems,' **MW**; 'Fast,' **DB**; 'Easy to find, easy to load,' **MB**; (● ●) Comments: 'Confusing dock,' **RM**; 'Militant, bolshie and un-cooperative,' **CS**; 'Too many lengthy breaks,' **GC**; 'Long-winded,' **ANW**; 'Lazy buggers,' **AJ**; 'Four to five hours to turn round,' **DAN**; 'Not interested,' **BW**; 'Long waiting periods,' **GL**; 'Slow — ex-London dockers,' **JLE**; 'Long delays, no facilities, no help,' **JHK**; 'Too much red tape,' **SL**; 'Union problems,' **CA**; 'Average time taken four hours,' **BA**; 'Too many strikes and too lazy,' **AM**; 'Very slow — too many tea breaks,' **DA**; 'Kept me five hours just to load,'**IW**; 'Badly organised,' **DG**; 'Slow,' **RR**; 'Lazy dockers, too much union,' **RK**; 'Militant restrictive practices,' **DV**; 'No help at all,' **DA**; 'The worst,' **RB**.

WATCHET, SOMERSET (★ ★) Comment: 'Exellent help,' **EB**.

WHARTON (Guiness) (★ ★)

WIVENHOE (★ ★)

STOP! POLICE CHECK

SMOKEY AND THE BANDITS

So how about Smokey and the Bandits, then? Well, it isn't exactly as it seems to be. Or, to be more precise, it isn't as it *sounds* to be. If you listen to the general chat about police, the impression you get is that it is the case of 'war, war' with the boys in the Jam Sandwiches, and not at all a matter of 'jaw, jaw' with them.

When drivers were questioned quietly — and soberly — about their relationships with the police (rumoured to be not good) by a very large majority they replied that they found them pretty good on the whole — and if not good to the point of commenting about it, good enough to consider the Smokies generally helpful and fair.

Admittedly, that could be that not so many Breakers are getting nicked nowadays because of the CB network and plenty of advance warning as to where trouble might lurk unexpectedly. But by and large, there seemed to be an affinity with the police rather than an antagonism. Does that surprise you? It surprised me and other people particularly in view of the deluge of complaints of harass-

'Personally, when I've got them in front of me and I'm travelling at 49mph and I can see everything they're up to — I regard them as guardian angels.'

127

ment which poured out on matters of the law earlier in the book.

At first glance it seems there is a serious contradiction in drivers' thinking about legal authorities: you cannot really say one minute that you are being harassed to distraction, and virtually in the same breath say that the harassers are pretty helpful and fair blokes.

Is it a question of 'the singer not the song'? Or put another musical way, 'don't shoot the piano player, he's doing his best'.

Among our several hundred respondents, perhaps driver **Frank Allington**, of West Malling, Kent, sums it up in the simplest way: 'They all have got a job to do.'

So they do it, and drivers, on the strength of their previous bitter comments, suffer while they still grin and bear it — though not exactly in stoical silence. Wherever drivers meet and talk the moans and groans reach a crescendo. Maybe if some enterprising truckstop built a Wailing Wall like the Jews have in Jerusalem, they would be on to a good thing; half an hour of serious atonement and bawling out the bricks and mortar after a stint on the road might be good for HGV men's souls — those who have them.

On the other hand, Mr **W.R. Lucas**, of Crofty, Swansea, may have the answer: 'They're all fair — unless they book you.' To follow that, and in quest of the truth about Smokey, let us listen to what you say about Her Majesty's Constabulary when you are talking about them behind their backs:

Hang about — is there a hint here that Mr **Lucas** has put the finger on an eternal truth: all police are good except the ones who have given you a hard time? Why else should Mr **Trevor Gray**, of Minster, Ramsgate, say that 'all do an excellent job — bar Somerset' and Richard Dembisky lament 'with two exceptions, all others are fair' and the CB-handle man, **Meandher**, pronounce them to be 'mostly helpful but with a little aggravation from those in Southampton'? Add to those Mr **Lawrence Higgins**, of Gloucester, whose experience is recorded: 'Humberside is antagonistic, all others are helpful.'

Fairness

'All are fair,' **T. Musgrove**, Stanford; **D.B. Emmerson**, Dumfries; **Ian McClachlan**, Dalbeatti; **TN**; **MW**. 'Police are very fair in general.' **Dennis Blacklock**, Carlisle — and that is a random selection from literally hundreds of replies to questions about the state of the police vis à vis drivers — surprising?

Helpfulness

'Most police are very helpful,' Driver, Bromsgrove; 'police in all areas are good, helpful and fair,' **R. Hutchins**, Stratford, London; 'Most police forces are helpful,' **M. Boyle**, of Cheddleton; 'To my mind, are very helpful,' **Roy Hudson**, of Sale, Cheshire; 'Everyone is helpful,' Mr **Friebel**, Nijmegan, Holland; 'I find the police throughout the country to be helpful rather than antagonistic,' **Paul Bonney**, St. Neots; 'All helpful,' **Gambler**, Gravesend; 'In general, all are helpful,' **A.J. Squire**, Cardiff — and that is a second random selection from a mass of documentation..

Reasonableness and attitude

'They are all reasonable,' **N. Powell**, Ross-on-Wye; 'Practically every force in Britain is good,' **L.M. McDonald**, Forfar; 'All are good,' Sheldon driver; 'No trouble with any of them,' **Malcolm Collins**, Basingstoke; 'No trouble with any of them because I am a good driver,' **R.P. Fell**, Cleethorpes; 'British police are all good,' **Memet Bayhan**, Turkey; 'They do a good job,' **Peter Mack**, Milton Keynes; 'No problems,' **W.** Belgium; 'No hassles... except in Birmingham,' **Tiger**, Stallam; 'Generally do a good job, especially when you are in trouble,' **Mick**, Chesterfield; 'All are fairly good, just the young ones are a bit sharp,' **Bob Morriss**, Norwich; 'All much of a muchness, the police are fair, traffic wardens are the ones to watch,' **Brian Pritchard**, Cannock: 'All vary, they are just doing their job,' **Ray Ramsey**, Failsworth, Manchester; 'Forces have good and bad days,' **Harry Bickley**, Hyde, Cheshire; 'No trouble, if spoken to properly,' **Sour Apple**, Walsall; 'I avoid them,' **M.D. Powell**, Basingstoke; 'Haven't met any yet,' Thirsk driver.

IT'S BIZARRE

no sitting on the fence

It was a bright idea, but it has its snags. A colleague of **Diesel Ringer**, from Monmouth, was having trouble getting the sheets off a high load so he figured that if he tied the sheet to a nearby fence and drove the truck forward his problem would be solved. He did — and pulled the fence down.

A real dumb blonde

Our informant from Rawtenstall, Lancashire, passed a car with a woman sitting very still in the passenger seat next to the driver and she appeared to be dressed only in her undies. He looked again and saw it was a life-size blow-up doll dressed in all the kinky gear. She was belted in.

Good lads

'They brought us coffee out of their own flask when we were snowed up near Bury St. Edmunds,' Swinton, Manchester, driver; 'Gwent police gave me a pen for safe driving,' **Trevor Fox**, Cambridgeshire.

Bad lads

'All are antagonistic,' Driver, Grimsby; 'Most are antagonistic, the rest are bastards,' Driver, Bradford; 'All bastards,' Drivers, Staines; 'They are all bastards,' Middleton driver; 'All forces are bad, especially Leeds,' Leighton Buzzard man; 'Ignorant gitts,' Basingstoke driver; 'Hampshire are swines,' Driver Weston-super-mare; 'Monmouth police are ruthless,' Liverpool driver; 'Dumfries — PIGS,' Scottish man; 'YUK!' Loper.

Out of a sample of just under 1,000 answers of which 844 named specific police forces and the rest gave general answers of the type listed above, you voted more than 3 to 1 in favour of the police.

One thing became quite apparent, you much prefer the police to the dockers — how about that?

Also revealed with startling clarity was the worst town in Britain for relations between police and drivers: *DUMFRIES*.

And the worst counties in Britain where the police are detested by most drivers: *LINCOLNSHIRE closely followed by ESSEX*.

There is a worst town in England — but dare I mention it? Yes, I'll be brave. It is that town which had a famous corner grocer's shop where a certain eminent person spent her childhood. And that, depending on the tortuous nature of your minds, may mean something: it is *GRANTHAM*. Grantham is a bad place for drivers — and so are nearby *SLEAFORD* and *WETHERBY*, in Yorkshire.

It is suggested that there are specific reasons for the last two mentioned: one is a training patch for traffic police and the other has the notorious weighbridge. But Grantham is just plain bloody-minded, so you say.

To get a direct fix on any particular police force is exceptionally difficult, if only because, self-evidently, drivers are mobile and passing through up to a dozen different areas in a day's work. Then there are contradictions: **Colin Hiorns**, of Timperley, thinks that town police are more antagonistic, yet another driver considers that town police are far more understanding and flexible than rural forces simply because they have to be allowing for the volume of traffic.

What does seem to emerge from the survey is that police forces' attitudes to drivers are spread over quite large geographical areas and not confined to isolated 'black spots' — with the obvious exception of Dumfries and Grantham, which do stand out.

Significantly, not a single complaint was registered against the motorway traffic police.

With that fact out of the way, I can concentrate on the rest and group them into areas such as the Midlands, East Anglia, the South East, the Metropolitan and large city areas and so on. Since this is a guide for HGV drivers and not an analysis of police operations, I can use a simple rule of thumb method to establish a 'rating' giving pluses and minuses to police forces you will meet on your journeys so that you will know when to take your foot off the pedal and not take unnecessary liberties — as if you ever would!

We asked drivers to state which police were *good*, *helpful*, *fair* or *antagonistic*: for each *good* registered I award three points, for each *helpful*, two points and for each *fair*, one point; for each *antagonistic*, minus four points is allotted. This system gives a balance in favour of the compliments, which seems the right thing to do. Then I subtract the 'bads' from the aggregate of the 'goods' and come up with a plus or minus 'rating'.

I hope that has confused you sufficiently. All you really need to know is that when you see a *minus* rating, watch it! When you see a *plus* rating, relax!

So here it is, our **SMOKEY AND THE BANDITS RATINGS:**
Your assessment of the police forces in descending order:

NORTH WEST rating +54
(Lancashire, Cheshire, Merseyside, Liverpool and area)

	Good	Helpful	Fair	Antagonistic
Sum	22	10	30	18

Remarks Driver commented: 'Real bastards round Clitheroe.'

LONDON rating +54
(Greater London and the City of London)

	Good	Helpful	Fair	Antagonistic
Sum	16	32	42	25

Remarks Driver commented: 'More sympathetic than rural forces.'

GREATER MANCHESTER rating +45

	Good	Helpful	Fair	Antagonistic
Sum	13	14	14	9

Remarks This force controls more urban motorway than any other and seems to have a more positively helpful attitude to HGVs to judge by the good and helpful responses.

EAST ANGLIA rating +38
(Cambridge, Suffolk, Norfolk and east of Peterborough)

	Good	Helpful	Fair	Antagonistic
Sum	17	7	21	12

Remarks Drivers comment particularly about chemical tanker checks on the A45 but are favourably impressed by help at the big ports.

MOTORWAYS rating +24
(Motorway routes all over Britain)

	Good	Helpful	Fair	Antagonistic
Sum	4	3	6	0

Remarks No hassle, no problems so little comment provoked. One driver commented: 'They do a bloody good job.'

THE MIDLANDS rating +23
(The vast area including Birmingham, the Black Country, Stafford, Nottingham and west towards Wales)

	Good	Helpful	Fair	Antagonistic
Sum	23	16	38	29

Remarks A unique blend of city, motorway and rural driving conditions. Driver **DA** commented about Stafford: 'The place is a pain in the bum.'

THE NORTH EAST rating +18
(Geordieland north of the Humber and up towards Scotland)

	Good	Helpful	Fair	Antagonistic
Sum	7	5	3	4

Remarks You can see where the traffic rolls nowadays from the answers recorded. A driver commented: 'Like the work, the traffic just goes through this area without stopping.'

THE SOUTH EAST rating +16
(The Home Counties and going south)

	Good	Helpful	Fair	Antagonistic
Sum	17	15	15	20

Remarks The prosperous, thriving part of Britain thick in jobs, money, houses, stockbroker belts, people and congestion; so perhaps the rating is much better than it first appears. A driver commented: 'The Kent police are hot on chemical tankers, and they are the best trained in the country, They really know their safety rules.' Yet to emphasise the entirely personal and subjective nature of these things, one driver's opinion was: 'THE WORST!'

YORKSHIRE rating +2

	Good	Helpful	Fair	Antagonistic
Sum	13	15	17	21

Remarks Yorkshire's rating is downgraded by certain black-spots like Leeds and Wetherby which drivers dislike intensely. One driver commented: 'They ambush you, they're very bad.' A second said: 'The weighbridge is a disgrace.' A third tempered the anger: 'They are helpful but very strict.'

HUMBERSIDE rating 0
(Big tanker and chemical country, Immingham, Grimsby and the south side of the Humber Bridge)

	Good	Helpful	Fair	Antagonistic
Sum	5	1	3	5

Remarks There isn't actually much opportunity to do a lot wrong in this area, the conditions are against it — say that Humberside police are very even-handed in their approach.

WEST COUNTRY rating −1
(Bristol, Avon, Cornwall, Devon, Somerset up towards Cheltenham)

	Good	Helpful	Fair	Antagonistic
Sum	8	10	7	13

Remarks Drivers comment: 'Cheltenham is very bad.'; 'I wish they'd pick up the slowest drivers as well as the fastest.'; 'They pick on HGVs.' 'They do not understand chemical tankers.'

NORTHAMPTONSHIRE rating −2
(Came up often as a special area for comment)

	Good	Helpful	Fair	Antagonistic
Sum	2	2	4	4

Remarks It is useful to see how a compact area shapes up in the survey but within the context of the Midlands generally.

THAMES VALLEY rating −4
(A very populous area but, strangely, seemingly not highly significant to HGV men)

	Good	Helpful	Fair	Antagonistic
Sum	3	0	4	6

Remarks A driver commented: 'They're all Evel Knievels.'

CUMBRIA rating −12
(All that area narth of Manchester conurbation and Lancashire)

	Good	Helpful	Fair	Antagonistic
Sum	5	1	2	8

Remarks A very important route for truckers. A driver commented: 'Carlisle — watch out, Mate!'

WALES rating −17
(The whole of the Principality)

	Good	Helpful	Fair	Antagonistic
Sum	10	5	11	17

Remarks Another case of selected black-spots downgrading a whole area. Gwent may give away pens to good drivers, but it came up very strongly as a potential danger spot for HGV men. Some of the observations about Gwent police were very rude — in English. Monmouth, the half-and-half Welsh town also got a pasting. Very mixed and, broadly speaking, hostile country.

SCOTLAND rating −32
(All of Scotland from the border upwards)

	Good	Helpful	Fair	Antagonistic
Sum	21	25	23	42

Remarks Out of 42 recorded antagonistic answers 18 replied to the question in the following terms about the Dumfries and Galloway police: 'Bastards,'; 'Ignorant gitts,' 'Pigs,' 'Shits,' 'Appalling.' No other place in Britain occasioned such an explosion of anger and vituperation. Not even the worst place in England, with a rating of −63, could match the unbridled rage and language evoked by this area. Could there be something wrong up there?

ESSEX rating −47
(East of London to the coast and East Coast ports, M11, M25 and Dartford Tunnel, and A12 country — very busy)

	Good	Helpful	Fair	Antagonistic
Sum	2	2	7	16

Remarks The Essex police have an unfortunate reputation for picking on HGVs often without apparent provocation and for no good reason. The A12 is notorious for unwarranted hold-ups — and consequently missing ferries at the East Coast ports. Perhaps Essex traffic police need a re-think of their approach. As the preponderance of drivers say, the police are just doing their job — so too are HGV drivers.

LINCOLNSHIRE rating −63
(North of Peterborough up virtually to the Humber and west to Nottingham, a big, sparsely populated area)

	Good	Helpful	Fair	Antagonistic
Sum	0	3	8	20

Remarks According to drivers, this huge county is a series of black holes in a big black spot. It is flat with good roads but bad truck-driving country peopled by police who, according to driver **AH**, are: 'A rare breed of bastards, apparently it is a training ground for motorway police so everything in sight is nicked to give them experience.' The towns of Grantham and Sleaford come in for bitter criticism, the latter with a suggestion, 'they are trying to cover the cost of the new weighbridge at Sleaford by nicking people on it. 'So the Lincolnshire constabulary wins the unenviable title of 'Least Loved Policemen in England.'

IT'S BIZARRE

A funny thing happened...
'In broad daylight on the A5 I watched a bright light hovering over Rugby radio station. Then two fighter aircraft arrived and it disappeared,' recounts **Peter Deakin**, who comes from Rugeley. He also tells how, after a hard day's driving, he arrived back at the depot and found his bicycle missing. After a frantic search he discovered it slung from the warehouse rafters with an attached message: 'ET rides again!'

Shanghaied...
There was a misunderstanding when **Barry Addlington**, of Hayes, Middlesex, was delivering to Argus, at Daventry. He heard a couple of thumps which he took to be a signal to go, so he drove off. But he was only half unloaded so he motored on with an Argus warehouseman and his pallet-truck still in the back.

Naturally, the answers to the questions tell you as much about drivers as they do about police. So judgement must be exercised in assessing the value of the results. On the weight of evidence that judgement should be that the vast majority of the police are *OK*, and the drivers are a responsible, law-abiding lot on the whole. The relationship between the two groups is very much better than would ever be imagined, to hear the talk, and the proverbial few 'bad eggs' taint the whole.

<u>*NOT*</u> THE GOOD
TIPPING GUIDE

It is the ever-recurring problem of the working day turned into the waiting day, and the waiting day into the wasted day, and the wasted day into the wageless day for the self-employed, and why the cock-up theory cocks-up more drivers than anybody else — and who organises this chaos anyway?

So we thought we would try to help by compiling a list of all the places where the tipping and loading is good *in your experience*, or not-so-hot, or could-be-better *when you have been there* — and to hell with the red faces.

'You'll have to back up to the camp commissariat at the end of this road ... but the rules state that you'll either have to strip off or wear a blindfold while you're on camp premises.'

The theory behind this was that it might do you a bit of good to be forewarned as to what to expect; but the practice would be that it wouldn't make a ha'p'orth of difference. You would either be tipped/loaded and rolling with speed and efficiency, or not tipped/loaded and left hanging about in the usual manner. So all you would gain would be the satisfaction of knowing what to expect and making arrangements accordingly for good or bad firms. The Stock Exchange could learn a lot from HGV drivers. It might pay one of those high-powered investment analysts to put a few pointed questions to truck drivers about the customers they visit. Few people know better than the truck driver in the dispatch or delivery bay the strength of a company: its efficiency and organisation hangs out at the back door like a line of washing in a suburban garden showing what goes on inside.

The plan did not work. No real, meaningful pattern resulted from your replies. All that emerged was an enormous list of good places to deliver to and load from, and an almost equally long list of bad places.

The lists themselves were fascinating in a Nosy Parker sort of way, household names cropped up frequently and were shown to be a bit of a shambles behind the scenes — and that is rather like reading the private lives of the famous and infamous in the scandal sheets, you might deplore it but you can't stop doing it.

In fact, some sort of pattern was beginning to form, though not strongly enough to put a firm finger on. It showed that companies which are famous for being in trouble, and a lot of those which have made take-over headlines, are the ones that have difficulties in getting their goods in and out of their places of business.

Others clearly brought joy to drivers' hearts. Like Ben Jonsons, of York. That was the spelling **Paul Taylor**, of Bradford, gave when he described them as : 'Brilliant, 20-tonnes loaded in half-an-hour.' Or Pfizer Chemicals, Widnes, of whom **Doug Vick** says 'magic.' LEICD, the container set-up in Barking, began to come up strongly, as did the Manchester International Freight Terminal, which also came out well in the docks section. Perhaps the best overall contenders for compliments were all divisions of ICI which came up a number of times, from fertilisers to bulk chemicals. Though Winsford and Billingham did come in for a bit of stick. Paper mills also came up well.

Those are but a few names out of hundreds. A great number of people have got it organised, according to the way our list was beginning to take shape, rather more than the ones who haven't. Though that still means a massive waste of time, effort and money because of those who fall into the latter category. It would have been nice to produce a comprehensive list clearly indicating good and bad. But this first survey of ours did not produce sufficient detail to be useful to the trucking fraternity as a whole. Well, you can't win 'em all.

What did become clear is what most drivers already know:

countless millions of the Gross National Effort as well as the Gross National Product are being frittered away in useless waiting at inefficient loading and delivery points. Economists are quick to point out how many man-hours are lost by industrial action; those would look like raindrops in an ocean if compared with the man-hours lost by sheer ineptitude. The difference is that industrial action is a self-inflicted wound, enforced industrial inaction is an arm and a leg cut off by somebody else's behaviour.

Let us be quite clear about this: it is a plain and simple industrial and commercial problem which should be a matter of concern for the **CBI**, Institute of Directors and suchlike organisations, and most of all for shareholders whose dividends are dribbling away at the loading bay because some warehouse manager can't get his act together.

That is the only way to get anything done about it: tell them it's costing them *money*.

Imagine the outrage at the annual general meeting if a finance director got up and said: 'Our transport costs are so sky-high because we had to pay these lorry drivers for sitting on their backsides in their cabs, reading Page Three of the *Sun*, for hours because the warehouse couldn't unload them — but they're nice lads, so we don't begrudge them the money.'

He might add: 'And Charlie, who runs the warehouse, is a bit past it anyway — as well as being a bit thick...'

Of course, it doesn't work like that. More often than not the person who pays for Charlie being a bit thick and past it is the lorry driver working on his own account. It's all very wrong — but still a fact of life on, or in this case, off the road.

What was revealed in your answers was what everybody expected to be revealed. I suppose there is some consolation in having confirmation of what you know. Thus:

IT'S BIZARRE

The early bird catches a cold

A keen lad, **P. Austin**, of Leeds, arrived at his tip very early and was well pleased with himself. It was 07.45 and he had to wait until 8 o'clock for the shop to open. He sat in his cab, dropped off until 11.30, spent the rest of the day making up three and three-quarter hours and explaining why he was late.

Short stay

After a motorway pile-up, three drivers stood at the Pearly Gates. St Peter scrutinised them: 'BRS — you come in. Goodyear — you come in. Ryder's Express — hang about, there's a back-load for you.'
D.J. Hendry, *Handsworth, Birmingham.*

SUPERMARKETS , all supermarkets but some more so than others, are a disaster area for truck drivers. There are a few, a very few, good ones which shine like lighthouses in a general thick fog of incompetence. It really is quite astonishing that such high-powered, aggressive, up-front retailers handling such sheer volume should be so bad at the back.

DIY STORES, this mushrooming sector of high street trade runs the conventional supermarkets a close second for driver aggravation.

FRUIT and VEGETABLE MARKETS vary enormously, but many are chaotic and utterly time-wasting.

In general, the retail trades tend to be messy from a driver's point of view. That, in part, is the nature of the business, though in the mid-1980s, in the middle of the great marketing boom era, you would have expected them to have sorted something out by now.

FARMS can age drivers before their time...

STEEL came up repeatedly on the black side of the survey, but why it should is difficult to understand. It is a straighforward commodity with no apparent difficulties in loading or unloading, except the weight, and it ought to be easy. But it isn't, not according to those of you who have to collect and cart the stuff around. The answer may lie in that provocative word nationalisation. Be that overtly political or not, it seems to be a fact; if it is or was nationalised, whatever it is it will be a pretty tricky, exasperating tip or pick-up.

BRITISH LEYLAND, in particular Austin-Rover at Longbridge, came in for a lot of criticism.

COLD STORES come in the categories of very good or awful. The bad ones never seem to have their cargoes ready, for some reason. It could be that the retail trade messes them about a lot.

FACTORIES and tanker men do not seem to have a happy relationship in many cases. A lot of this is due to industry converting to oil as an energy source. It appears that oil tanks are placed in the most inaccessible spots as a matter of course. This accounts for some tanker drivers' conceit, they regard themselves as undisputed champions of the road because of the places they have to squeeze into when delivering to factories. Very often each run is a test of skill and initiative in putting a motorised camel through the eye of an industrial needle. They are, quite rightly, proud of their achievements in this field.

What it boils down to is that the infrastructure of the country has not changed or advanced as rapidly as the modern, huge, sophisticated HGV, it hasn't expanded rapidly enough to accomodate 38-tonners and more. And it is going to take a long time for buildings to catch up with vehicles now in common use.

But you are a skilled driver and you can handle your truck like a mini...

TOP OF THE CAFÉ
POPS CHART

It is all a question of taste — and a little bit of what you fancy does you good. Well, you can't fancy *that* all the time, so we'll talk about food and sustenance. Whether they are junk food, fast food, health food or plain good food freaks, what all drivers have in common is that they are value-for-money fanatics. And this is reflected in the persistent and insistent cries from all drivers we questioned: 'Motorway services charges are exorbitant and the quality is awful.'

You might be like **Peter Austin**, of Bramley, Leeds, who answered the question 'Name your best café' with the reply 'My Mum's Kitchen, Leeds.' Mind you, if there is a café called that, congratulations to them for a great name. But there is a risk that Mrs Austin might get a flood of unexpected guests, so we will withhold the address. On the other hand, you might be of the same mind as **K Nine**, of Somewhere in the South, who answered the question 'Name your worst overnight stop' with the terse reply: 'Home!'

But individual tastes apart, the test of a good café is how many people use and then recommend it. An advertisement or a standard guide book will tell you what the place has to offer, where it is and what the proprietors would like you to think about it. The basis of our guide to good grub and *proper* prices is what *drivers* say — and only drivers.

So we have compiled two lists for readers: the first is our *Top of the Café Pops Chart* which comes in the order of most popular, most recommended and most used on drivers' say-so. In the second list (see page 187) we place the cafés by county in index form.

There is however a slight sting in the tail: we also list what drivers consider to be the worst cafés. That does not mean at all that they are necessarily bad eating or staying places; quite a few of those in the very top popularity bracket are named by some of you as right at the bottom of the heap — ah well, it is all a question of taste, and you can be very choosy indeed.

The approach is flawed because numbers alone cannot really count in assessing quality; the great life-lines of the nation run north to south so café-customers are thick on the ground on those routes, sparser going east or west. But numbers do give a guide, a good name spreads rapidly in this close-knit fraternity. We seek no five-star accolades, but just what *you* like. Such as:

THE HOLLIES A5　　　　　　　　　Tel: (0543) 53435

Situation* On the A5, Watling Street, M6 junction 12 a quarter of a mile away. Perfect access.

Services Overnight accommodation for 40, truck park for 200 on three sides of the building; Ultramar diesel.

Food Highly commended and good prices, dining-room seating 200.

Amenities A notedly friendly staff of 30: 'Really friendly people, a very friendly atmosphere,' **K. McDowell**, Birmingham; television; a few yards up the road is the 16th-century inn, The Four Crosses, selling Bank's Old Ale, providing live entertainment and very popular with drivers.

Proprietor Derek Curtis is a fastidious man who took over a tea-place shack 29 years ago and built it to its present state. His approach is: 'I eat in the place myself, and if the food isn't good enough for me, it isn't good enough for the drivers. And I am a very fussy man. I buy all the food fresh when available. We had new potatoes, a drivers' favourite, on the menu when they came on the market at 80p a pound. Even with items like baked beans, I won't buy until I've tasted them. I buy Danish bacon, and that has got to be right. I buy only the best, and I keep the prices right.'

Recommended by: **B. Burnage**, Kettering; **F.S. Lowe**, Derby; **Peter Mack**, Milton Keynes; **N. Powell**, Ross-on-Wye; Driver, Bolton; **Derek Lenton**, Queenborough; Driver, Rochdale; Dennis Blacklock, Carlisle; **Plastic Cap**, Wigan; **Loper**; **B.R. Gammon**, Ashford, Kent; **W.R. Lucas**, Swansea; **Gwyn Latcham**, Tonypandy; **P. Enery**, Warrington; **S.W. Laffam**, Chorley; **J. Hughes** Leyland; Driver, Southampton; **J. Knest**, Exeter:

A funny thing happened...

Bryan Williams, of Leigh-on-sea, recalls the day he delivered to a builder in Lincolnshire: 'He was really ignorant. I arrived at the site just as he was going home. Rudely he snarled, 'Put them there, or take them back.' He pointed at a spot on the site, signed for them and stormed off. I put nine packs of bricks into a 6-foot square, they looked like a tower. I hope he had a ladder.'

---

*We have given as much and as detailed information as we could regarding the situation of the cafés listed. In some cases, this was not available. If in difficulty, we suggest you telephone for directions.

'I like it here, it's a very homely atmosphere.'

Frank Allington, East Malling; Driver, London; **T. Newman**, Brackley, Northants; **W. Morriss**, Hull; **Derek Gordon**, South Shields; **D. Cresswell**, Basildon; **P.O.P.** Hawley, Basildon; **Drunken Duck**, Wigan; **Steve Newall**, Leigh; **Steve Hoggard**, Wigan; **J. Mennie**, Friocheim, Angus; **E. Tearle**, Ramsgate; **J. Aylett**, Blyth; Driver, Wisbech; **R.E. Parry**, Anglesea; **Geoff Lomax**, Stockport; Driver, Oldham; **Trevor J.S. Gray**, Ramsgate; **John L. Evans**, Slough; **Mick**, Chesterfield; **Reg Sowman**, Kirkaldy; Mr. **Gorrett**, Crediton; **Tiger**, Stallam; **Geoffrey Nelson**, Wyrill, York; **D. Sherrington**, Maidenhead; **M. Foster**, Cannock; **Alan Arrowsmith**, Sandbatch; **Michael Weaver**, Standish; Driver, Alyth; **Ken Masters**, Woking, 'Very good food.' Driver, Manchester; Driver, Slough; **Jim Young**, Peterborough; **Sandy Gordon**, Kirkbride; **Lawrence Higgins**; Gloucester; **R. Mallinson**, Corby; **Ron Hetherington**, Blackburn; **Dennis Copeland**, Sheffield; Driver, Blackpool; Driver, Trafford Park; Driver, Romsey, Hants.; Driver, Sale; **Richard Buckley**, Worseley; Driver, Manchester; **Kevin Seaton**, Biggleswade; **S.Links**, Hendon; **R. Flint**, Richmond, Yorks: **Simon Tandy**, Ledbury; **Montague Murrell**, Basildon; **Bernard Cawston**, Dursley; **Chris Clark**, Ipswich; **Neptune**, Ipswich; **A. Stewart**, St. Boswells, 'Good food, reasonably priced.'; **D. Ellicott**, Swansea, 'Good value for money.'; **A. Dunn**, Skellow; **Ronald Balmer**, Appleby; Driver, Portadown; **J.Ousby**, 'Good food and value for money.' **Green Eagle**, Stallam; Mr **Walker**, Penrith; Mr **Pratt**, Swindon; **Alexander McNicol**, Aberdeen; **R.J. Chandler**, London; **Cinder Man**, Ayr; **John Wheatley**, Sutton Coalfield; **Lawrence Higgins**, Hardwick; **Malcolm Cow**, Hyde; Driver, Liverpool; **Pop Rivet**, Aspatria; **Richard Beddingfield**, Tydesley; **Drew Cook**, Liverpool; **R. Scott**, Kilwinning; **T.T. Hardman**, Warrington; **P. Thompson**, Widnes; **Colin Shaw**, Essex; Driver, Rochdale; **David Simmonds**, Gloucester; **Dave Hayter**, Bristol; Driver, Widnes; **P. Butterworth**, Shaw; **S. Mulvaney**, Audenshaw; **D. Davis**, Ystalyfera; **J. Lay**, Bedford; **A. Bell**, Anglesea; **K. Stedman**, Old Woking; **L. Dunn**, County Durham.

Now that formidable list of recommendations says a number of things: it says first that if you are interested enough and take the trouble to answer our questions, then we will take good note — except that we did not expect you to be so single-minded in your choices. But there you are, drivers are an awkward bunch of cusses at the best of times. It also says loud and clear that somebody has got it just about right when it comes to catering for the men on the long-haul trips: out of the mouths of drivers comes the message that Derek Curtis, of The Hollies, is putting the right thing into the mouths of drivers at a price that is also tasty to them.

There are about a dozen such places up and down the country, and they have all come out strongly in our listings. So we will print them with your recommendations in full.

SUNSET HOTEL M6   Tel: (078) 571 2283

Situation Wolverhampton Road, Penkridge, between Stafford and Wolverhampton; come off the M6 at junction 12 or 13; very good access with three entrances at the front, one at the rear.

Services 100 single bedrooms, sleeper-cab facilities; six showers, two on each floor and being extended; three pay-phones; garage adjoins truck park.

Food restaurant for 85, all home cooking by women cooks; all pies, puddings and tarts are home-made, and all food is bought in fresh; an overnight stay will cost you £9.95 including parking, three-course evening meal and light breakfast; for sleeper-cabs, £7.95 but including the meals — and there are reduced rates in summer.

Amenities full bar, live entertainment — Country and Western and cabaret artists five nights a week in winter, three nights in summer; a separate video-room, pool table and 26 staff to attend to your needs. Staff and guests are kept in order by Mrs Tricia Slade, a former WRAC — so stand by your beds.

Companionship always a crowd in, all truckers. Open 24 hours daily. Truck park is hard-standing on concrete and hard-core.

Recommended by: **Stanley Hunter**, Burtonwood; **Pat Finnigan**, Stirling; **David Simmonds**, Gloucester; **Alex Main**, Preston: Mr **Webster**, Teignmouth; **H. Hills**, Folkestone: **T. Barrigan**, Kirkby; **D. Cotteringham**, Ashford, Middlesex; **Diesel Ringer**, Monmouth; **Barley Bree**, Stirling; **A. Stewart**, Blairgowrie; **D. Littlewood**, York; **Cave Man**, Welwyn, Herts; Driver, Widnes; **Corsair**, Welwyn, Herts: Driver, Liverpool; **T. Newman**, Brackley, Northants; **L. McDonald**, Forfar, Angus; **M. Rooney**, Liverpool; Driver, Edinburgh; **John Paul Batty**, Droylesden, Manchester; **Dave Partington**, Bolton; **Arthur Hughes**, Liverpool; **Larry Mealy**, Liverpool; **Jim McNally**, Kirkby, Mr **May**, Liverpool; **John Cook**, Edmonton, London; **Stanley Hunter**, Burtonwood; **Riverboat**, Leyland; **Terrence Lane**, Barkingside; **Malcolm Dickinson**, Erith; **Cruiser One**, Cardiff; Driver, London; **T. Roberts**, Liverpool; **Roy Hudson**, Sale; Driver, Bristol; Driver, Liverpool; **R. Hutchins**, Stratford, London, London; **John (Foxy) Cunningham**, Prestonpans; **W. Cockram**, Liverpool; Driver, Chadwell Heath; **Rob Madden**, Denton, Manchester.

Note on the value The live entertainment costs more than £50 a night. When they say: 'Put your hands together for...' They should say: 'Put your hands together for a bargain!'

IT'S THE WAY YOU TELL'EM

A yolk

One egg in the saucepan to the other: 'By heck, it's hot in here!' The second replied: 'Wait till you get out, they'll smash your head in.'
Bryan Williams, *Leigh-on-sea, Essex.*

DEPUTY DOG'S A45   Tel: (0284) 810994

Situation On the A45 at Bury St. Edmunds with parking for 85 trucks.
Services Open 6 a.m. to 10 p.m. for full meals, and you will be all right for light refreshments until midnight; washrooms for drivers. Tony Doggett drove HGV for 40 years until he bought this café in 1982. He also bought the orchard next door and extended the truck park.

Deputy Dog's is ideally placed to serve the boat and docks trade at Felixstowe and Harwich. In the four years since it was begun it has proved its necessity. With the enormous developments planned at those two busy East Coast ports, and now with the 30,000-tonnes super-luxury ferry Koningin Beatrix in service from Harwich, its importance to truckers will steadily increase.

Food He serves all home-cooked food prepared by his wife Olwen: 'We supply every range of breakfast. The rest of the day there are roasts of beef, lamb and pork; lamb chops, gammon and our speciality is liver — a big demand for that. But we also have a full range of home-made pies of every sort. We don't go in for fast food. I didn't like it when I was driving, so I don't serve it.'

Amenities The drivers' bar, run by daughter Nicola, is a lounge as well. A staff of nine and Shell diesel complete the service. Once there were seven cafés between Felixstowe and Cambridge — now two: Deputy Dog's is still expanding.

Recommended by: **Davie Young**, Glasgow; **Jan de Koster**, Zwyndrecht, Holland; **Gordon Clark**, Lincoln; **Ron Bergmout**, Puttershoek, Holland; **Kiwi**, Tamworth; Driver, Warrington; **F.S Lowe**, Derby; Driver, Bolton; **J. Abbott**, Peterborough; Driver, Warrington, **Ian McClachan**, Dalbeatti; **Derek Gordon**, South Shields; **D.B. Emmerson**, Dumfries; **Roger Kindred**, Colchester; **Ian Bannister**, Cupar, Fife; **M Foster**, Cannock; Driver, Widnes; **P.L. Macinally**, Felixstowe; **Stewart McClure**, Scunthorpe; **Malcolm Hotterwell**, Doncaster; **David Knight**, Aylesbury; **Phil Keeble**, Felixstowe; **Derek**, Teeside; **Kevin**, Welwyn; **Kevin Howard**, Peterborough; Driver, Hull; **J. Bull**, Colchester; **S. Links**, Hendon; **J. Seddon**, Hyde; **Cliff McInnes**, Aberdeen; **Bert Wilson**, Forfar; **Hans Leeuwesteijn**, Bladel, Holland; **T. Barrigan**, Kirkby; **Colin Stanford**, Trimley St. Mary, 'Bar, video, TV, and pool-table.'; **Don Morley**, Ashton-in-Makerfield; **Tom Morley**, Runcorn; Mr **Flapper**, Wisbech; **Kevin Clark**, Braintree.

CHECKLEY REST AND STATION (A50)   Tel: (0538) 722307

Situation on the main A50 at Tean, Stoke-on-Trent, Staffordshire; the truckstop is now bypassed but is signposted from both ends of the bypass road; perfect access with three 100m-wide entrances.

Services 30 bedrooms and room for 70 sleeper-cabs, three showers, eight wash-basins and ten toilets; pay-phone in private room and pay-phone in café; bunkering on BP, Shell, National, Access and Barclaycards.

Food City and Guilds trained chef, three dining rooms seating a total of 94; an overnight stop with parking, single room, evening meal (starter, steak, gammon or mixed grill, sweet), breakfast included will cost you £10.50; on the chef's day off, proprietor Barry Brash cooks, and he is also C & G trained; open from 6.00 a.m., and you can still eat if you arrive at midnight.

Amenities full bar, TV and video, pool tables and live entertainment, exotic dancer, cabaret artist, some nights.

Companionship 100 truckers a day. Open five days Monday to Friday; telephone Friday for weekend beds. *Now a Routiers restaurant.*

Barry and Stuart Brash's father built the truckstop from scratch in 1936 when they had to dig a well to get water. Like the famous Windmill Theatre in London, during the war they never closed. An aunt ran the café while Mr Brash, Sr. was a prisoner-of-war. When the bypass opened, trade slumped 50 per cent. Now they are busier than ever and voted one of the best old-style transport cafés. All clients receive a Checkley card which is stamped for each stay. On the sixth stay, parking is free and a new card commences. Truck-park all hard-standing, fully tarmaced; they have their own bulldozer for maintenance work and snow clearing in winter.

Recommended by: **Brian Howard**, Putson, Hereford; **Colin Hill**, Peterborough; **Trevor Bostock**, Heanor, Derbyshire; **Charles Youles** , Southend; **Dipstick**, Uxbridge; **David Wood**, Lincoln; **E.A. Johnson**, Wisbech; **Rawhide**, Beverley; **Stephen Taylor**, Staines; **Harry Newstead**, Norwich; **Steve Handsley**, Littlecover, Derby; **Cruiser**, St. Andrews; **Andy Hall**, Sudbury, Derbyshire; **Drumstick**, Edgware; **Tiger**, Stallam, Catfield; **W.G. Gray**, Dagenham; **Mal Grimes**, Downham Market; **Alex Main**, Preston; **J. Fiddes**, Cowley; **Brian Chambers**, Ruskington; **Gordon Clark**, Lincoln; Driver, Rawtenstall; **R. Sudale**, Louth; **Mick Butcher**, Downham Market; **Ivan William Shipp**, Southey, Norfolk; **G. Moat**, Colchester; **Green Eagle**, Stallam; **Roy Coupier**, Bradford; Driver, Liverpool; **Charlie Armstrong**, Southampton; **S. Crawford**, Macclesfield; **Raymond Bosson**, Mackworth; **Roger Gadd**, Sleaford; **Robert Greenaway**, Rainham; **Brian Saville**, Burstall, W. Yorkshire; **Tommy Hosker**, Prescott; **William Cameron**, Edinburgh;

IT'S BIZARRE

A cautionary tale
A colleague of **Tony Reynolds**' swerved to avoid one sheep, ran off the road and killed seven others instead.

PENRITH TRUCKSTOP (M6)   Tel: (0768) 66995

Situation Penrith M6 junction 40 with A66. Access purpose-built and perfect.

Services 50 bedrooms, singles or twins, all with private bathrooms; showers and toilets free for sleeper-cab drivers; telephones, shop and film shows; Shell diesel station, retail, agency and fuel bunkering. Park for £3.00 or £4.00 with a £1.00 food voucher; a room is £6.00 with b & w TV, £6.75 with colour, video relayed to all rooms.

Food à la carte with a choice of 50 dishes from £1.00, or a three-egg omelette for £1.75, or an eight-ounce Scotch steak all in at £4.00 — the menu includes six chef's specials a day which can run to boeuf Stroganoff; a full breakfast, egg, bacon, sausage and tomatoes, £1.50, and lunch, £1.95.

Amenities full bar, lounge for 100, games room with pool tables, TV and video, live entertainment on Thursday at no extra charge.

Companionship 3,000 truckers a week, so there is always somebody to talk to. Truck park for 200 is fully enclosed and all hard-standing — it is on a metre and a half of hard-core with three inches of road-planings rolled. No pot-holes, they spend £12,000 a year maintaining the surface.

Penrith Truckstop has a pedigree and a touch of class; its chairman is the Earl of Lonsdale — so watch out, his family provides the boxing belts. John Mason has run it for five years. He says: 'The locals approached Lord Lonsdale to keep truckers out of the town. So he built the truckstop on this estate. It was built as a hotel to hotel standards, the rooms are fully carpeted, there are private bathrooms and TV or colour-TV in all. It was built with truckers only in mind to provide them with a complete service. The aim is to provide the very, very best value and service. And to try to understand truckers' needs. For instance, they find it difficult to get a haircut. We now have a Vidal Sassoon trained hairdresser on site, Sara Rawlinson, she's very popular. Before she came here she was in Paris. We don't have much live entertainment because our particular customers don't want it. In the other sites we are developing, we will have a second bar where we can stage entertainment for those who do want it.'

But a truckstop of this standard doesn't happen at the flick of an aristocratic finger, no matter how well-intentioned. Lord Lonsdale packed his bags and went to America to see how they do it there, then he studied the Continental approach. He is a truckers' champion and campaigns on their behalf. But he doesn't just talk, he does something about it — like building Penrith. Impress your neighbours, tell them: 'I've just been staying at Lord Lonsdale's place in the Lakes.' Well, it's no lie, is it?

Recommended by: **George Ross Sharp**, Alness; **J.H. Bickerton**, Wallasey; **D. Ainscough**, Chorley; **D. Littlewood**, York; **Willie Carson**, Kirkintiloch; **Derek Gordon**, South Shields; **Ian Bannister**, Springfield-by-Cupar, Fyfe; **Robert Greenaway**, Rainham; **Joseph Frank**

Bagot, Hyde; **D.B. Emmerson**, Dumfries; **Richard J. Williams**, Edinburgh; Driver, Stranraer; **Colin Pedlow**, Portadown; **Ian Angus**, Alness, Ross; **I. Beevers**, York; **Bert Wilson**, Forfar; **Jonathan North**, Bourne, Lincs; Driver, Melksham; **Drumstick**, Edgware; **M. Foster**, Cannock; **Gordon Milne**, Forfar; **Michael Weaver**, Standish; **Matchstick Man**, Oldham; **A. Alexander**, Aberdeen; **R. Beaumont**, Speke; **David Simmonds**, Gloucester; Driver, Workington; **T.M. Cullen**, Huddersfield; **Drifter**, Macclesfield; **John Lucy**, Melling, Merseyside; **Jan de Coster**, Zwyndrecht, Holland; **M. Stewart**, Haltwhistle; **Reinhard Stoll**, Rennigen, Holland; **J.Fiddes**, Cowley; **A. Taylor**, Letchworth; Driver, Hastings;

LINCOLN FARM CAFÉ (A452)   Tel: (067 55) 2301 or 2769

Situated Kenilworth Road, Hampton-in-Arden, West Midlands, on the A452 to Kenilworth and Warwickshire; to get there from the M6/M1 leave at junction 4 and take the A446 to Kenilworth, cross the A45 island, cross the second island and it is on the right — 4 miles from the motorways, and obviously, less from the A45.

Services 65 single cubicles, all newly furnished, new beds, carpets and curtains; 12 private cubicle showers and two baths, 20 wash-basins and eight loos to accommodate the sleeper-cab contingent; three telephones, fully floodlit truck park, no diesel on site; parking £3.50 including a £1.00 or 50p voucher depending on time, but for £6.50 you get parking, a full meal and a bed.

Food meals served 24 hours a day.

Amenities full bar, five-foot TV screen so all can see, videos and films; live entertainment in season, cabaret, singers, comedian and strippers sometimes but the customers felt the attraction had worn bare; shop; full-sized snooker table and darts.

IT'S THE WAY YOU TELL'EM

> **Mindless**
> 'You've got the brains of an idiot,' the furious transport manager told his defaulting driver. 'I know,' the defaulter admitted, 'do you want them back?'
> **Chris Smith**, *Bettws*.

Companionship always a good turn out. Truck park all hard-standing.

There is an old photograph of Lincoln Farm with folk in the garden surrounded by cows when it was a tea-house. Ray Wilcox has run it for 19 years and built it to its present size. He has strong views on subjects like hygiene and cleanliness and his aim is to win the top health award for the area in the face of competition from Birmingham's top hotels. He also has strong views on how a guide like this should be constructed. 'You ought to go into the places, see the kitchens, see the toilets and wash rooms, and see that they are kept clean for 24 hours a day not just for the visit. You ought to award marks for quality. I don't go into a panic when the health inspector is coming, I ask him to come to advise us what to do.' In answer to all that, I say to Mr Wilcox that we would like to do that, probably we will. But in the meantime we have to rely on customers' recommendations. But there is strong assurance in Mr Wilcox's assertion: 'Hygiene ought to play a big part in rating transport cafés. In that respect we are in the lead.'

Good news indeed for truckers are Ray Wilcox's plans. Planning permission has been granted for a £4-million development of a truckstop on the site and work is to begin in 1987. 'First I'm going to America to study how it's done there. They don't keep truckers segregated as if they are unfit to mix with the general public. We intend to do something similar here. New truckstops are going up but they put them in terrible places, on industrial estates and the like. I wonder what the directors of transport companies would think if they had to wake up to the outlook they expect the drivers to.'

Recommended by **Andy Berryman**, Portsmouth; **Richard Hawkins**, Canterbury; Mr **Nixon**, Northwich; **John Cunningham**, Prestonpans; **J. Hughes**, Leyland; **William Cameron**, Edinburgh; Driver, Rochdale; **A. Crossin**, Harbury; **Jeff Newell**, Warwick; **David Wrathall**, Bishop's Stortford; **K.Stedman**, Old Woking; **Eric Fielding**, Broseley, Salop; Driver, Birmingham; **Mr Rotton**, West Bromwich; **C.J. Smith**, Bristol; **Johnny Cartwright**, Coventry; **Scott Hillier**, Leamington Spa; **A. Stewart**, Blairgowrie; **Steve Moore**, Bishop's Stortford; Driver, anon; **Christopher Crombie**, Reading; Driver, Liverpool; **Colin Shaw**, Essex; **W.Cockram**, Liverpool; **J.H. Bickerton**, Wallasey; Driver, Hastings; Driver, Abingdon; Driver, Slough; **John J. Westwell**, Oswaldwhistle; **M. Rooney**, Liverpool; Driver, Widnes; Anon, Rochdale; **R. Beaumont**, Speke; **Joseph Bagot**, Hyde; **Sour Apple**, Walsall; **H. Hills**, Folkestone.

NUNEATON LORRY PARK (M6)   Tel: (0203) 370663

Situation Nuneaton, Leicestershire, M6 junction 4, take the A444 to Nuneaton and follow the signs — very well signposted. Access is purpose-built and perfect.

Services First-class bedrooms for 18 with all modern facilities; separate shower units for sleeper-cab contingent — male and female facilities; five acres to park in and expanding; Shell diesel unit and the Shell Derv-serve service; three telephones; the parking is £4.50 with a breakfast voucher if needed; a room is £6.00.

Food especially highly commended for quality, quantity and variety; everything is made in-house; a buffet salad, any type — a Waldorf — pile it on for £2.50 and a very popular meal, T-bone or rump steak, just ask; they also have barbecues; the fruit salad is *fresh* fruit salad; curries and exotic dishes are home-cooked.

Amenities a full bar and a complete club atmosphere; films every night, a disco and live entertainment which is often spectacular. Where else would you get Flowers and Gloucester Brass Band? It brought the house down. Entertainment is advertised in advance so you don't miss the best shows; also a shop and, of course, the barbecue party nights.

147

Companionship plenty about, and lively with it. Truck park is all hard-standing.

Behold, this is life-style 1987 and onwards for truckers. In one year proprietors Les Duerdon and Stewart Gibbons have put Nuneaton in the top of the truck popularity lists and made this stop-over a sign of things to come in the road haulage industry. Note — and don't screw up your faces like that, please — the facilities for females. OK, not many of them at the moment, but they are coming on to the scene. Les Duerdon says: 'We can blow our own trumpet about the food, that is something we are proud of. Drivers are sophisticated people nowadays and the time is coming when they will not stand for less than the standards we try to provide. Sometimes it is difficult to know what they will stand for or what they want, but all we can do is try to meet it.' There is a curious similarity between Nuneaton and Penrith: both came about because local people considered lorries to be a damned nuisance. Les Duerdon was secretary of the local chamber of trade when the complaints arose and somebody demanded: 'Open a lorry park.' 'A what?' Les queried and then discovered what they meant. He also discovered that the expertise to do the job lay within his own family and circle of friends. By profession he is an accountant — so don't try to fiddle the bill, he'll tie you up in knots — with his wife he'd done outside catering as a second string; Stewart Gibbons was in the furnishing trade, another friend was a builder. From our point of view, the important thing is that they kept their minds firmly on the truck trade. They have put in the quality and have pulled out success. Now they have a place you could proudly take a wife to stay at — preferably your own, for convention's sake.

Recommended by: Clive Nuttall, Rawtenstall, Manchester; Mr **Bright**, Kesgrave, Ipswich; **Richard Williams**, Edinburgh; **Gary Cooper**, Pitsea, Basildon; **P.A. Chapman**, Dartford; Mr **Mills**, Ipswich; **Kevin Simpson**, Folkestone; H.S. Jeffrey, Wigan; **D. Littlewood**, York; **Mrs P. Edmonds**, Ashill, Thetford; **John Brame**, Claydon; **Allen Mossman**, Basildon; **T. Thatcher**, Leyton, London; **Neil Evans**, Oswestry; Mr **Pratt**, Swindon; **K. Garratt**, Ironville; **David L. Lowe**, Pennistone; **David Simmonds**, Gloucester; **Fred Flower**, Staines; Mr **Addison**, Rainham; **D. Cotteringham**, Ashford, Middlesex; **J. Bull**, Colchester; **J.H.J. Baker**, Woodbridge; **Barry Addlington**, Hayes; **Terence Archbold**, Purfleet; Driver, Shepton Mallet; **D.J. Wiffen**, Aveley; **S. Trimmer**, Wisbech; **G. Flight**, Pentney, Norfolk; **Danny Woods**, Edinburgh; Driver, Workington; **John Cunningham**, Prestonpans; **Jeffrey John Harmycz**, Cressex, High Wycombe; **Peter Austin**, Leeds; **A. Tarmey**, Sunderland; Mr **Jones**, Glossop.

〰〰〰〰〰〰〰〰〰〰 **IT'S BIZARRE** 〰〰〰〰〰〰〰〰〰〰

Yes, it's a shaggy-dog story

In Ilford, Mr **Gordon**, of Aylesbury, saw a dog standing by a zebra crossing and apparently watching the traffic, so he stopped. The dog walked to the centre of the road, paused, looked in the other direction, the traffic stopped and the dog completed its crossing.

TRAFFORD PARK TRUCKSTOP (M63 and 62)

Situation Trafford Wharf Road, Manchester 17. Perfect access from M63 and M62, 1½ miles.

Services no accommodation, sleeper-cabs only; three showers, five wash-basins, constant hot water, heated room in winter, shaver sockets; three coin telephones; bunkering by Key Fuels;

Food café run by ex-trucker Bill Bradbury, his wife, Pauline, her sister and brother-in-law, Sally and Peter Beardsmoor; open from 5.30 a.m. until 9.00 p.m.; full breakfast, bacon, sausage, egg or tomato, beans, bread, butter and tea, £1.80; sausage, egg, beans, £1.00; three-course evening meal, £3.50; £4.00 parking fee includes a £1.25 meal voucher;

Amenities Welcome Inn, run by Mary Callaghan, live entertainment four nights a week, strippers.

Companionship 80–100 truckers a night. Truck park all hard-standing, fully concreted. Seven days. Harry Caine and his brother bought the run-down site in 1982, and pumped in money, improved the services and won the trade.

Recommended by: **Paul Raymond**, Isleham; **Tony Smith**, Fleet, Spalding; **Cliff Eater**, Cheshunt; **Paul Taylor**, Bradford; **Terence Archbold**, Purfleet; **D. Cotteringham**, Middlesex; **Cobra**, Suffolk; **David Beech**, Northampton; **I. Beevers**, York; **Andy Miller**, Bonnybridge, 'Much improved.'; **Cliff McInnes**, Aberdeen, 'Food could be better and cheaper.'; **Gwyn Latcham**, Tonypandy; **Albert Machtelineks**, Eindhoven, Netherlands; Mr **Jones**, Glossop; **Lawrence Higgins**, Gloucester; **Jan de Kosta**, Zwyndrecht, Netherlands; **Davy Young**, Glasgow; **Richard Hawkins**, Canterbury; **M. Foster**, Cannock; **Frederick E. Wilderston**, Slatney, Chester; **R.B. Marsden**, Wellingborough; **Arthur Dieton**, Den Haag, Netherlands; **S.W. Poole**, Farningham, Surrey; **Kurt Rossnagl**, Vienna; Mr **Gorrett**, Crediton, Devon; **R. Beard**, Carwell Bank.

THE KERNEL (A34)   Tel: (0922) 475182 and 492793

Situation On the A34 between Walsall and Cannock; come off the M6 at junction 11, Sharehill, take the Bloxwich road and it is down the third road left, Long Lane, then turn left and you are there. Access could not be better.

Services Accommodation for 60 singles, 20 doubles, baths and showers, separate shower block for sleeper-cabs, rooms held for late-comers; three telephones; diesel garage next door; parking £3.25, single room £6.20, room and breakfast £7.40.

Food Dining room for 70 open from 6.00 a.m. until 7.00 p.m.; breakfast £1.20 or more if you eat more, main meal: a popular steak and kidney pudding dinner at £1.25, equally popular gammon, egg, chips and peas at £1.89 or a rump steak dinner at £3.14 — book with your room and you get the big breakfast.

Amenities Naturally, television, billiards, snooker, pool, darts and cards, plus a night-club on site. The night-club is separate from the hotel but all truckers are welcomed. A good night is Monday for the

Over 30s' Disco, a great time for £1, live entertainment.
Companionship Always a good crowd. 'We're inundated with truckers, which is how we like it,' says Philip Hardwick. Truck park all hard-standing.

Come in and be one of the family — and there could hardly be more family. Until Ralph died it was Ralph, Betty and sons Gar, Keith and Philip, a fourth son is a shareholder but not in the business. Ralph and Betty bought a grocery shop in Newtown village 33 years ago and opened a tea-shop café at the back of the store. Then they bought two and a half acres of land opposite when it became available and put up a long wooden café building as a transport café. Son Keith explains: 'It took a lot of bottle to expand and build the place up.' The family lived in a detached house next to the shop. Whenever they wanted to expand, they sold the house to raise the money and took the family to live in a caravan. Keith lived in caravans for two or three years. They sold the house and bought it back twice and watched the business grow. They are very proud of their parents and very proud of the place. Younger brother Philip says: 'I think we've got just the right mix now. And it is pulling in the customers. We have always thought that you've got to treat the drivers with importance.' Keith adds: 'I've grown up with half the customers here, we've had people coming regularly for twenty years or more.' The night-club runs as an independent entity but is a great attraction for truckers. It is called Hardy's because that is an abbreviation of Hardwick and it is based on an Oliver Hardy 'bowler-hat' theme. There is a separate telephone number for the club: (0922) 409898.

Recommended by: Mr **Beaumont**, Speke, Liverpool; **Gambler**, Gravesend; **Brian Pritchard**, Cannock; **Tony Squires**, Poole, Dorset; **K. Doran**, Newcastle; **Arthur Hughes**, Liverpool; Driver, Wisbech; **J.H. Kelly**, Durham; **Drifter**, Macclesfield; Driver, Uttoxeter; **Bear**, Reading; Driver, Leeds, Driver, London; **Angus Smith**, Bristol; **A.A. Parker**, Helsby; Mr **Jones**, Glossop; **Drew Cook**, Liverpool; **Cinder Man**, Ayr; Driver, Melksham; Driver, Rawtenstall; **R.J. Chandler**, London; **Arthur Penbridge**, Llandridno, Powys; **Dennis Copeland**, Sheffield; **Jim Young**, Peterborough; **William Cameron**, Edinburgh; **Curly**, Sheffield; Driver, King's Lynn.

IT'S BIZARRE

Fall from grace

It was rough justice but **Ian Norrie**, of Fettercairn, thought it fair when the policeman flagging him down for speeding stepped back and toppled down the embankment behind.

Anchors aweigh

It cannot happen often and **R. Mallinson**, of Corby, thought it odd when a driver backed his truck into a ship at the docks. Did his accident report read: 'Collided with ocean-going vessel?'

CARLISLE TRUCK INN MOTEL (M6)   Tel: (0228) 34192

Situation M6 junction 44, Carlisle. Access purpose-built.

Services Accommodation is 95 bedrooms single and twin, all bedrooms with own shower and bath, shaver plugs, £6.00 single, £6.00 each twin, £7.00 with colour TV, two washrooms on park; floodlit and supervised parking for 180 on 9 acres — by the way, forget the Nigel Mansell touches, you're ripping the asphalt up — parking £3.00; shop; diesel.

Food from crack o' dawn until midnight, and a wide selection.

Amenities Colour TV room, games room, pool, bandits and videos; cabaret and dancing to live bands — in all, the complete modern purpose-built truckstop — there is even a vehicle wash, so both you and your truck can put cleanliness next to godliness.

Companionship Superb, mix with the crowd which shares your personal taste for either a quiet evening or a rave-up. Truck park all hard-standing.

Ring a carillon for Geoff Bell, he knows the game. 'We are the best in the business, second to none,' he peals with justification. He does indeed know the business, he was a haulier himself for 20 years beginning with one truck and building to a fleet of 14. Then, ten years ago, the company building the motel went bust when it was half finished. Geoff, needing more room for his trucking business, stepped in and bought the site. He finished the building and became engrossed in the truckstop operation which he has developed to its splendid present state. 'These lads have £12 a night to spend, it's not a lot,' he says, and knowing the business he pleads the truckers' case, 'as an employer, I know that if I pay my drivers more than £12 a night they have to pay tax on it. That is all wrong. Ministry of Defence drivers are allowed £25, the BBC gives its people £30, company reps spend £40 a night in a hotel and put it down to the company, and some big petrol companies pay £15 to £20 — I'll bet none of them pay tax on any of that.' That is quite a point and, of course, it is true. So Geoff packs in the value. 'We are top of the list for quality. We must be getting it right because the lads keep coming in droves.' But please slow down a bit in his truck park, you're playing havoc with his asphalt. I know it is 9 acres, but it has just cost him £2,500 to fill in the ruts some Formula One aspirants have torn out.

Recommended by: **Raymond Bosson**, Mackworth; **Arthur Van Dieten**, Den Haag, Holland; **Jan de Koster**, Zwyndrecht, Holland; **Alex Farries**, Glasgow; **Chris Walls**, Burton-on-Trent; **John J. Westwell**, Oswaldtwistle; **Geoff Hyams**, Leyland, Lancashire; **Christopher Andrew Crombie**, Reading; Mr **Nixon**, Northwich; **John Lucy**, Melling, Merseyside; **Glyn Porter**, Burton-on-Trent; **Watty Dewar**, Fife; **Joseph Frank Bagot**, Hyde, Cheshire; **M. Foster**, Cannock; **H.S. Jeffry**, not specified; **F. Griffiths**, Cwmbran, Gwent; **Martin Handley**, Pyle, Port Talbot; Mr **Jones**, Glossop; **T. Thatcher**, Leyton, London; **D. Cottingham**, Ashford, Middlesex; **Richard J. Williams**, Edinburgh; Driver, Basingstoke; **Brian Pritchard**, Cannock; **Sour Apple**, Walsall.

KATE'S CABIN CAFÉ (A1) Tel: (0733) 233286

Situation A1, the Great North Road, at Alwalton, 4 miles north of Peterborough. Access good.

Services Accommodation is 40 bedrooms, two washrooms with showers for sleeper-cabs' use; telephones; diesel.

Food Dining-room for 100, all home cooking by mother, Mavis Sykes, and daughter, Karon Sykes, assisted by 25 staff; breakfast comes at £1.25 and a main meal is £1.40; parking is £3.00, £1.50 on Sundays; the £7.00 for a bedroom includes a meal. Diesel on site.

Amenities TV, pool and bar; live entertainment on the electric organ and a good old sing-song now and again.

Companionship On average 30 to 40 guests a night.

A real old-type truckstop which has kept up with the times and is much loved for style and atmosphere by many. It could not be more family orientated, grandfather began it all then leased to a third party for a time until the present father, mother and daughter combination took over. It has been a good pull-up for travellers for a long time; its name derives from the fact that Dick Turpin used to meet his girl friend Kate here. Well, times have changed, nowadays used-car dealers are the direct lineal descendants of horse-thieves, and highwaymen come in crisp, white ministry coats or flat-'ats with chequered hat-bands, but it is pleasant to rest awhile in a historical atmosphere. On the basis of the better the day, the better the deed, not only do you pay half price for parking on Sunday, there is also a free bar-snack thrown in. You can meet a few characters at Kate's Cabin: one driver's boss allowed 75p for lunch, the driver handed him his meal chit for £1.58. 'God Almighty,' exploded the boss, 'I'm not standing you a bottle of wine with your dinner as well.' Truck park all hard-standing.

IT'S THE WAY YOU TELL'EM

Gourmet
The driver stopped at the motorway services check out and demanded: 'Give us a pair of scissors, it's cheaper to eat money.'
Gareth Williams, *Pontadulais, Morfa.*

Recommended by: **Geoffrey Nelson Wyrill**, York; **L. McDonald**, Forfar, Angus; **Allen Mossman**, Basildon; Driver, Worksop; **Cinder Man**, Ayr; **Stewart McClure**, Scunthorpe, 'Happy Hour six to seven, beer half-price, good facilities'; **J. Seddon**, Hyde; **Graham Mogford**, Stonebroom, Derbyshire; **Derek**, Teeside; **Kevin**, Welwyn Garden City; Driver, Alfreton; **D. Cottingham**, Ashford, Middlesex; **Malcolm Hotterwell**, Doncaster; **Paul Taylor**, Bradford; **Peter Austin**, Leeds; **David L. Lowe**, Pennistone; **John Howard**, Penrith; **Paul Bonney**, Huntingdon; **Ronald Balner**, Appleby, Yorkshire; **Alex Maine**, Preston; Driver, Bolton; **Jan de Koster**, Zwyndrecht, Holland.

WHITWOOD TRUCKSTOP (M62)   Tel: (0977) 517690

Situation M62 junction 31, at Castleford, halfway between A1M and the M1. Access purpose-built.

Services Sleeper-cabs only; three pay-phones; washroom with four showers, separate female ablutions; Ultramar quick-fill service but all comers can be served; parking is £4.00, give or take a bit.

Food Cafeteria for 84 but with full restaurant licence; breakfast for £1.90 is two eggs, bacon, two sausages, beans, tomato, fried bread, tea or coffee (and breakfast goes on all day for late risers), dinner from 10.30 a.m. for early eaters, liver and bacon, liver and onions, lamb or pork chops, roast pork, beef, roast or boiled potatoes in the £1.40 range, omelettes £1.60, up to the mixed grill at £2.40 — or combinations to your taste; open at 6.00 a.m. and meals until 9.30 p.m., light suppers until 11.30 for overnighters.

Amenities Video lounge and two pool tables; live entertainment is by proprietor Stuart Wardell, or partner John Mulheir, or both together as a double turn — side-splitting. When they opened two years ago the local Castleford council, true Yorkshiremen all ruled: 'No live entertainment on't industrial estate, ther's t'time and t'place for everything.' Thus Stuart and John found themselves on Ilkley Moor bart t'acts. So like t'food, t'fun is home-cooked. Well, thi gets more of it to t'pound. **Companionship** There's a lot about.

While John Mulheir was driving trucks for 17 years, Stuart Wardell was swanning away his time in the Bahamas and Florida for 15 years. Then, for Stuart, good sense prevailed and he came back to Yorkshire — and lost his shirt, literally. Before the bar opened at Whitwood, they used to run drivers down to the local pub. One group decided they wanted to go on to a night-club in Wakefield, but none of them were wearing shirts. Shirts were borrowed from those not going on the razzle but at the end of the evening there was one shirt missing. Stuart had been to a business meeting and was clad in snappy pin-stripe suit and matching shirt, the latter he gave to a shirtless driver. Returning home, his wife asked: 'Where's your shirt?' Takes some explaining when you arrive home bare-chested. That sets the atmosphere for the place, but they *do* give service. A distress call came over the CB from a driver who had been broken down on the M62 for five hours. He was starving. Stuart took him a hot sausage butty. He stopped his Porsche by the truck, handed over the food, and told the driver: 'Room service.'

'How much?' the driver asked. 'The food is free but the delivery is £10,' joked Whitwood boss.

IT'S THE WAY YOU TELL'EM

Recommended by: Driver, Bedlington: **T.T. Hardman**, Warrington; Driver, Hull; **Joseph Frank Bagot**, Hyde, Cheshire; **Terence Archbold**, Purfleet; **K. Garrett**, Ironville; **Tony Smith**, Fleet, Spalding; **A. Taylor**, Letchworth; **D.J. Wiffen.**, Aveley; **T. Cable**, Ipswich; **Ron Hawkins**, Lambourne; **Kevin Simpson**, Folkstone; **Dennis King**, Bury St. Edmunds; **L. McDonald**, Forfar, Angus; Driver, Wisbech; **John Lucy**, Melling, Merseyside; **Davey Paterson**, Hamilton, Strathclyde; Driver, Hastings; **Derek Gordon**, South Shields; Driver, Hull; **P. Thompson** Widnes.

THE POPLAR TRUCKSTOP (A50)   Tel: (0925) 756522

Situation on the Knutsford to Warrington road but 1 minute off the motorway M56, junction 9, and M6, junction 20; superbly sited halfway between Scotland and the South. Access excellent.

Services developing all the time but so far parking for 140; no accommodation, sleeper-cabs only; 6 wash-basins, 3 showers, separate female washroom and shower; parking is £3.00 with a bonus of a free weekly draw with 8 prizes and a monthly snowball; diesel on site; open 24 hours from 6.00 a.m. Monday until midday Saturday, with a special opening from 4.00 until 10.00 p.m. for the benefit of Scottish truckers.

Food prepared under the direction of Andy Schumacher who accepted the challenge to put on something really good for truckers. Here you will get priority treatment; there is some car trade but it isn't encouraged. If a trucker on a tacho-break arrives he goes to the head of the queue. Breakfast comes at £1.85, every day there are chef's specials at £2.00 up to £2.25, which is the charge for roasts with vegetables. The specials change daily.

Amenities a full pub licence but the bar opens in the evenings only and is being improved all the time as development continues.

Companionship as much as you want any time. Truck park is part hard-standing, three-foot of the road-stone surfaced with motorway planings and kept pot-hole free.

You have heard of fast food — well, this is fast café provision to a degree. Brian Lever took over the keys at four o'clock one Friday when the then café was closing for the weekend; he moved in with an army of cleaners, painters, builders and at six o'clock on Sunday customers walked in, stopped in their tracks and began to walk out saying: 'We're in the wrong place.' That was three years ago and the place was a 'bomb-site'. The new truckstop came about almost by accident. Brian had been in the petrol station business for 20 years and somebody suggested this as a suitable site. 'Hopeless,' Brian proclaimed, 'absolutely useless.' He saw the old, ramshackle café and suddenly got a gut feeling about it even though it was derelict and in an appalling condition. He began to think about truckers and their requirements. His secretary was married to a driver, so he sat him down and talked; then he went to America, like others, to see how they did it; next he travelled 3,000 miles in his car to question British drivers. Finally he was convinced. He took over the Poplar Café and wrote a personal letter to all drivers to be handed out along the road asking what they wanted, welcoming ideas and criticisms. Bill Meakin joined him and they evolved a philosophy expressed by Bill: 'Truckers have been left out of it for far too long. We think of a trucker as a professional man and try to provide what he requires. That is why a trucker gets first service at the Poplar. He's under pressure, if he's got an hour's break on the tacho, he's in a hurry, we cater for that.' Brian says: 'We must be doing something right, it seems to meet with approval.' They came in green and the truck-bug bit them. 'It's a fantastic business, we love it and we enjoy it,' is how Brian Lever explains his views, 'we give what they want and what they haven't thought of before.' All the money goes back into the business because they're putting a lot of thought into it — and putting thought into bricks and mortar costs cash. Watch for big developments.

Recommended by: **A.A. Parker**, Helsby; **Cliff McInnes**, Aberdeen; **Richard J. Williams**, Edinburgh; **Drifter**, Macclesfield; Driver, Sheldon; **Neil Evans**, Oswestry; **D.B. Emmerson**, Dumfries; **David Lowndes**, Cumnock; **Davie Young**, Glasgow; **John Howard**, Penrith; **Ron Hetherington**, **Ian McClachlan**, Dalbeattie; **Simon Tandy**, Ledbury; **Steve Newall**, Leigh; **Steve Hoggard**, Wigan; **S. Crawford**, Macclesfield; **Terence Archbold**, Purfleet; **Derek Stead**, Leeds; **Flying Ted**, Minster, Ramsgate; **Ian Bannister**, Cupar, Fife; **Christopher Andrew Crombie**, Reading.

THE COMPASS (A1)   Tel: (0476) 860336

Situation A1 eight miles south of Grantham on the Colsterworth roundabout, so available from both north and south. Access is easy.
Services all being rigorously revamped at the time of writing; parking for 30 to be extended to handle 100; showers at the present 'inadequate' says the owner, but a shower block is planned with private cubicles comprising wash-basin, WC and shower; two pay-telephones; diesel garage opposite but probably on site soon.
Food dining-room for 60, breakfast costs £1.25 or the special £1.95, main meals for meat, potatoes, three vegetables the price is £2.15; open 24 hours daily from 6.00 a.m. Monday until 5.00 p.m. Saturday, and from 10 a.m. until 7.00 p.m. Sunday.
Amenities TV and video room.

This is a place in a prime and useful situation which is about to blossom as Jonathan Rundle and his mother make plans for it. Somewhat neglected until now, it looks like coming good from early 1987. Now there is dormitory accommodation soon to be converted into five bedrooms. But as it stands a lot of people like it well enough. Various factors have held back its development but those now seem to be overcome. Taste the pies: Gwen, the manageress, does all the pastry cooking.

Recommended by: **F.S. Lowe**, Derby; unnamed driver; **Ian Hooks**, Great Oakly; **Tom Cook**, Spalding; **Davie Yound**, Glasgow; Driver, Liverpool; Driver, Bedlington; **Steven Wood**, York; **Derek Stead**, Leeds; **Cliff McInnes**, Aberdeen; **John Whitehurst**, York; Driver, Swinderby; **Colin Roadnight**, Bradford; **Alex Main**, Preston; **Geoff Hyams**, Leyland; **R.B. Marsden**, Wellingborough; Driver, Alfreton; **Tom Morley**, Runcorn; **G. Stockton**, Middleton; **Stephen McErlean**, Stretford, Manchester.

THE WOODLANDS MOTEL (A1)   Tel: (0532) 864806

Situation on the old Great North Road at the south end of Micklefield village, 50 yards off the A1 and well signposted. Access, the site has been a filling station since petrol was invented, so it is good.

Services 30-plus beds, singles and shared rooms; Five-star washing facilities, this motel was the first to provide washroom and showers for sleeper-cab men, and it is probably the only fully-attended toilet area on the network. An ex-BRS trucker looks after the washrooms and keeps them spotless, you need a parking ticket or £1.00 to use them. A £50,000 extention to the motel was opened in autumn last year; park for £2.50 with a free tea: two telephones; room and breakfast, single £8.00, shared £7.00.

Food all food is fresh and home-cooked except the fish which comes frozen, sausages are 100 per cent meat, cakes and scones are made to home recipes, breakfasts are £1.20 or £1.80 and main meals run from £1.15 for sausage and chips or similar to £3.00 for a slap-up steak meal.

Amenities bar, video room, pool tables, darts and a relaxed atmosphere.

IT'S THE WAY YOU TELL'EM

Chestnut corner

What's the best thing to come out of Scotland? The road back to England.

'Mummy, is daddy dead?' 'No darling, he works for Halfords, he gets a day off next month.'

Sportsman, *Redditch.*

Companionship 100 overnight and many say: 'It's like being at home. Why, you can even get nagged for going to the club.' Truck park is hard-standing with gravel surface.

Here is a place with a truck history. It began with the horseless-carriage, turned into a tin-roofed wooden structure, and then burned down. In the late 1960s, a different attitude prevailed at the Ministry of Transport, they decided that lorry drivers deserved better accommodation and 'good-quality digs' became the current phrase. Remarkably, the ministry helped design the new motel, they laid down the rules about the sizes of rooms, bathrooms and so on. When the new establishment opened tea was served on silver trays and it didn't work. Then it became the site office for building the new A1 which bypassed the village. Later a group took it over but fell out among themselves about how to run it. It was pretty run-down when Gordon and Nadine Braithwaite took it over in 1979. They were actually looking for a pub to run at the time and the university-educated Gordon gasped: 'Crikey, a *transport* café!' Within two months success was so complete that he had to give up his job in

textiles to help Nadine cope. Once in it, they liked the business —
and the business liked them. Their objective, which succeeds, is to
make it 'as much like going home as possible'. There is a niggle, a
thorn in the side. Every year since they took over never less than
£25,000 has been reinvested in the business for improvements. But
Micklefield is a former mining village right in the heart of the
Yorkshire working man's clubs area; many drivers grab the facilities
offered by Woodlands then drink in the neighbouring subsidised
club for the sake of 6p a pint cheaper. I suggest there is food for
thought there for fair-minded drivers. After all, there are bitter
complaints enough when transport café owners sell out to Little
Chefs — like Markham Moor, which is not too far away.

Recommended by: **W.G. Gray, Dagenham; T.M. Cullen**, Widnes; **Driver**, Hull; **David Thomson**, Musselburg; **D. Ellicott**, Swansea; **Driver**, Liverpool; **John (Foxy) Cunningham**, Prestonpans; **Steven Wood**, York; **Driver**, Hornsey; **Steve Hoggard**, Wigan; **Steve Newall**, Leigh; **H. Hills**, Folkestone; **Richard J. Williams**, Edinburgh; **Kevin Taylor**, Richmond, Yorkshire; **Driver**, Bedlington; Robert Greenaway, Rainham; Mr **Rotton**, West Bromwich; Driver, Hull; **W.R. Lucas**, Swansea.

IT'S BIZARRE

The long way round
As **Pete Robinson**, of Colne, Lancashire, made his way
round the roundabout and down the southbound entrance
to the M6, he spotted a hitch-hiker with a placard asking to
be taken to Carlisle.

LONDONDERRY LODGE (A1)　　　Tel: (0677) 22143

Situation A1 at Londonderry, 12 miles south of Scotch Corner, 50
yards off the road. Access is purpose-built.
Services parking for 45 on the motel's own park and 70 on the official
park behind the lodge; shower for sleeper-cab men; three telephones including one Continental; accommodation for 46 and the
price includes everything, parking, evening meal, bed and breakfast,
singles £9.40, shared £8.90, all top quality new slumberland beds
and all rooms with hot water and radiators plus shaver points; day
sleepers are accommodated as well as night and the early call
system operates throughout the night every half-hour if required;
diesel is available for 24 hours and parking is £3.20 with a £1.50 meal
voucher.
Food a full 24-hour service, breakfasts come from double egg on
toast at 98p to sausage, bacon, egg, beans, tomato, two toasts and
marmalade at £2.27, main meals — if breakfast wasn't enough —
range from home-made pies with chips at £1.65 to roasts with
potatoes, Yorkshire pudding and vegetables at £2.30 and a full range
of salads.

Stay in Lane

Amenities full bar, TV, fruit machines, darts and a particularly homely lounge — count the atmosphere as an amenity.

Companionship always plenty about. Truck park is hard-standing on nine inches of concrete and the space is being constantly enlarged.

This truckstop is housed in a class 2 listed building, two sides of it, so it has been around for a long time. But it is the old, now familiar story: it was virtually derelict until Maurice and Margaret Gill took it over nine years ago. Maurice was an owner-driver himself who lived locally and took over the café when it became available. It is a good business now and largely due to the fact that profits have been ploughed back into it — last year £15,000 on extending the concrete in the truck park. Maurice knows 90 per cent of the customers from past experience and the atmosphere is welcoming, friendly and homely because of this. Margaret Gill says: 'The lounge is immaculate because that is the way the drivers keep it. They see it as home from home. This is a place where their families can come and often do.' So with confidence put Londonderry Lodge in the list of those facilities which are improving conditions on the road because they are run by people who know drivers' needs.

Recommended by: Bluebeard, Crawley; **Alex Main**, Preston; **J.J. Coleman**, Darlington; **Wattie Dewar**, Fife; **A. Stewart**, Blairgowrie; Driver, Bedlington; **W.R. Lucas**, Swansea; Driver, Liverpool; **Ian McClachlan**, Dalbeattie; **D.B. Emmerson**, Dumfries; **Ian Bannister**, Cupar, Fife; **D. Ellicott**, Swansea; **Riverboat**, Leyland; Driver, Basingstoke; **R.J. Chandler**, London; **Sandy Gordon**, Kirkbride; **Ronald Cavanagh**, Caddishead.

IT'S THE WAY YOU TELL'EM

Counsel's opinion
It will be no use telling the magistrates that though you knew unlawful meant breaking the law, you honestly thought illegal was a sick bird.
Richard Dembizki, Scunthorpe.

THE RENDEZVOUS (A5)   Tel: (0788) 65165

Situation A5 on Watling Street, at Lilbourne, near Rugby, Northamptonshire, come off the M6 at junction 1, Rugby turn-off, and off the M1 at junction 18, Crick. Access good.

Services parking for 100, self-service diesel; 18 bedrooms, day and night sleepers; two shower units; two telephones, incoming and outgoing; parking is £5.00, a bed is £7.00 which includes an evening meal and breakfast; open 24 hours daily until midday Saturday, begins again at 10.00 a.m. Sunday, but if you arrive earlier, knock.

Food breakfast is £1.50 and consists of bacon, egg, two sausages, beans or tomatoes, fried slice, bread and butter and tea; the main meal is £1.95 for, say, roast beef, Yorkshire pudding and three vegetables, with sweet and a cup of tea £2.50.

Amenities so far a video room and TV, but it is another case of 'watch this space' as plans are afoot.

Companionship they are coming back in droves.

We seem to be compiling this book at a time of great renaissance of the British truckstop. This popular one is under the new management of Trevor Matthews and his wife Barbara, and since they took over in March 1986 things have looked up and customers returned in numbers. The changes he is bringing about include plans for a self-service diesel unit on site and a licenced club house. So watch for developments.

Recommended by: **Adrian Dennis**, Sandown, Isle of Wight; **Manwell**, Stranraer; **G. Seltock**, Leighton Buzzard; **Frank Allington**, East Malling; **Stewart Shepley**, Clifton; **W. King**, Liverpool; **S. Handy**, Coventry; **Malcolm Murray**, Manchester; **Sal Chester**, Leeds; **A.T**, Rugby; **Dave Partington**, Bolton; Driver, Blackpool; **T. Stamford**, Redditch; **E. Tearle**, Ramsgate; **Harry Philby**, Stoke Aldermoor; **W.P. Smith**, Bedford; **M. Stone**, Walsall.

'Look, mate — your voucher's for a meal not a nibble!'

TRUCKERS' PARADISE (A45)   Tel: (0480) 54141

Situation Godmanchester, Huntingdon, A45 and take the slip-road A604 into Godmanchester and it is just before the town. Access is purpose-built.

Services parking for 60 extending to 120 by the time you read this; two showers, four by the time this reaches you; two telephones as above; no accommodation, sleeper-cabs only; diesel on site.

Food they are 'proud of it' because it is all freshly cooked every day, the 'very pleasant restaurant' seats 62 and they are open 24 hours for six days with Saturdays from 8.00 a.m. until 8.00 p.m.; breakfast of sausage, back bacon, fried bread, egg, beans or tomato, two slices of toast, tea or coffee, is £1.65, a main meal comes at £1.85 for a home-made shepherd's pie with two vegetables, to £2.45 for a large braised steak all in.

Amenities pool tables, bar, video room and two TVs. Live entertainment on Mondays and Fridays.

Companionship the cognoscenti gather here. Truck park road-stone and rolled planings.

In eleven months Truckers' Paradise came up from nothing to top-rating and firmly established itself as a part of the new truck philosophy. Since Truckers' Catering took it over in 1984 and began to give drivers what they want, trade has soared. It is actually in a very good prime spot: a few minutes off the A1, a trundle down the road to the A45 for Ipswich, Felixstowe and Harwich and the M11, and it could fit into running and tacho schedules very well indeed. Norman Small is an unlikely manager since he comes strictly from the 'carriage trade' side of the business. He was an hotelier before he was persuaded to help his friend at the old Lodge Transport Café — now sold out to Little Chef. At the Lodge he liked the trade so much that he stayed for three years as manager. Old acquaintances in the hotel trade rather sneered when he insisted in staying in the trucking business after the Lodge closed. But he explains it: 'Everything depends on how you welcome your truckers. It's not a job really, it is something you have got to believe in what you are doing. Truckers have had a bad time for too long. If you are working for them, they will come back to you. A reputation depends on word of mouth, they can make you or break you on the CB.'

In head office, where the money comes from, there is strong support; director Mr Alan Sears is a pro-truck man very firmly on the truckers' side.

Recommended by: **Derek Gordon**, South Shields; **Derek Stead**, Leeds; **David L. Lowe**, Pennistone; **Pop Hawley**, Basildon; **Herbert E. Johnson**, Peterborough; **D.B. Emmerson**, Dumfries; **I. Beevers**, York; Driver, Bedlington; **Jonathan North**, Bourne, Lincolnshire; **J.H.J Baker**, Woodbridge; **Ian McClachlan**, Dalbeattie; **Ranger**, South Luffenham; **Reinhard Stoll**, Rennigen, Holland; **Roy Coupier**, Basildon, Bradford; **G. Stockton**, Middleton; **David Thomson**, Musselburg; **N. Powell**, Ross-on-Wye; **G. Flight**, Pentney, Norfolk.

THE ROSE CAFÉ, CHELMSFORD (A12)   Tel: (0245) 252260

Situation on the westbound carriageway of the A12 between the Widford roundabout and Margaretting. Eastbound traffic pull into the lay-by and walk across the wooded central reservation — dozens do so every day.

Amenities and services prize-winning food, a phone and toilets. This is a departure from our usual style because The Rose Café is unique — it opens from 5.30 in the morning until 2.00 p.m. and 6.00 a.m. Saturday until midday. Seats for 40 diners.

One woman's passion is one hundred men's pleasure every day. The woman is blonde Pauline Stevens and her appetite is insatiable — you name a new dish which isn't on her menu and it will be there the following morning! Yes, her burning, overriding passion is cooking, she simply loves cooking food. So she has turned her kitchen at home into a connoisseur's library of cuisine — that is the theory side of her vocation, the practical is served at the Rose Café every day, and it has won her awards from all quarters. Her husband, Terry, explains: 'If somebody orders food we haven't got on the menu, the next day it is on. That's the way Pauline works.'

The Rose Café is itself a 'slice of Old England' — it is a genuine old-fashioned transport 'caff' with no frills and fewer pretentions. And it is *popular* — they queue to get in because the value and quality is universally recognised.

IT'S BIZARRE

A bum note

In the town of the ancient Roman bridge and International Eisteddfod, Llangollen, in North Wales, **Neil Evans**, of Oswestry, heard a driver asking the puzzled inhabitants for a distinctive street name. Neil knew the place well enough — it was in Cardiff.

The Stevens have run it for three years and during that time it has boomed. 'Packed out all the time,' says Terry. A lot of thought and attention has gone into the menu. They looked at all the bakers in the county, and beyond, until they 'got on to the right bread'. And they did the same with the hams until they found just the right one in Cambridge. 'The best gammon ham you can get on the road,' is the proud claim. Where the breads and hams come from is kept a tight secret but their fame has spread. Scottish drivers stop on the way down and order whole hams to take back home on their return.

Fame came with breakfast and the awards they have won for it. 'The Trucker's Breakfast is the biggest you can buy on the road. Not many drivers can actually eat it,' Terry says. And it comes with coffee or tea on 'the hot side'. In Terry's view: 'Nothing is worse than a cold cup of tea or coffee.'

Altogether there are twelve menu boards displayed including 'Toasties' and sandwiches. But study these examples as a guide. All home-made dinners include new potatoes, cabbage, peas, carrots and gravy. Braised steak is the most expensive at £2.00; and then at an inclusive £1.60 they offer: pork chops and Yorkshire pudding; two lamb chops and Yorkshire pudding; steak and kidney pie; steak and kidney pudding; liver and bacon casserole; cottage pie; beef stew and dumplings; chicken curry and rice or chips; bacon and onion roll; two stuffed hearts and dumplings; sausage toad-in-the-hole; two sausages and onions; breadcrumbed cod, peas and chips; pizza and chips or potatoes.

See the size of the helpings and then, if you feel you can cope, try a home-made sweet, all of which are served with cream or icecream at 40p: gooseberry pie; syrup pudding; jam pudding; apple pie; spotted Dick; apple and raspberry pie; apple crumble; cherry crumble; cherry pie; apple and cherry crumble; jam tart; mince tart; bread pudding.

Terry Stevens is tarting up the old place — putting on a new roof, decorating and widening the parking lot — but not enough to spoil the flavour.

Recommended by: **Richard Berry**, Kelsale; **S. Links**, Hendon; **Steve Brown**, Martlesham Heath; **Paul R. Smith**, Ipswich; **Roger Kindred**, West Mersea, Colchester; **Colin Stanford**, Trimley-St-Mary, 'Very good food, good value'; **John Brame**, Claydon; **T. Cable**, Ipswich; **Phil Keeble**, Felixstowe, 'Best breakfast on the A12'; **Kevin Clarke**, Braintree; **Tony Smith**, Fleet, Spalding; **N.B. Whitworth**, Holbeach; **Chris Clark**, Ipswich; **Gwyn Latcham**, Tonypandy; **Colin Roadnight**, Bradford.

JOCK'S CAFÉ at Colnbrook on the Slough bypass

This is where Jock's came in the popularity list but by the time you read about it Jock's will be no more. After 52 years' service the Lowden family has sold out and the property is to be redeveloped as high-tech offices. It leaves a big gap in that neck of the woods.

IT'S BIZARRE

How to get a quick rise
D.J. Wiffen, of Aveley, reports on how to go up in the world with the least effort. The wagon was carrying a container and went under the crane to have it lifted off. But the twist-locks weren't opened properly so container, wagon, driver and all took an unexpected airborne trip.

Browned off
My Pakistani neighbour claimed he was better off than me because he didn't have a Paki living next door to him.
Frank Baker, *St. Helens, Liverpool.*

TAYSIDE TRUCKSTOP (A85)   Tel: (0382) 621941

Situation Dundee, Scotland, on the A85 Dundee ring-road from Perth to Aberdeen, well signposted. Access could not be better.

Services parking for 100, diesel on site; accommodation is three doubles and three singles priced at £5.00 single and £4.00 shared; four showers available for sleeper-cab men; parking is £3.50 with a 50p meal voucher; special services are a public weighbridge and maintenance on site — DAFs especially (they are DAF agents).

Food the special breakfast of bacon, sausage, egg, beans, toast and tea is £1.75, main meals are served from 4.30 p.m. and the standard is home-made soup, dish of the day and sweet for £2.85, from the à la carte take a lasagne at £2.30 to a T-bone steak at £3.75; the restaurant opens at 5.45 a.m. and closes at 9.00 p.m. flexible; tea is available for residents until 11.00 p.m. which is also when the bar closes.

Amenities bar, video and special room for pool and darts.

Companionship it is becoming very popular. Truck park is all metalled.

There used to be another truckstop in Dundee until, guess what — no, it wasn't a Little Chef or Happy Eater this time, the Scottish Development Association took it over to turn into a tourists' hotel. then, of course, they had problems with trucks until the Ridgeway family stepped in. The Ridgeways are brothers Philip and Donald with wives Sheila and Maureen; the wives naturally do all the work — in the truckstop. You probably recognise the name from your travels, the menfolk run a fleet of 50 or more trucks, so they do know a bit about the business. To make the truckstop they took over one of their workshops and converted it, which is why there is full maintenance on site and the services are tailor-made for truckers.

Recommended by: Richard Dembizky, Scunthorpe; **S.W. Poole**, Farningham, Surrey; **Simon Tandy**, Ledbury; **D. Littlewood**, York; **A. Stewart**, Blairgowrie; **K. Allison**, South Queensferry; **J.H. Bickerton**, Wallasey; **J.H. Kelly**, Durham; **Michael Chandler**, Lambourne; **A. Taylor**, Letchworth; **Roy Coupier**, Basildon, Bradford; **Jan de Koster**, Zwindrecht, Holland; **Pop Rivet**, Aspatria; **R. Austin**, South Queensferry.

IT'S BIZARRE

Sporty performance on the M25

After a hard day's trucking, **The Wagonmaster**, of Summersome, thought it was a Fiesta for sore eyes on the M25 — the lady driver was topless.

Lame duck

Flogging up a motorway hill, the ultimate humiliation for **Rob Madden**, of Denton, came when he was passed by an invalid tricycle.

FIVE WAYS CAFÉ (A41)   Tel: (0926) 87278

Situation on the A41, Waseley, it is the Birmingham to Warwick road, at the Five Ways roundabout take the Warwick road and find the café between Hatton and Knowle. Access good.

Services a 1.6-acre surfaced truck park; diesel from adjoining garage; accommodation for five in a three-roomed dormitory with own kitchen and shower; pay-telephone.

Food café is open from 7.00 a.m. until 5.00 p.m. but overnighters get late three-course meals; breakfasts are bacon and egg, two slices of bread and a half-pint mug of tea for £1.19 or the full bacon, egg, two sausages, tomatoes, fried bread, two slices of bread and butter and a mug of tea for £1.65; main meals come in the same range, two eggs and beefburger at £1.95 or the ham, corned beef and so on with chips at £1.55 and sandwiches at 50p. Different from other truckstops, the parking is £2.00 for those staying, £1.00 to leave the truck and not stay, and £6.00 parking, bed and breakfast with tea at any time.

Amenities colour TV and amusement machines in the café, the pub across the road called The Case is Altered is very popular.

This is a case of the singer not the song: because it hasn't the full facilities and cannot offer the same privacy, Five Ways charges less to stay. But its popularity stems from proprietors Sam and Yvonne Gorton — 'great personalities'. It is very attractive, there was a scare among drivers that they were selling out when solid oak tables and chairs were installed, a great stone fireplace built, new solid oak doors were added to keep in style with the bay-windowed frontage. But there was no need to worry, they were just improving the place for customers' comfort and pleasure. Over a period of 18 years the Gortons have attracted a steady clientèle.

Recommended by:M.D. Howell, Basingstoke; **A. Robbins**, Southampton; **Meandher**, Chandlers' Ford; **A. Willoughby**, Pangbourne; **Joseph Frank Bagot**, Hyde, Cheshire; **D. Ainscough**, Chorley; **Peter Kerry**, Aylesbury; **Geraint Thomas**, Conway, North Wales; **J.W. Jackson**, Stalybridge; **J. Cooke**, Denton, Manchester; Driver, Rawtenstall; **A. Crossin**, Harbury; **Graham Elgar**, Oxford; **Stephen Taylor**, Staines.

FARM CAFÉ TRUCKSTOP (A17)   Tel: (0406) 23652

Situation On the A17 at Fleet Hargate, two miles from Holbeach on the eastbound carriageway.

Services parking for 60 trucks on five feet of hardcore and gravel — 'Hold anything'; changing rooms and showers, 12 toilets and wash-basins; five telephones, two private call boxes for incoming calls; possibly Shell diesel on site soon.

Food the café seats 400 and is open from 6.15 a.m. until midnight with 18 staff in attendance, breakfast is £1.50 and there are 50 meals to choose from ranging from £1.50 up to a 10-oz. T-bone steak at

IT'S THURSDAY...
I'M IN BIRMINGHAM...
SHE MUST BE BERYL!

£6.50; opening times on Saturday are 6 a.m. until 8 p.m. and on Sundays, 7 a.m. until 9 p.m.

Amenities shop, fruit shop, two pool tables and a spectacular TV lounge.

Companionship 600 to 700 trucks a day call at the Farm, so among that lot there should be somebody to talk to.

About that TV lounge; it is the only lounge for truckers which I have come across that is furnished with £32,000-worth of antiques. The programmes may be rubbish, but you watch in style. And such style is part of the approach of proprietor Bill Pyne who runs the café with his wife, Patricia Anne, and his mother. He says: 'We built the lounge bar specially for lorry drivers, and people couldn't believe it was for them.' So the furnishing is as much part of the conversation as the antics of 'Dirty Den' in Eastenders and, from a trucker's point of view, the Farm is a sort of Antiques Road Show. Part of the same philosophy is Bill Payne's assertion: 'We look after them 100 per cent, if there is anything wrong, it is put right immediately.' That could sound like big talk, but there is big talk and there is word of mouth, the second is what drivers rely on and what has put The Farm so high on drivers' lists, so that 600 to 700 call every day. If

165

anybody doubted that catering for truckers can be big business, this café proves that it is. Coaches and private motorists are queuing to get in on the act; a national brass band festival is held in the locality, one Friday the organisers booked 2,600 meals for contestants travelling from the north — that is some catering. 'But,' says Bill Payne, 'transport is our business, we built up from nothing on transport and truckers always get top priority and always will.'

Recommended by: Driver, Rochdale; **P. Edmonds**, Thetford; Driver, Rochdale; **Mike Lambert**, Ramsey; **L. Williams**, Widnes; Driver, Bedlington; **N.B. Whitworth**, Holbeach; Driver, Swinderby; **Mad Monk**, Spalding; **Tony Pearson**, Middlesborough; **Daniel McDonald**, Middleton, 'Good overnight parking, nice café with waiter service, nice, pleasant bar with bar staff.' **R. Beckett**, Great Yarmouth; **Geoff Hyams**, Leyland; **Graham Elgar**, Oxford; **Ronald Cavanagh**, Caddishead.

NELL'S CAFÉ (A2) Tel: (0474) 352136

Situation Gravesend, Kent, on the south bank of the Thames and in one of the most useful sites in the country on the A2 five miles from the Dartford end of the M25 tunnel and just before the M2 proper begins leading to the Channel ports. Take the Gravesend east turn-off. The café has no parking of its own but there are *free* Kent County Council lorry parks either side. It fits beautifully into many a time schedule.

Services eight to twelve individual bedrooms were being built to be ready by early 1987; two showers in private cubicles; pay-telephone; diesel nearby.

Amenities television.

Food big, busy restaurant open from 6.30 a.m. until 9.30 p.m.; breakfast is £1.60 and main meals come up to £2.50.

This is one of those 'watch this space' transport cafés which is 'upwardly mobile' in all senses. For instance, they came in the top four in the national 'Best British Breakfast' contest against all comers, top hotels included. The winner of that contest prepared about 40 breakfasts a day — compared with Nell's 400 — and came top on presentation, not quality. Laurie and Ann Yeomans took over four years ago and the improvements followed. Laurie is a trained chef who learned his trade in the best hotels like the Waldorf and Dorchester in London. He quit the 'carriagetrade' end of the business because the unsocial hours got him down, so he then ran a chip shop which somewhat restricted his skills. Now he caters for 1,500 a day. Most are HGV men but private motorists are increasingly attracted by the food — truckers are guaranteed priority. After the breakfast, steak and kidney pud rates very highly.

Recommended by: **Sal Chester**, Leeds; **Loper**; **Trevor J. Gray**, Ramsgate; **I. Beevers**, York; **E. Tearle**, Ramsgate; **Gambler**, Gravesend; **Derek Lenton**, Queenborough; **John Marshall**, Dorset; **Dennis Blacklock**, Carlisle; **Malcolm Murray**, Manchester; **R.A. Hall**, Swansea; **Pete Spicer**, St. Paul's Cray;

QUERNHOW CAFÉ (A1)   Tel: (0845) 567221

Situation On the A1 three miles north of the Baldersby roundabout/
flyover, and 14 miles south of Scotch Corner — entrance only on the
northbound side.

Services a good tarmacadamed and concrete truck park for 50 − 60
vehicles; large toilet block, male and female, two showers in the
male section, one in the women's part, and open all day; one
pay-phone outside and a second in the café; the filling station
adjoining the site has been closed and may become a Little Chef; the
café seats 85 and is open from 7 a.m. until 7.30 p.m.; a touring
caravan site is attached to the site.

They are in a bit of a cleft stick at the Quernhow: they have applied
for planning permission to extend and build extra accommodation,
but until they can enlarge the truck park, they cannot extend the
premises. Yet the café grows more popular all the time. Bryan and
Maureen Lye put it down to 23 years' hard work in the place. A
possible extra reason for the surge in popularity is Winifred
Simpson, the cook for the last two years — which brings us to the
Food breakfast, full English with two slices of toast and a mug of tea,
£2.00; the ever popular steak and kidney pies, £1.85; and Winifred's
Yorkshire puddings are a smash hit, hundreds are sold and now you
can get them as a starter with onion sauce.

Recommended by: Driver, Hornsea; **Derek Gordon**, South Shields; **Pete Spicer**, St.
Paul's Cray; **A. Stewart**, St. Boswells, 'Good food reasonably priced.'; **J. Kelly**, Durham;
J. Blunt, Wednesfield; **T.M. Cullen**, Huddersfield; Driver, Newcastle; **Brian Saville**,
Birstall, West Yorks; **John O'Connor**, Openshaw, Manchester; **D. Archbold**, Jarrow;
Stuart Dunn, Morpeth.

IT'S BIZARRE

Stripped for action

Driver, from St Neots, took a second look in astonishment.
Pedalling furiously down the road was a stripped-down
cyclist — all the man was wearing was a woolly hat.

JAYNE'S PLACE   Tel: (090 076) 776

Situation Blyth, Nottinghamshire, 100 yards off the A1 on the Bawtry
Road.

Services The truck park is small, the owner explains, with room for
40, he could do with a much larger area, and it is only a park; once
they had sleeping accommodation for 21, but with the advent of
sleeper-cabs, that is closed; there are washrooms for males and
females but, as yet, no showers, and there is a telephone in the café.

Food This is home cooked and good enough to go into the Egon Ronay food guides, and that is an exceptionally high recommendation; breakfasts range from bacon, egg, and tomatoes at £1.25 to the special with bacon, egg, sausage, fried potatoes, black pudding and mushrooms at £1.65; top of the range main meals are braised steak, roasts of beef or pork, with apple sauce and stuffing, at £1.50, then home-made meat pies or liver and onions at £1.30: 'And for that you get a real dinner-plate full.' Open from 6.00 a.m. until 8.00 p.m. and for

Companionship They are packed out all the time.

For pride in the job and the product you cannot beat Ernest Woodiwiss, he has earned a reputation with Jayne's Place and is rightly proud of it. For the sheer pleasure of an old-type transport café which has moved with the times and been brought up to standard you will have to look far and wide for a better one than this family business. It has been a café for 70 years and until five years ago was known as Tom's. Ernest and Ann Woodiwiss renamed it Jayne's Place in honour of daughter Jayne who is now an integral part of the business — and a big attraction in her own right. Ernest Woodiwiss left the regular army and was a lorry driver for 30 years until he bought the old Tom's café, a wooden shack. 'You wouldn't have kept a dog in it,' he comments. So up went the brick building and the place was put into army-order and cleanliness.

From his army days, Mr Woodiwiss knew about discipline and how to run things. He must know how to do it properly because his staff have been with him for 10 years. 'It is kept spotless,' he proclaims, 'anybody can inspect my kitchens any time.' He says that you can't mop around people's legs while they are sitting at the immaculate tables, but he gives the impression he would like to if so much as a crumb fell to the floor. The result is that drivers bring their wives and families in when they are passing on recreational jaunts, and regulars have been coming for 15 years. Wife Ann does all the pastry and pies cooking. 'Nothing frozen whatsoever, it's got to be the proper stuff or none at all,' says the proprietor, and adds, 'I tell a lie, we do keep a bag of frozen chips in case of emergencies or for when a rush of children come in and want chip butties. 'He does not sell fish and chips, he sold them only once, on a Good Friday. 'Beautiful fish,' he recalls, 'but it smelled the place out. You can't get rid of the smell — and I'm never asked for them, anyway.'

They do have neighbour problems, being near the residential estate, which meant that they had to stop opening all night because the noise of trucks arriving and leaving disturbed the peace. Until 1986 they were on septic tank drainage, hence no showers. But mains drainage was due and with it showers and further amenities were planned. And then came Jayne...say no more, they changed the name. All around Little Chefs and Happy Eaters have been buying up transport cafés. 'I will not sell,' says Mr Woodiwiss, 'they've approached me, but I've been a lorry driver and I know what it's like. If you eat at of one of those places you come away hungry.

'But at Jayne's Place you get a proper dinner-plateful.

Recommended by: **Brian Sylvester**, Sleaford; **Doga**, Thirsk; **Paul Mason**, North Kyme; **J.J. Sylvester**, Sleaford; **M. Thorpe**, Pudsey, West Yorkshire; **John Barrie Ducker**, Knarborough; **C.W. Grainger**, Stamford; **Roger Kindred**, West Mersea, Colchester; Driver, Wisbech; **W. Mackney**, Huntingdon; **P. Thobald**, Denton, Manchester; **Paul Sharples**, Droylesden, Manchester.

IT'S THE WAY YOU TELL'EM

R.I.P.
Tentatively, the child asked: 'Mummy, is Daddy dead?' 'No darling, he's picking up a load at Dover docks.'
John Barrie Ducker, *Narborough, Norfolk.*

GEORGE's CAFÉ, alias: CRICK COMMERCIAL CAFE alias: THE CHATTERBOX (A5)   Tel: (0788) 823247

(The last is the latest name and the one it will be known by, but drivers will still call it George's, I'll bet.)
Situation: On the A5 but just off the M1, half a mile from junction 18, look for the Halfway House pub, then Crick Commercial Trucks site.
Services: Parking for 250 trucks, diesel and repairs are on site — and the whole new, expanding café complex awaits you. Planning permission gained and the work in progess (at the time of writing) and the café will have doubled in size to seat 140, two new toilets and showers will be in use and 'The Chatterbox' will be on its way. *Open* 24 *hours* daily until 1 p.m. Saturday, then open again at tea time Sunday.
Food: Breakfast is £1.65 and main meals are £1.80, all meat is bought in daily and everything is home-made, tea is 15p with a second cup for 10p, coffee is 18p with a second cup for 13p.
Amenities: TV and video, pool, and the Halfway House pub is a ahort walk away and well used by visiting drivers.

Behind this explosion of activity in a much loved haunt is Mrs Eve Williams. You may remember her, she came into transport catering by running a caravan snack bar until George's came on the market. Until then she had been at the receiving end of transport cafés. Her husband, Michael, drove for North West Freighters, Haydock, and she often travelled with him. 'I saw some of the cafés he had to eat in and I was appalled. That is why I wanted to get into the business, to make it better,' explains Mrs Williams. So far she has succeeded well enough to be able to break into our 'Top 40' list after only a few months in the game. She has relied on word of mouth to spread the fame of the café, which is the same principle as this book is written on. What the drivers say is all that matters in the long run to all café and truckstop proprietors.

GILL'S CAFÉ, ANDOVER (A303)   Tel: (0246) 23037

Situation one mile from the centre of Andover on the A303 at the old Weyhill roundabout which is now an intersection on the extension of the Andover bypass; follow the brown and white truck and eating signs; down the slip-road, over the bridge and you see the large Shell canopy, the white building is the truckstop.

Service, parking for 100 trucks and Shell diesel facility; 23 beds, each room with wash-basin; three showers with separate one for women; pool room, fruit machines and juke box; shop on site; telephone in entrance; fifty yards away is the popular Why Not? inn; parking £4.00 with a £1.00 voucher; a bed is £7.00.; fuel from 6.00 a.m. until 11.00 p.m.

Food all meals home cooked and range from £1.50 to £2.50 with always six daily dishes on the menu; restaurant opens from 7.00 a.m. until 9.30 p.m..

Amenities as mentioned above, but you can hire a Godfrey Davis self-drive car if you feel like a busman's holiday.

Companionship meet lots of old friends, some regulars have been coming for 30 years.

Gill's is all shipshape and Bristol-fashion because proprietor John Gill is a former Royal Navy officer — catch him on a good day and he might split the mainbrace — actually, I don't know how many good days they have in Andover, so you might have to settle for a cup of tea. After his naval service on frigates, aircraft carriers and minesweepers he and his wife, Linda, joined his father Harold in the more dangerous minefield of running a truckstop. It was a difficult transition for the first few years, as you can imagine, until he got the bug and put his heart into it.

The Gills had raised the café to a pretty good standard so that in the early 1970s they came in the Top Ten in the Egon Ronay survey and they went to a reception in the Houses of Parliament to represent the transport café side of the catering industry.

Since they took over the business, John and Linda Gill have doubled the size of the truckstop. But not without some concern from the regular clientèle. John says: 'They saw the improvements being made and suspected that we were going to sell out to the Little Chef or Happy Eater chains. For 40 years we have made our business from the transport trade and we wouldn't have it any other way. There is a valid market out there and we want to keep our share of it. Facilities for truck drivers are on the wane. As soon as leases run out or premises become available, the Little Chefs and Happy

Eaters move in and that is the end of trucks. The way they look at it, one truck takes up the space of four cars; four cars carry a potential 16 people, a truck has the one driver — so it is goodbye to the truck.'

So it looks as if Gill's is pretty well anchored where it is for the foreseeable future.

Recommended by: **Malcolm Collins**, Basingstoke; **Arnold William Pearce**, Par, Cornwall; **G. Moat**, Colchester; Driver, Andover; Mr. **Gorrett**, Crediton, Devon; **K.M. Mallett**, Bristol; **P. Butterworth**, Shaw, Lancs.; **Cave Man**, Welwyn; **Corsair**, Welwyn; **Trevor J.S. Gray**, Ramsgate; **John Marshall**, Dorset.

A funny thing happened...

'I promise you, it is absolutely true,' vouches **Dennis Blacklock**, of Carlisle, 'there was this pink elephant rolling slowly towards me down the slow lane of the motorway — it had fallen off the back of a van in front.'

THE CHEERIO CAFÉ (A17)   Tel: (0529) 8694

Situation On the A17 at South Rauceby, two miles on the Newark side of Sleaford and near RAF Cranwell.

Services home from home accommodation in a detached bungalow next to the café, two drivers per room, bathroom en suite, TV, kettle — what more could you want for £6.00 a night? As a unique service the proprietor has a DROT international with a four-in-one bucket which comes in useful when drivers need a tow or a slipped load straightening — it is used more often then you'd imagine.

Food breakfast at £1.75 and main meals at £1.80, room for 60 in the café which opens from 6 a.m. until 8 p.m., seven days a week.

This is an old-style popular café of the type which is rapidly disappearing or being bought out — there's a Little Chef next door. Trevor and Monica Marsh have run the 'Cheerio' for eight years. The café goes back 60 years when it began as a wooden hut and they carried the water from a well two miles away. All the food is home baked and service comes from a staff of ten. Parking can be a bit tight, but there is room for 30 trucks if they are 'parked prettily' — naturally, one private car can ruin the prettiness. 'You see them everywhere else parked neatly, they come in here and abandon them,' says the proprietor. This café is one of those which is in a natural good spot for a great number of drivers, just at the right place for a break or a stop-over. Sleeper-cabs are charged £1.00 plus 15p VAT.

Recommended by: **W. Sellers**, Barrow Hill; **Roger Thurlby**, Boston; **Brian Sylvester**, Sleaford; **John Howard**, Penrith; **John Barrie Ducker**, Knaresborough; **Ronald Balmer**, Appleby, Yorks; **Ivan William Shipp**, Norfolk; **L. Holmes**, Thetford; **Steve Hoggard**, Wigan, Lancs; **Steve Newall**, Wigan; **J.J. Sylvester**, Sleaford; **Roger Gadd**, Sleaford.

BOB's CAFÉ (A45)   Tel: (0203) 542704

Situation on the A45 at Stretton-on-Dunsmore about four miles from Coventry.

Services parking for approximately 60 trucks; 22 single beds, two showers, two telephones, £6.00 the bed including meal, £5.00 for sleeper-cabs, £1.50 ordinary parking.

Food a big breakfast with all the usual plus black-pudding, mushrooms, tomatoes — £1.60, main meals at £1.55 and £1.85, puddings 65p, open from 6 a.m. until midnight, Saturdays until 8 p.m. and Sundays from 11 a.m. until midnight.

Amenities lounge, bar and TV plus video. And all home cooking, not a thing bought in.

This is another of Dr Rundle's establishments — see the Sunset, Rendezvous and Ace Cafés. They certainly have a strong attraction for truckers and regulars will not desert them. Jean Roberts, manageress, says: 'This is a pretty dead part of the A45 nowadays, but they come from quite a way to stay here.' So the

Companionship factor is strong with 20 or 30 overnighters in attendance most times. You will probably recognise Jean Roberts, when she was 18 she began her truckstop life in the old Tubby's Café which became the Rendezvous. Then she took factory jobs for a while until the trucking trade lured her back. 'Live entertainment?' she queried, 'only when I give a party — we have quite a few party nights.'

Recommended by: Mr **Beaumont**, Speke; **Alex Main**, Preston; Driver, Rawtenstall; **AT**, Rugby; **Frank Baker**, St. Helens; **Frank Allington**, East Malling; **Reg Sowman**, Kirkaldy; **T. Roberts**, Liverpool; **K. Stedman**, Old Woking.

BARTON LORRY PARK (A1)   Tel: (0325) 77777 or 77778

Situation on the A1 one mile north of Scotch Corner. Access perfect.

Services parking for 100 vehicles and a comprehensive range of diesel facilities including Ultramar Quickfill, K-Fuels electronic systems and cash bunkering; accommodation is 19 single rooms; three showers for sleeper-cab men; parking £3.50 with £1.00 voucher, bed is £5.50 with £1.00 voucher.

Food a full breakfast is £1.90, there is a great range of main meals at £2.90 — 'Any meal you like.' Open from 6.00 a.m. until midnight on Mondays to Fridays, and from 6.00 a.m. until 5.00 p.m. (2.00 p.m. in winter) on Saturdays; 2.00 p.m. until 10.00 p.m. on Sundays. And the food is all home cooked.

Amenities full bar, gaming machines, pool and darts room, video and TV lounge, live entertainment.

Companionship you will find plenty of kindred spirits.

Barton Lorry Park is another truckstop in the process of expanding and progressing. The resident managing director is Michael Burgess who likes to push the business along. Already it has won a reputation as a 'specially homely place' which is what the lads seem to want and this management strives to provide. Actually, it should be encouraging for drivers, this is another place which has pulled itself up by its boot-laces from a near fatal decline. It is a classic case of when one door closes, another opens: the old-style cafés are biting the dust, particularly along the A1, but new ones are springing up. Michael Burgess's approach is that if you don't give drivers what they want, they don't come. Four years ago he had no connection with the trucking industry and he had to learn by 'common sense' and keeping his eyes and ears open. Obviously, he learnt well, they now have plans for considerable expansion and improvement.

Recommended by: **D. Littlewood**, York; **Dave Partington**, Edinburgh; **Ronald Cavanagh**, Caddishead; **M. Pratt**, Swindon; **P. Kent**, Norwich; Mr. **Newell**, Swinton, Manchester; **S.J. Fulge**, Bristol; **Charlie Braham**, Haydock.

IT'S BIZARRE

It's an ill wind
You hear the warnings, sometimes you see the results, but you don't often witness it happen. There was a howling gale blowing the day **Frank Allingham**, of East Malling, Kent, watched an approaching van suddenly take off and fly, landing upside down in a field.

NORMAN'S CAFÉ AND MOTEL (A1)   Tel: (0977) 82444

Situation an A1 pull-up but on the old Great North Road at Brotherton, near Ferrybridge. The northbound approach is easy, just turn into the village; southbound turn at the Brotherton Fox pub and cross the fly-over bridge. Access is good.

Services truck park for 100. and diesel should be available on site in 1987; three showers and a new washroom with five showers and wash-basins in the pipe-line; accommodation for 50 in the process of being refurbished; telephone; parking is £3.00 and an evening meal, bed and breakfast is £8.00.

Food all home cooked by Mary McNally which is an attraction, as explained later; breakfast of two rashers of bacon, two sausages, an egg, beans, tomato and special black pudding plus two slices of bread and butter is £1.65, tea is 18p, main meals of steak and kidney puddings are £1.72 plus the tea. They are particular about the bread for sandwiches, it comes thick. Opening hours are from 5.00 a.m. until midnight weekdays, until 4.00 p.m. Saturdays, and from 8.00 a.m. until 10.00 p.m. on Sundays, and they open on Bank Holidays.

Amenities a bit sparse at the moment but planned to be much improved as planning permissions and money allows; there is a good pub nearby and a 26-inch colour TV in the lounge; novel features are five daily newspaper vending machines and a chilled drinks dispenser.

Companionship it is popular. Truck park is hard-standing on rolled tarmac planings.

Yes, it is another 'new wave' truckstop under development and, like others, created from the ashes of an old-style one. Norman's secret weapon is Mary McNally who achieved fame and popularity at the Woodlands where she was renowned for her generous portions of food. With husband Hugh and son Hugh Thomas, she took over in 1985 and the difference was soon noted by drivers who remarked: 'What a change,' when they saw the new stainless steel kitchens and fittings. Has all the makings of a good 'un.

Recommended by: **N. Powell**, Ross-on-Wye; **Malcolm Crawford**, Haltwistle; **Paul Bonney**, Huntingdon; Mr **Hammond**, Walsall; Driver, Stamford, Lincs; **Alex Main**, Preston; **J.H. Kelly**, Durham; **Billy Huntley**, Durham; Driver, Darlington; **A. Tarmey**, Sunderland.

A funny thing happened...

'I finished unloading two tonnes of stuff and handed in the delivery note. The man looked at it puzzled and said, "I'm sorry, chum, you've brought it to the wrong address".' When **P.A. Chapman** told us this sad little tale, he forgot to say where he came from — well, what else would you expect?

THE ACE CAFÉ (A45)   Tel: (0327) 40405

Situation On the A45 at Weedon. Four miles from junction 16 on the M1, nine miles from junction 18. Come off on the A45 driving away from Northampton towards Daventry, where the A5 crosses the A45 at the bottom of the hill, the Ace Café is at the top of the hill — easy.

Services very good access, parking for 60, a bit bumpy but firm; diesel adjoining site; pay-telephone.

Food Café seats 65, breakfast is £1.30, main meals of steak and kidney pie, liver and onions are £1.65 and roast beef or chicken are £1.85 — all meals are under £2.00. Open from 6 a.m. until 10.30 p.m. daily, Saturday closes at 3.30 p.m. Sunday; 9.30 a.m. to 3.30 p.m.

Amenities TV and video feature-film every night.

The Ace has had its ups and downs but Jane Ainsley is back and it is on an *up*. Still the regulars remain faithful. One thing they like is that it is a quiet spot and they get an unbroken good night's sleep. For those in the know, there was a time when the Spirit was willing but the Level caused a bit of aggro. Improvements are pending.

Recommended by: Mr **Peadon**, Coventry; **Charles Youles**, Southend; **Dave Broomfield**, Maidstone; **T. Beetham**, Wirral; **Charlie Braham**, Haydock; **M. Stewart**, Haltwistle; **Malcolm Collins**, Basingstoke; **Pete Spicer**, St. Paul's Cray; **D. Sherrington**, Maidenhead; **R. Hutchings**, Stratford, London.

CHESTERFIELD B.R.S. TRUCKSTOP (M1)
Tel: (0246) 851414/852836

Open to everybody

Situation Holmewood Industrial Estate, Holmewood, near Chesterfield, junction 29 on the M1, south side of Chesterfield.

Services everything a trucker could want — tarmacked parking for 120 trucks, floodlit, night security; power points for fridge vehicles; repairs, breakdowns and return loads available through Datafreight; all services within the security area; showers; fuel — all agency cards; telephones; even a fork-lift truck on hand.

Food the restaurant seats 60, breakfast is £1.90 to £2.20, there are four main meals to choose from daily at £2.50, and 'call orders' of eight to ten special dishes up to a T-bone steak — reckon about £3.50 — £3.90.

Amenities truckers' shop, 45-inch TV and video with latest films; bar and games.

Now they discover that they should have built it bigger. Completely trucker-orientated, built by truckers for truckers, they questioned drivers about the standards of service given. And one reply came: 'Staff too helpful.' Jock Graham, a former driver and now the manager, asked what the man meant. He was told: 'If they see you hanging about, they assume you're lost and come up to help — you might just be looking, or finding things out for yourself.' The philosophy of the place is stated as 'service and civility' and the staff stick to it — too much, apparently, for one driver. The main thing is that they have got the attitude and atmosphere right. That is clear because mid-week they are full to overflowing. So the second part of the philosophy is that nobody is ever turned away. Overflow drivers are parked on adjoining BRS land. A look at the map shows that it is another 'natural' as a site, it is exactly halfway between north and south and so perfect for trunkers. It has one other unique advantage — it is signposted from the motorway. And that took some arm-twisting. 'One thing about truckers,' says John Graham,' is that they will tell you the truth. If anybody has a grumble or a grouse we always listen.' The way you lot go on, I wonder if he has time for anything else.

Recommended by: **Paul Taylor**, Bradford; **D. Cottingham**, Ashford, Middlesex; **M. Foster**, Cannock; **B. Taylor**, Amersham; **Roy Hudson**, Sale; **David L. Lowe**, Pennistone; **A. Willoughby**, Pangbourne; **Sour Apple**, Walsall; **S.W. Poole**, Farningham, Surrey.

TRUCKERS FINDERN (A35)   Tel: (0332) 517401
(THE OLD ATKINS CAFÉ, LONG FAMOUS.)

Situation On the A38 near Derby, access from northbound carriageway with footbridge from southbound.

Services parking for 120 trucks at £3.00 a night with a 50p voucher for bedrooms; diesel both sides of road, agency cards — Dial, Overdrive and Diners Club — but no credit cards in restaurant.
Accommodation seven single, seven double bedrooms bookable in advance, sleeper-cabs.
Food fully licenced restaurant and bar — read on...

This is now the first *Les Routiers* appointed truckstop in Britain and a leader in the new generation of truck motels catering for transport. If you want to know the style and charges refer back to *Truckers Paradise*, this is one of the same group and part of the 'great leap forward' in services for HGV men. A third is on the A40 at *Whitchurch*, near *Ross-on-Wye*. These splendid places are opening under the banner '*TRUCKERS* — are driving up standards' but they place us in a dilemma because they are really too new to register on our survey. One thing is certain, they will rise in the list.

Recommended by: **Roy Purcell**, Derby; **David Duncalf**, Warsop; **Antony Millen**, Sheffield; **Stewart Dearden**, Chard; **D. Ellicott**, Swansea; **Brian Watson**, Cleveland; **Raymond Bosson**, Mackworth; **W. Lucas**, Swansea.

IT'S BIZARRE

Enterprising old crock

Astonished to see an invalid carriage trundling along the M63, it didn't take **John Marshall**, of Yeovil, long to deduce that the invalid had also travelled the length of the M62 to get where he was.

The last five cafés/truckstops in our Top 40 come with equal popularity ratings, so we present them in alphabetical order:

CORONATION CAFÉ (A5)   Tel: (0543) 53544

Situation On the A5, at Churchbridge, about a mile from the M6 junction 12 roundabout. The café is set well back from the road behind a line of big poplar trees which the guv'nor, Les Grogan, says are older than him and his dad, John Leslie Grogan, who have run the place for generations.
Services there are one and a quarter acres to park in and it is such hard-standing that Pickfords put an 80-tonnes load on and didn't ruffle the surface. Sleeper-cabs have a special priority. Les Grogan says: 'We close at weekends, but the lads are welcome to use the place. A lot of them park and leave before we open, then pay us when they come back. I believe in give and take.' The charge is £3.75 overnight.
Food Two breakfasts, a jumbo at £2.25 and a lighter one at £1.35; all breakfasts get two eggs, the jumbo gets three, and both include tea and bread butter. 'I've been serving the jumbo for 28 years,' Les tells,

'and they still keep coming back for it. So there can't be much wrong.' Open daily from about twenty past seven in the morning until quarter past six in the evening, closed Saturdays and Sundays, but you are welcome to use the park.

Recommended by: Mr **Somerfield**, Rednal; **M. Boyle**, Cheddleton; Driver, Liverpool; **J.H. Bickerton**, Wallasey; **T. Chaplin**, Leigh; **R. Beaumont**, Speke; Driver, Mansfield.

DUNKIRK CAFÉ (A5117)   Tel: (0244) 851655

Situation At Great Mollington, on the A5117, 400 yards from the beginning of the M56, the café is on the Queensferry bypass.

Services Parking for 75 overnight and 50-60 daily visitors on good hard stone; diesel from adjoining garage; pay-phones.

Food Breakfast £1.65 and main meals at £1.99, some drivers take three meals a day in the restaurant. Open 24 hours daily, Saturday until 5 p.m. and Sundays from 8 a.m. until 5 p.m. The hours are important because for years the nearest all-night cafés were at Cannock and Cardiff. Now The Populars at Lymm is also open.

The owners are partners, Mr Reno Perruzza nand Mrs Joan Shaw. Mrs Shaw used to run the Sale Hotel and then the Royal Thorn Hotel at the other end of the M56. Alas for her, the police have objected to a bar at the Dunkirk. Planning permission has been granted for a new café, and the intention was to build a social club as well and turn the old café into a toilet block — it may yet come. Meanwhile these are the

Amenities TV, videos, pool, juke-box and fruit machines. Many old hands, hearing of the plans, pleaded: 'Don't pull down the old café, it will spoil the happy atmosphere.'

Recomended by: **A. Williams**, Wrexham; **Roy**, Halkin; **T.M. Cullen**, Huddersfield; Driver, Trafford Park; **Andy Hall**, Sudbury, Derbyshire; **Tom Runathan**, Liverpool; **R.E. Parry**, Anglesey.

ENTERPRISE CAFÉ (A45)   Tel: (0954) 210383

Situation On the A45 at Hardwick, west of Cambridge and just at the beginning of the northern bypass to the city.

Services Parking for 80 on hard-standing; shower; pay call-box; 20 beds, two to a room; diesel is coming — may be there by now — the charges are £3.50 overnight and £5.50 for a bedroom.

Food Breakfast is £1.90, inclusive of tea and bread and butter, main meals are £1.80 plus 20p for tea. Café is open from 6.30 a.m. until 7 p.m., the bar is open from 7 p.m. until 11 p.m. every night; Saturdays, café: 7 a.m. until 10.30 a.m.

Roger Merritt and his wife, Sally, run the establishment. He says: 'I'm not the cheapest on the road, but we've always had a policy of providing decent food. If it isn't good enough to eat ourselves, then it isn't good enough to serve.' If you are approaching from the St. Neots side, it is at the second roundabout.

Recommended by: **G. Flight**, Pentney, Norfolk; **Roy Gilbert**, Ipswich, 'Good breakfast, opens at 7 a.m.' **J.H.J. Baker**, Woodbridge; **T. Cable**, Ipswich; Mr **Nixon**, Northwich; **Harry Bickley**, Hyde; Anon, Warrington.

IT'S BIZARRE

A fast moving story
Loper, who drives anywhere but often to London and the North East, looked down from his cab one day at an overtaking car and saw the driver reading a book propped against the steering-wheel.

MOLLY'S PLACE (M8)   Tel: (0501) 51264

Situation At Harthill, a spit away from junction 5 on the M8, if you can spit 1,000 yards.
Service Parking for 70 trucks on firm hard-core. The £4.50 parking charge includes a three-course meal; accommodation for nine, four beds in one room, three in another, bed, breakfast and meal is £7.50; two showers; phones.
Food Breakfast with two eggs is £1.40, main meals are £1.50 and a steak will rush you £2.50.
Amenities Bar, videos and live entertainment.

Graham and Janet Wright now run the café. They took it over from Graham's mother. She bought it when it was the Burnside Transport Café — you guessed? Her name was Molly and the drivers re-christened the place. The café seats 70 and is open from 6.30 a.m. on weekdays and from 10 a.m. until 11 p.m. on Saturdays and Sundays. It is well liked and popular with all travellers but truckers get priority at all times.

Recommended by: **Dave Partington**, Edinburgh; **Alex Farries**, Glasgow; **Susan Stringer**, Blakeley; **Michael Chandler**, Lambourne; **R. Beaumont**, Speke; **B. Taylor**, Amersham; **J.H. Bickerton**, Wallasey.

THE STAR CAFÉ (A74)   Tel: (0555) 892557

Situation On the A74 at Lesmahagow — pity the poor old Star, but do not forget it. Just as it was becoming popular they cut it off by opening the M74 extension. Now the way to get to the café is off the motorway one mile south or five miles north. They have put a few sharp corners into the road because of the motorway construction, but regulars soon began drifting back. Jim and Sheila Rossiter opened The Star in 1982 with little to offer but a warm welcome, a homely atmosphere and a solid respect for the trucking fraternity. 'Salt of the earth,' says Jim. They turned a shack into a friendly stop-over. And there are plans: 'We are going to provide the proper facilities truckers deserve. We will have accommodation and a complete truckstop by May 1987,' the Rossiters assert. When it comes to hospitality, Mr Rossiter knows a thing or two about it, before taking over The Star he was in the 'afore ye go' business as area manager for a whisky company.

Food Full breakfast £1.90, three-course meal £2.10.

Recommended by: **J. Hughes**, Leyland; **Matchstick Man**, Oldham; **A. Taylor**, Letchworth; **Alex Main**, Preston; **S.W. Laffam**, Chorley; **K. Anderson**, Aldershot; Driver, Hornsey.

Those are the 40 truckstops and cafés out of nearly 400 which you voted by your recommendations to be the best of the lot. Anybody in the list is doing a job which pleases the drivers. We are not saying that they are the only ones, all we are saying is that they are the ones which you like to use. If you know any others, tell us. But please be precise. Some of the following cafés are not as detailed as they could be. I mean, 'Café on the A1' isn't much of a guide. Nor is: 'The café in Birmingham, y'know, just off the M6.' And while we are in Birmingham it was an acerbic Birmingham transport manager with a jaundiced view of drivers who said: 'Believe me, the trouble is that half these b*****s don't know where they're going, where they've been or where they are half the time!' Cheeky!

IT'S BIZARRE

Excelsior
'My old unit and trailer trying to climb a steep hill.' — **Ronald Cavanagh**, Manchester.

Let's now look at those cafés which are just knocking at the door to get into the 'Top 40':

ALVESTON MOTORWAYS TRANSPORT MOTEL
(A38/M4/M5)   Tel: (0454) 413344

Situation Note that this is the *Avon* Alveston, not the one in Warwickshire; on the A38 four miles north of the M4 and M5, come off the M5 at junction 14 or 15 going west, junction 16 going east, or junction 20 on the M4. Alveston is on the A38, some people prefer to say the truckstop is near Thornbury.

Services Ample parking, beds, bar and video. It is now very well spoken of and a boon to West Country travellers.

Recommended by: **G. Moat**, Colchester; **A. Stewart**, St, Boswells, 'Good food, reasonably priced.' Driver, Manchester; **Alex Main**, Preston; **Harry Bickley**, Hyde.

BIRTLEY TRUXSTOP (A1)　　　　Tel: (091) 4109617

Situation Portobello Road, Birtley, Tyne and Wear. On the A1(M) northbound at the junction where the A69 branches left and the A1 continues to the Tyne Tunnel; take the tunnel road to the Washington slip road, take another left, back over the A69 and the entrance is on your left.

Services Supervised 10-acre truck park, bedrooms, restaurant, showers, bar and TV room, games room, phones and fuel.

Recommended by: **Ian Bannister**, Cupar, Fife; **Kevin Simpson**, Folkstone; **Malcolm Hotterwell**, Doncaster; Driver, Washington; **Stewart McLure**, Scunthorpe, 'Video and good facilities.'; **Richard J. Williams**, Edinburgh.

BRIAN'S CAFÉ (M50)

Situation At the Worcester turn-off of the M50 — some say it is at Tewkesbury — well, it must be there because you say it is, but nobody except the drivers who recommend it seems able to place it exactly. The police don't know, they think it might actually be called The Little Hut. But that's not in the phone book or any other reference book. The more exact you can be, the more helpful it will be to others. Anyway, take pot-luck.

Recommended by: **Michael Meak**, Parkend; **N. Wallis**, Swansea; **Alan Marsh**, Dinas Powys; **S. Gallagher**, Abercrave, Powys; **Gwyn Latchem**, Tonypandy.

THE COPPER KETTLE (A5)

Situation On the A5 Atherstone to Nuneaton road. This is where the Atherstone police say it is: coming out of Atherstone, go past the big Mancetter/Withersley island and the Copper Kettle is a caravan 200 yards down the road — look for The Bull pub on the left, and it's about there.

Recommended by: **T.**; **Chaplin**, Leigh; **George Stubbs**, Sale; **R. Scott**, Kilwinning; **John O'Connor**, Openshaw, Manchester; **FC**, Colne.

IT'S THE WAY YOU TELL'EM

Use your loaf

The Irishman came off the ferry, went into the pub and ordered a pint. 'Whitbread?' The barman queried. 'T'ank you, two slices,' said the Irishman.
Big A, *Chalvedon Pitsea, Essex.*

ED'S CAFÉ (A11) Incorporated in BRECKLAND LODGE
Tel: (0953) 455202

Situation At Attleborough, at the south end of the new bypass on the A11 between Thetford and Norwich.

Services Parking for 25 on solid concrete, showers, shaving rooms — absolutely full facilities.

Food Superb breakfast for £2.00, meal-of-the-day, a choice from three or four, £2.50, café open from 6.30 until 7.30 in the evening, but meals still available in the pub on site until 9.30 p.m..

Following after the Copper Kettle — but with absolutely no disparagement intended — this is moving from the ridiculous to the sublime. Ed's requires a special mention because it is the first of its type to be opened in Britain — the complete motoring complex, for ALL motorists. Ed's began as an old log-cabin café and expanded under Ted and Doreen Devlin's guidance, and later with son Ed and his wife Maureen's assistance. Then came the bypass! That could have scuppered the whole thing from a transport point of view. But the Devlin family met the challenge and decided to develop the site to match the new conditions, and do it in the Continental style with a family restaurant, an à la carte restaurant, transport café, shop and pub — The Stag — all in one complex. Says Ed: 'We've put in the finest facilities. The days of transport drivers roughing it are coming to an end. We believe that this is the first of the new style services in the country.' There is more than a spin-off for truckers in a development like this, Breckland Lodge now employs 60 local staff in an area where there isn't too much work about. But still they cannot get the place sign-posted. Ed laments: 'The local council must have a yard full of unofficial signs I've put up and they've pulled down.' Ed's came up strongly in our survey, but too early yet for its impact to have been fully registered.

Recommended by: **Tiger**, Catfield, Stallam; **W.G.Gray**, Dagenham; **R. Beckett**, King's Lynn; **Green Eagle**, Stallam; **Charles Youles**, Southend; **Robert Greenaway** , Rainham.

IT'S BIZARRE

The nature of an accident
All precautions duly taken, all care being properly exercised and still unforeseen incidents can cause devastating accidents and the distress is extreme. **Ken Hickman**, a Manchester driver, was being towed after a breakdown. The two vehicles had to stop. An elderly lady shambled between them and fell over the tow-rope. Ken leapt from his cab to help her and drag her clear. At that moment the towing vehicle moved off pulling an unmanned, uncontrolled truck behind it. The result was mayhem and untold damage.

THE GARWICK CAFÉ (A17)   Tel: (0529) 605504

Situation On the A17, 7 miles east of Sleaford and just east of the Heckington bypass.

Services Parking for 20 trucks and meals from 7 a.m. until 4 p.m..

Food Breakfast is £1.60 and main meals with four vegetables and home-made sweets are £2.10 to £2.20. The café has been on this main coast road since 1946. Patrick Price bought it in 1983, the old staff stays on, all local ladies. The proprietor knows about driving — and its irritations — he drove a London bus for years.

Recommended by: **Dennis King**, Bury St. Edmunds; **Roger Gadd**, Sleaford; **Richard Levitt**, King's Lynn; **Dawn Fox**, Holbeach; **Paul Mason**, North Kyme.

THE HEATHERGHYLL MOTEL (A74)   Tel: (086 42) 641

Situation On the A74 at Crawford, one hour's drive from Glasgow. Crawford is only a tiny place, population 300/400, say the local police, but it caters in a big way for truckers, it used to be a big change-over place for them. William Holmes has run the motel for 14 years. He can park 40 wagons, there is a shower and phones; food in the café comes at £1.90 for a full breakfast and £3.00 for the three-course evening meal — they love their soup in Scotland. A well-regarded spot.

Recommended by: **Stanley Hunter**, Burtonwood; **Curley**, Sheffield; Driver, Liverpool; **Bear**, Reading; **J. Martin**, Clacton.

JACKS HILL CAFÉ (A5)   Tel: (0327) 50522/50154

Situation On the A5 trunk road one mile north of Towcester and 8 miles from junctions 15 and 16 on the M1.

Services Plenty of parking, £3.00; diesel on site; 40 beds, £4.50; showers and phones.

Food The café seats 100 and is open from 6 a.m. until 10 p.m. every weekday, from 6 a.m. until 3 p.m. on Saturdays and 10 a.m. until 6 p.m. on Sundays; breakfasts come in great variety: standard at £1.76 which includes tea and bread and butter, bumper with more on the plate but bread and tea extra, and the super at £2.60 — you could be there all day eating it. Main meals range from £1.50 to steaks at £2.87. Barry Freeman has run the place for 25 years and survived the coming of the M1 which diverted the trade from his doorstep. Now he faces a new bypass opening at Towcester, he'll survive that — drivers like the place.

Amenities bar, and TV.

Recommended by: **Stewart McLure**, Scunthorpe; **Peter Kerry**, Aylesbury; Driver, Romsey; **David Beech**, Northampton; **J.H. Kelly**, Durham.

MONTS CAFÉ (A38)   Tel: (0626) 82333

Situation On the old A38 at Liverton, near Newton Abbot. There is easy access from the A38/Heathfield Industrial Estate, follow the 'Local Services' signs.

Services Parking for 30 comfortably, 50 if they park properly; shower and washing facilities open all night, £3.00; accommodation for 5 at £9.00 which includes evening meal and breakfast.

Food You can have English at £1.35 or American, with more on the plate, at £1.40, main meals are £1.80 with a choice of six dishes with three vegetables; potatoes are boiled, roast, chipped or jacket.

Amenities TV — and the welcome stranger pub is five minutes walk away — but there are other attractions as well.

Monts has been around for 30 years but Vern Oxley has run it for the last four years. He finds that drivers are becoming food and health conscious and are cutting out the fried grub after breakfast time — now he is bringing in wholemeal bread. His big speciality is CB, which he supplies and fits, and is renowned for it. Add to that Country and Western supplies: buy your gun, holster and shirts here — and have your photograph done, that's a new line for a truckstop.

Recommended by: **David Simmonds**, Gloucester; **Trevor Gray**, Ramsgate; **J. Knest**, Exeter; **John Marshall**, Dorset; **A. Stewart**, St. Boswells, 'Good food, reasonably priced.'

MORGAN'S CAFÉ (A38/M5)   Tel: (0823) 672273

Situation On the A38 between Exeter and Taunton, to be precise, between junctions 26 and 27 on the M5.

Services parking for 30 trucks, beds for 10 in double rooms, two showers; parking is £2.50, including breakfast, and beds are £7,00 including evening meal and breakfast.

Food the large breakfast is £1.49 but there are permutations from 85p upwards, main meals like roasts are £1.50; open 6.00 until 7 p.m. daily, until 10 p.m. on Saturdays and closed on Sunday.

Amenities bar, TV room, darts and snooker.

Derek Webber has been at Morgans for ten years and has run it for the last five. He took it over from his wife's uncle, so the family connection stretches back more than 30 years. A strong bond has grown up between the regulars and the café.

Recommended by: **J. Knest**, Wellington; **N. Powell**, Ross-on-Wye, **Diesel Jockey**, Bristol; **Diesel Ringer**, Monmouth; Mr **Gorrett**, Crediton, Devon.

IT'S THE WAY YOU TELL'EM

Solution
Why did the hen cross the road? It was the chicken's day off.
S. Mulvany, *Audenshaw, Manchester.*

THE MOSS CAFÉ (A74/M6)   Tel: 022874 216

Situation on the A74 at Todhill, five miles from Carlisle and just before the start of the M6...hmmm, five drivers named the café, so in fairness to them I will list it too. But I found the management unforthcoming when I requested information about the establishment − prickly even. So I have reservations. A condition of my recommendation for any catering establishment is a welcome on the doormat, not a flea in the ear.

Recommended by: **Kevin Taylor**, Richmond, Yorks.; **Driver, Melksham**; Driver, **Bolton**; **James Murdoch**, Stranraer; **Frank Baker**, St Helens.

IT'S BIZARRE

Three-legged race

The drama was intense and the din was terrific; lights were flashing, the 'shrieker' was splitting the air and traffic swerved out of the way. So did **Dennis Copeland**, of Millhouses, Sheffield: it was a flat-out, high-speed police chase down the M62. Then Mr Copeland saw that the police car had a flat tyre.

THE RAVEN CAFÉ (A41/A49)   Tel: 0948 2570

Situation easy to find at the junction of the A41 and A49, at Press Heath, 3 miles south of Whitchurch, Shropshire.

Services parking for 40, with a second park opposite to take 60, all tarmacadamed; four showers and two bathrooms; beds for 25, doubles and singles; parking costs £2.00 and bed and breakfast is £6.00.

Food breakfast from £1.00 up to £1.80 and main meals, pudding included, are £2.20; open from 06.00 hours until 8 o'clock in the evening every day, seven days a week:

Amenities TV, darts, dominoes, two pool tables − and The Raven Pub next door.

Seven years ago The Raven was a wooden hut café which had closed down. Farmer Cedric Wilkes bought the place and built the present café which he runs with his wife, Susan. It is a family business and between them they own six pubs − sister Anne runs the one next to the café. Mr Wilkes still farms, so the food should be field−fresh.

Recommended by: **Tony Reynolds**, Flint; **T. Beetham**, Wirral; **A. Bell**, Anglesey; **P. Butterworth**, Shaw; **R. Dyke**, Stevenage.

THE RIGGEND CAFÉ (A73)　　　　　　Tel: 023 683 219

Situation at Riggend on the A73, three miles south of Cumbernauld.
Services parking for 60 trucks, diesel; 2 showers; 3 double
bedrooms, 2 singles and still a dormitory for 6, 2 singles in the
adjoining bungalow if needed; parking charge is £3.00 and an
evening meal, bed and breakfast will set you back £6.50:
Food breakfast is £1.90 and main meals range from £1.65 to T-bone
steak or Scampi mornay at £6.50; they are open from 6.30 a.m. until
10 p.m. on Saturday night, Sundays from 7.00 a.m. until 10.00 p.m.,
Saturday and Sunday night off, the transport café seats 30, the
tourist café 45; drivers use the tourist café as a lounge and TV room
at night; the bar is good, popular and flexible. (It has appeared in
Egon Ronay.)

Gordon McPherson has run the Riggend Café for 23 years. At one
time he accommodated 66 drivers a night until sleeper-cabs came
on the scene. One of the few cafés open at weekends and
southbound drivers stock up for the barren run through England.

Recommended by: **Ron Hetherington**, Blackburn; **L. McDonald**, Forfar, Angus; **Michael
Meak**, Parkend; **Sandy Tandy**, Ledbury; **William McWatt**, Denny, Stirling.

THE SALT BOX CAFÉ (A50/A516)　　　Tel: 0283 813189

Situation on the Derby to Stoke road at the junction of the A50 and
A516 roads. It is at Hatton, the lorry park is at the rear of the café and
there is space for 36; there is a park for private motorists at the front.
Services it is a café pure and simple, open from 7 o'clock in the
morning until 7 in the evening daily, 2.30 p.m. Saturdays, closed on
Sundays; sleeper-cabs can stay overnight for £2.45, which includes
a meal voucher − it's a give-away.
Food breakfasts, in several permutations, £1.70, with tea and bread
and butter; main meals: home-made pies, £1.22, roasts £1.56.

A real old-fashioned, unchanged café of thirty years good
standing; it is so well liked that they are terrified to change. It has
been in the Egan family for 20 years and is now run by Jim and
Margaret Egan, and Jim's brother, Hugh. Both brothers are caterers,
Jim trained in London hotels and at the Leofric, in Coventry. He's
never set foot inside a truck, and doesn't want to. 'I feed them, that's
my job,' he insists. They haven't changed the menu for 20 years.
That worries Jim, but he dare not change because that is the way the
lads like it. It's all fresh food, served up for the past 20 years by their
cook, Dolly Seamark, and the grill cook, Patricia Komenda. When
you go to the Salt Box, you can be sure what you're going to get in
the way you prefer.

Recommended by: **S. Mulvaney**, Audenshaw, Manchester; **H.S. Jeffrey**, (no address
given); **George Stubbs**, Sale; **P. Butterworth**, Shaw; **T. Beetham**, Bebington, Wirral.

SUPER LADY'S CARAVAN (A1) — on C.B., handle, Super Lady.

Situation on the A1, in the lay-by approaching Worksop — very well known and appreciated. If you have read the club section of the book, you'll know quite a bit about Super Lady and company. She is one of the founders of the A1 Club. The caravan became an information centre as well as a café with the advent of C.B. you could say the June Southworth — C.B. handle, Super Lady — was the pip in the grape of the grapevine. And, as we said before, Super Lady's has its moments. 'You should see us at Cabaret time,' said June. Remember.

Recommended by: **George Bishop**, March; **I. Watson**, Wisbech; **David Wood**, Lincoln; **Christopher Briggs**, Peterborough; **M. Bright**, Lincoln, who adds: 'A beautiful bacon sandwich.'

IT'S THE WAY YOU TELL'EM

Ever-helpful

The distraught lady driver in the lay-by had the bonnet of her VW Beetle up when a second lady Beetle driver pulled up to offer assistance. The first lady sobbed: 'I've lost my engine.' The second replied: 'Don't worry, they put a spare one in my boot, you can have that.'
R. Allison, *South Queensferry*.

A suitable case for treatment

I have nothing against women drivers. Actually, they are just like any other normal psychopaths.
Manwell, *Stranraer*.

OTHER OF YOUR FAVOURITE TRUCKSTOPS

Along the highways and byways of the land there are certain quiet hide-aways known to the *cognoscenti* and those who like a gentle skive to ease the rigours of the day — and a good meal. This list includes many such places and some might just fit the bill for you. They are not the popular well-known stops but places one or two of you favour and recommend.

There is a problem however: in some cases those who have recommended the cafés have not been exactly specific in locating them. So, in a way, this is a DIY section of the guide — if you can find the hide-away, you might do yourself a favour. And when you do, please let us know the exact location and we will be more helpful next time.

The places are listed alphabetically, but it might help if you also looked down the right-hand column which gives the road where the cafés are said to be so that if you are travelling down that way you can keep a look-out for them.

The same rules apply in this list as in the detailed section. Nobody can be published here unless recommended in writing by a working HGV licence holder.

A1 Café, North Circular Road   **A406**
Recommended by: **Bugs Bunny**, Hitchen.

Airport Café, Burton-on-Trent   **A38**
Recommended by: **A.T. Maddow**, Bristol; **S.J. Fulge**, Bristol.

Alex's Café, Bradford   **A6036**
Recommended by: **Kevin Simpson**, Folkestone.

Andover Café   **A303**
Recommended by: **Jacques Boeking**, Berck-sur-mer, France.

Annie's Café, West Bulney, King's Lynn   **A47**
Recommended by: **Green Eagle**, Stallam; **Tiger**, Catfield.

Ann's Café, Derby/Uttoxeter A516
Recommended by: **Brian Saville**, Burstall, W. Yorks.

Arthur's Café, East Lancs Road A57
Recommended by: **Larry Mealey**, Liverpool.

Ashgrove Café, Inverness to Aberdeen road A96
Recommended by: **Ian Angus**, Alness, Ross.

Autostop, just off A14 Godmanchester to A603/A14
Royston, 603 is a turn-off to Grantchester
Recommended by: **Kevin Seaton**, Biggleswade.

Badger's Mount, Bruce's Café at Orpington A21/A224
Recommended by: **Richard Futter**, King's Lynn.

Bagshot Café, between Sunningdale and Camberley A30
Recommended by: **Stephen Priest**, Woking.

Ballinluig Services, 20 Miles north of Perth A9
Recommended by: **Ian Angus**, Alness, Ross; **Driver**, Andover;
George Ross Sharp, Aless.

Bank Foot Café, Perthshire, Scotland A9
Recommended by: **L. Holmes**, Thetford; **Andy Miller**, Bonnybridge,
'Egon Ronay recommend it too.'

Barnaby Top, Barnaby, just off A1 A1
Recommended by: **M. Holmes**, Helborough.

Burgermaster, Hull to Leeds road A63
Recommended by: **Bob Key**, Evesham.

Birch Services, Granada motorway services M62
Recommended by: **Welter**, Eupen, Belgium; **Geoff Mayston**, Altrincham.

Blue Star A74
Recommended by: **Gambler**, Kent.

Blue and White Café, south of Ashford, Kent, A20
take the *old* road.
Recommended by: **B.R. Gammon**, Ashford, Kent

Bob's Café, East Lancs Road A57
Recommended by: **Driver**, Leeds.

Bob's Café, off junction 20, M1 on the A427 A427
road to Market Harborough
Recommended by: **Peter Austin**, Leeds.

Bob's Café, Rochester, Kent A2
Recommended by: **Chris Cesana**, Margate; Mr **F. Loates**. Chatham.

Bob's Café, Winchester Road, Popham   **A31**
Recommended by: **Rob Roy**, Greenhithe.

Boot and Shoe, Wetherby, southbound A1 at   **A1**
Ferrybridge
Recommended by: **Derek**, Teeside; **Kevin**, Welwyn Garden City;
Tony Pearson, Middlesborough.

Brent Knoylle   **M5**
Recommended by: **Mervyn G. Thomas**, Cardiff.

Bruce's Café, *see* Badger's Mount, Orpington   **A224/A21**
Recommended by: **Driver**, Rye.

Bungalow Café, just outside Indian Queens on the A30   **A30**
Recommended by: **Jeffrey John Harmycz**, High Wycombe.

Cara Café, Eccles, Manchester   **A57**
on the A57 at Eccles, Manchester.
Recommended by: **Gerard Harrison**, Bolton; **A. Robbins**, Southampton;
Driver, Manchester; **T.M. Cullen**, Huddersfield.

Carlton Café, one mile east of Basildon, Essex   **A127**
Recommended by: **Bryan Williams**, Leigh-on-Sea

Carmen's Café, Wantage to Didcot, turn off A34   **34**
to Wantage, next roundabout, turn right, 200 yards on left.
Full breakfast £1.50
Recommended by: **Mad Monk**, Spalding.

Carol's Café, Skellow, Doncaster   **A1**
Recommended by: **L. Dunn**, Shildon, County Durham.

Charnock Richard Services,   **M6**
Recommended by: **M. Taylor**, Burnley

Chatfield's Café, Wrotham Hill, Kent   **A20**
Recommended by: **Rob Roy**, Greenhithe.

Chris's Café, High Wycombe — on the old A40,   **A40**
running parallel with M40, at West Wycombe.
Recommended by: **T.M. Cullen**, Huddersfield; **Kevin Simpson**, Folkestone;
Graham Elgar, Oxford; **Bugs Bunny**, Hitchin; Driver, Abingdon.

Cliff Café, Llangollen   **A5**
Recommended by: **Gwyn Latcham**, Tonypandy.

Coatesgate Café, on the northbound carriageway   **A74**
it is one of Egon Ronay's 'Top Ten' for food and
accommodation.
Recommended by: **Willie Carson**, Kirkintilloch; Driver, Newcastle;
Frank Baker, St. Helens.

Comfort Café, A11, near A11/A604 roundabout **A11/A604**
Recommended by: R.V., Euston, Thetford.

Corner Café, on the A61 at Queensbury **A61**
Recommended by: **John Wheatley**, Sutton Coldfield; **Albert Machtelinecks**, Eidhoven, Holland; **Colin Roadnight**, Bradford.

Coveney Heath Café **A449**
Recommended by: **Joseph Frank Bagot**, Hyde, Cheshire.

Coventry Truck Stop **A444**
Recommended by: **Driver**, Rawtenstall; **Driver**, Manchester, **Richard Neill**, Boston.

Crawford BP Services, on the A74 at Crawford **A74**
Recommended by: **Ronald Cavanagh**, Caddishead; **Driver**, Liverpool; Mr **Muldoon**, Paisley.

The Cup, on the main road from Bristol to Avonmouth **A4**
'Excellent.'
Recommended by: **Mark J. Taylor**, Radstock.

Dalwhinnie Café **A9**
Recommended by: **George Ross Sharp, Ian Angus**, Alness.

Darrington Café **A1**
Recommended by: **Driver**, Wisbech; **P. Kent**, Norwich.

Dennis's Café, Preston **A49**
Recommended by: **Dennis Copeland**, Sheffield.

Derek's Café, Bodell Wyddyn **A55**
Recommended by: **Geraint Thomas**, Conway, N. Wales.

Dingle Café, Grindley Brook, Whitchurch **A41**
Recommended by: **Mark Seymour**, Hendon, London.

Dunker Café, Bollington, off the A523 or **A523/A5002**
the A5002
Recommended by: **W. King**, Liverpool.

Eaves Café, Crick **A5**
Recommended by: **Chris Walls**, Burton-on-Trent.

Elvanfoot Café, just south of Crawford on the A74 **A74**
Recommended by: **Andy Miller**, Bonnybridge; 'Food very good, staff pleasant and helpful especially Big Maggie.' **William McWatt**, Denny, Stirling; **John Martin**, Clacton: 'Crawford is the best town in Britain for truckers.'

Ferrybridge Café **A1**
Recommended by: **N. Holmes**, Helborough.

Flowerpot Café, Shardlow, on the A6 near M1 junction 24 **A6**
Recommended by: **Steve Handsley**, Littlecover, Derby.

Fordal Café, Dalkeith   **A68**
Recommended by: **Rambling Jack**; King of the Road.

Forton Services, Lancaster   **M6**
Recommended by: **Humphrey Eng**, LLanharan; **Ian Whiteside**, Wigan;
J. Ousby, Penrith.

Fountain Café, Wellesbourne   **A423**
Recommended by: **M. Pratt**, Swindon.

Four Wheel Café, Penrith   **A74/M6**
Recommended by: **Leslie Merriman**, Lancashire.

Furline Café, Stibbington, near Peterborough   **A1**
Recommended by: **Derek Gordon**, South Shields

Gate Café, Beattock   **A74**
Recommended by: **Mac**, Chesterfield

Gate Café, Dover   **A2**
Recommended by: **R.B. Marsden**, Wellingborough; **Dave Smith**, Mansfield;
Mr **Nixon**, Northwich.

Gatwick Café, Heckmondwike   **A47**
Recommended by: **D.J. Rimmer**, Ormskirk

Gedney Café, Gedney, near Long Sutton   **A17**
Recommended by: **John Shortland**, Spalding.

George Café, on the Leek to Buxton road
Recommended by: **T. Kinnerton**, Shrewsbury

Graham's Café, on the A38 at North Petherton   **A38/M5**
just off the M5
Recommended by: **P. Pegler, K.M. Mallett, Dave Hayter**, Bristol;
B.R. Gammon, Ashford, Kent.

Green Dragon, Welton   **A157**
Recommended by: **R.P. Fell**, Cleethorpes.

Gull's Nest, at North Berwick on the A1   **A1**
Recommended by: **Richard Dembizky**, Scunthorpe.

Halfway Café, Ternhill,
on the A41 in the   **A41**
Market Drayton area. Ternhill is the village at the junction of the A41
and A53.
Recommended by: **Tony Reynolds**, Flint.

Happy Hour, at Bassett's Pole, just north   **A38/A453**
of Sutton Coldfield almost at the junction of the A38
and A453 — a slip road seems to link the two.
Recommended by: **Stewart Deardon**, Chard.

Harold's Café, at Fleet, which we assume is the Lincolnshire Fleet because the driver is a Norwich man — which puts it on the A17   **A17**
Recommended by: **Harry Newstead**, Norwich.

Haydock Café, on the A580 where it crosses the A58 in East Lancs.   **A580**
Recommended by: **Driver**, Bedlington.

Headlight Café   **A27**
Recommended by: **Cinderman**, Ayr.

Highway Café, just before the town at Norwich   **A47**
Recommended by: **D.J. Rimmer**, Ormskirk.

High Littleton Café, at High Littleton, west of Bath and north of Midsomer Norton   **A39**
Recommended by: **C. Reynolds**, Bristol

Hillington Park, at Atherstone on the A5   **A5**
Recommended by: **S.W. Poole**, Farningham, Surrey.

Hungry Horse, East Dereham   **A47**
Recommended by: **Mark Seymour**, Hendon, London.

The Hut, Tewkesbury and Worcester A38   **A38**
Recommended by: **Diesel Ringer**, Monmouth; **Driver**, Shepton Mallet.

Island Café, East Lancs Road   **A580**
Recommended by: **Gwyn Latcham**, Tonypandy.

Ivy's Café, outside Leeds on the A64   **A64**
Recommended by: **Dennis Copeland**:

Jet, near Rugby on the A5, near to junction 18, M1   **A5**
Recommended by: **Steve Newall**, Leigh; **Steve Hoggard**, Wigan.

Jim's Tea Bar, West Walton Highway on the A47   **A47**
Recommended by: **Christopher Briggs**: Peterborough; **I. Watson**, Wisbech; **George Bishop**, Match.

Juggernaut Café, Horsham to Crawley road, Sussex   **A264**
Recommended by: **Blue Beard**, Crawley.

Keele Services   **M6**
Recommended by: **Stanley Hunter**, Burtonwood; **Geoff Hayston**, Altrincham; **Nick Thorley**, Sale, Cheshire.

Kirtlebridge Café, Dumfriesshire   **A74**
Recommended by: **Stewart Shepley**, Clifton; **Charlie Armstrong**, Southampton.

Knayton Café, Knayton, Yorks.   **A19**
Recommended by: **Driver**, Darlington

Leek Motorway Café, Charnock Richards, near Wigan   **M6**
Recommended by: **Stanley Hunter**, Burtonwood.

Leeming Bar   **A1**
Recommended by: **Cinder Man**, Ayr.

Lewdown Service Staion, Launceston, near
Oakhampton   **A30**
Recommended by: **Arnold William Pearce**, Par; **Ian Elliot**, Bournemouth.

Lindsay Towers   **A47**
Recommended by: **Stanley Hunter**, Burtonwood.

Little Bistro, near Boroughbridge   **A1**
Rcommended by: **Derek Gordon**, South Shields.

London House Café, at Kirkpatrick, Fleming, in the main   **A74**
street, just off A74
Recommended by: **William McWatt**, Stirling; **L. McDonald**, Forfar.

Magno Café, West Thurrock, near Dartford tunnel   **A126**
Recommended by: **Driver**, Cambridge.

Maple Cross Café, near Rickmansworth, M25   **A405**
and A405
Recommended by: **Adrian Dennis**, Sandown; **Dipstick**, Uxbridge;
Alan Jones, Southampton.

Marsh Barton Café, Exeter, on A30, first junction M5.   **A30**
Recommended by: **Eric Stanway**, St. Ives.

May's Café, Brentwood on the A12   **A12**
Recommended by: **J. Lay**, Bedford; **P.I. MacInally**, Felixstowe.

Merlindale Café, Crawford   **A74**
Recommended by: **Larry Mealey**, Liverpool; **Frank Baker**, St Helens;
Harry Bickley, Hyde.

Merry Chest, Greenhithe, Kent   **A2**
Recommended by: **Gambler**, Gravesend.

Mid Cornwall Services, Bodmin, on the A30   **A30**
Recommended by: **D. Johnson**, Rossendale.

Midway Café, at Whitchurch, on the A41 between   **A41**
Chester and Telford
Recommended by: **John Braine**, Claydon; **Eric Fielding**, Brosely, Salop;
Driver, Uckfield.

Monmouth Truckers   **A449**
Recommended by: Mr **Bickley**, Hednessford.

Mountnessing Café, on the A12 eastbound   **A12**
Recommended by: **Colin Stamford**, Trimley St. Mary.

New Island Café, Loughton, Leigh A580 east **A580**
to Manchester
Recommended by: **Steve Newall** and **Steve Hoggard**, Wigan.

Noakes Café, Rainham, in Essex **A13**
Recommended by: **Charlie Braham**, Haydock; **S.J. Fulge**, Bristol;
Colin Short, Swansea; **A.T. Maddow**, Bristol.

Norton Fitzwarren Café, at Norton Fitzwarren, west **A361**
of Taunton
Recommended by: **S.J. Fulge**, Bristol.

Nunney Catch Café, west of Frome **A361**
Recommended by: **Driver**, Wincanton.

O.K. Café, eastbound at Kelverdon, between **A12**
Chelmsford and Witham.
Recommended by: **Bryan Williams**, Leigh-on-sea; **M. Whitemoor**,
Southampton; **J. Knest**, Exeter; **Colin Stamferd**, Trimley St. Mary.

Oak Café, Amesbury **A303**
Recommended by: **J. Knest**, Exeter.

Oakdene Café, below Brand's Hatch, junction 2a **M26/A227**
Recommended by: **Dougie Vick**, Cheltenham Spa.

Oaklands Café, Wrotham, Kent **A20**
Recommended by: **Driver**, Rye.

Odsal Café, Odsal roundabout, half a mile from **M606**
the M606, Bradford
Recommended by: **Paul Taylor**, Bradford.

Out Of Town Café, Andover, **A303/A343**
just off the A303/A343
Recommended by: **Driver**, St. Neots.

Paddy's Café, on the A2, left at Gravesend, left and **A12**
left again on to park
Recommended by: **F. Loates**, Chatham.

Penny-Farthing Café, Ringwood, Hampshire. **A31**
Recommended by: **Tony Squires**, Poole, Dorset.

Peter's Café, Hatfield, on the Barnet bypass **A1**
on the A1 southbound
Recommended by: **Bluebeard**, Crawley; **Stanley Hunter**, Burtonwood.

Petts Truckstop, King's Lynn **A47**
Recommended by: **R. Beckett**, Great Yarmouth.

Plain Jane Café, at North Thetford **A134**
Recommended by: **Paul Raymond Smith**, Ipswich.

Ponderosa Café, at Crick   A5
Recommended by: **Driver**, Skelmersdale.

Pop's Café, Lymm, Cheshire   A5
Recommended by: **R. Walshaw**, Eccleston; **T. Roberts**, Liverpool;
J. Blunt, Wednesfield.

Portbury Dock, adjoining Portishead   M5/A369
Recommended by: **Mel Taskor**, Weston Super Mare.

Pott's Café, junction 20   M6
Recommended by: **R. Hull**, Macclesfield.

Punchbowl Inn
Churchtown, near Preston, from Manchester M602, M62,
M61, M6 to M55 junction, pick up A6 through Garstang,
about 2-miles up is the signpost to Churchtown
Recommended by: **G. Clayton**, Audenshaw, Manchester.

Raglan Café   A449
Recommended by: Mr **Appleyard**, Stafford.

Rainham Lights, at Rainham, Essex   A13
Recommended by: **Big A**, Pitsea.

Ralph's Café, Tewkesbury, Glos   A38
Recommended by: **L. Williams**, Widnes.
Recommended by: **M. Foster**, Cannock; **T.T. Hardman**, Warrington;
P. Thompson, Widnes; **Alan Ball**, St. Helens, Lancs.

Red Lion, Dumfries   A74
Recommended by: **T.T. Hardman**, Warrington.

The Red Lodge, Freckenham, off the A11   A11
Recommended by: **J. Lynes**, Norwich; **Gordon**, Aylesbury.

The Retreat Motel, Orpington, Kent, at junction 4   M25
Recommended by: **Tony Sqires**, Poole; **Malcolm Dickinson**, Erith.

The Roca, Purfleet/Grays, Essex   A13
Recommended by: **Allen Mossman**, Basildon.

Rosa Café, Chapel-en-le-Frith, Derbyshire   A6
Recommended by: **Driver**, Salford.

Sabrina's Café, Blythe   A614
Recommended by: **Colin Hill**, Peterborough.

Sally's Café, High Littleton   A39
Recommended by: **A.T. Maddow**, Bristol.

Sally's Café, Plympton   A374
Recommended by: **L. Williams**, Widnes.

Santa Rowsley, Chapel-en-le-Frith
A6
Recommended by: **Antony Millen**, Sheffield.

Savlon Grill, Cheltenham, junction 11
M5
Recommended by: **Alexander McNicol**, Newton Stuart.

Silver Ball, Royston
A10
Recommended by: **Brian and J.J. Silvester**, Sleaford; **Paul Mason**, North Kyme.

Sleepy Sausage, on the Daventry to Coventry section
A45
Recommended by: **R. Beaumont**, Speke; **Driver**, Bromsgrove; **J.H.Bickerton**, Wallasey.

St. George's Café, Ogbourne St. George
A345
Recommended by: **Driver**, Romsey, Hampshire.

Standeford Café, Coven, near Birmingham
A449
Recommended by: **A. Stewart**, St. Boswells.

Stanlow Café, at the Stanlow picnic area
M56
Recommended by: **David Vickers**, Bolton; **Stephen Andrews**, Manchester; **Tom Runathan**, Liverpool.

Staverton Grill, at Mecklesham, near Gloucester
A38
Recommended by: **Driver**, Walton.

Stradishall Café, at Stradishall, Suffolk
A143
Recommended by: **Driver**, Suffolk.

Sugar's Café, Newark, on the A1 Northbound
A1
Recommended by: **Driver**, Portadown.

Swift's Red House Café, via the M62 to junction 36
M62
near Goole
Recommended by: **Dougie Vick**, Cheltenham Spa.

Symond's Yat Truckstop, near Ross-on-Wye
A40
Recommended by: **Pete Redditch**, Birmingham; **N. Powell**, Ross-on-Wye.

Talbot Café, cut across on the side roads,
M54/A442
near Telford
Recommended by: **Friebel**, Nijmegen, Holland.

Taylor's Café, Pelsall Road, Brownhills
A5
Recommended by: Mr **Twist**, Burntwood; **Jockey**, Llangobe.

Telford, near Crawford
A74
Recommended by: **Scania Man**, Crieff.

Thornbury Motor Service
A38
Recommended by: **J.W. Foulkes Bill**, Alfreton; **Larry Mealey**, Liverpool; **Bernard Cawston**, Dursley.

Tilla's Café, Foston
A1
Recommended by: **Roy Coupier**, Basildon, Bradford.

Tinsley Café, Tinsley junction, Sheffield
M1
Recommended by, **R. Flint**, Richmond, Yorks.

Toddington Services
M1
Recommended by: **Stephen Priest**, Woking; **Gary Mazzone**, Chichester.

Toby Jug
A17
Recommended by: **Paul Sharples**, Droylesden; **George Stubbs**, Sale.

Tony's Café, an A1 café at Grantham
A1
Recommended by: **Oil Baron**, Stevenage.

Tomm's Café, off the A1 at Bluth, at the A1M roundabout
A1
Recommended by: **A. Tarmey**, Sunderland.

Tony's and Dot's Café, Bristol Road, Gloucester
A38
Recommended by: **Robert Sin**, Nailsworth, **Richard Asters**, Gloucester.

Trafford Park, Third Avenue Café, universally known as *Dave and Vals,* Third Avenue, Trafford Park, Manchester
Recommended by: **Stephen McErlean**, Stretford, Manchester; **Richard Berry**, Kelsale; **J.H.J. Baker**, Woodbridge; **David Rogers**, Felixstowe; **Ray Ramsey**, Failsworth, Manchester.

Transport Café, Crawford
A74
Recommended by: **Peter Deaking**, Rugeley.

Treble 4, Coventry, off the M6
M6
Recommended by: **B. Taylor**, Amersham.

Trewint Services, on the A30 at the beginning of Bodmin Moor National Park, Launceston end, on the Bodmin road
A30
Recommended by: **K. Garrett**, Ironville; **S.W. Poole**, Farningham.

Truckers Monmouth, on the A449 northbound
A449
Recommended by: **Ian Williams**, Bridgend; **Gwyn Latcham**, Tonypandy; **David Duncalf**, Warsop.

Truckers Rest, Oakhampton
A30
Recommended by: **Driver**, Bristol.

Ulceby Truckstop, South Humberside, just off the A180 for those using the M18 and M180
A180
Recommended by: **Frederick E. Wilderston**, Saltney, Chester; **N. Holmes**, Helborough.

The Vale Café, Evesham
A439
Recommended by: **T. Stamford**, Redditch;

Valley Café, on Whitchurch to Warrington road   A49
Recommended by: **T. Kinnerston**, Shrewsbury.

Venture Café, on the A20 Southbound   A20
Recommended by: **Frank Allington**, East Malling; **Dave Broomfield**, Maidstone.

Watford Gap Services   M1
Recommended by: **Alan Ball**, St. Helens, Lancs; **Gambler**, Gravesend; **Pop Hawley**, Basildon.

Watling Street Café, on Dunstable road on the A5, from junction 9, M1   A5
Recommended by: **Trevor Gray**, Ramsgate; **Peter Mack**, Milton Keynes; **John Marshall,Dorset**.

Wayside Café, on the Exeter to Honiton road at Exeter   A41
Recommended by: **Brian Howard**, Putson, Hereford.

Wayside Café,   A1
Recommended by: **John Cook**, Edmonton, London; **G. Mills**, Bristol.

The White House Café, one mile north of Oakhampton on the A30   A30
Recommended by: Arnold William Pearce, Par,Cornwall.

Willows Café, at Lichfield   A5
Recommended by: **Dave Roberts**, Hull.

Windy Ridge Café, in Cornwall at Trerule Foot, a few miles west of Saltash   A38
Recommended by: **J. Guest**, Exeter; **D. Johnson**, Rossendale; **Jim McNally**, Kirkby.

Wishing Well Café, on the Litchfield to Rugeley road   A51
Recommended by: **Peter Deakin**, Rugeley; Mr **Bickley**, Hednessford; **Driver**, Leeds.

Woodbrook Café,   A6
Woodbrook, Mountsorrel, Leicester, north of Leicester
Recommended by: **D. Littlewood**, York.

Works Canteen ICI Telford
Recommended by:
Ken Hickman, Middleton, Manchester.

Wrotham Heath Café, at the bottom of Wrotham Hill, Kent.   M20/M25
Recommended by: **Dougie Vick**, Cheltenham Spa; **George Mindham**, Paisley.

APPENDIX: TYRES

Since they sponsored the book, I'll give Bandag a puff. Their depots are listed below. I can also promise you that I have personally watched the whole process in operation and can vouch for the incredible care and attention paid to each tyre.

'I don't care how fond you are of her, we only retread truck tyres here!'

Aberdeen: Tel: (0224) 639730

Bishop Auckland: Tel: (0388) 605121

Bristol: Unit 110, Burcott Road, Severnside Ind. Est., Avonmouth.
Tel: (0272) 826847

Cardiff: Tel: (0222) 27922

Cheltenham: Tel:(024267) 5937

Exeter: Tel: (0392) 36203

Lancaster: Tel: (0524) 54081

Maidstone: Bircholt Road, Parkwood, Maidstone.
Tel: (0622) 50048

Norwich: Tel: (0953) 607098

Nottingham: Tel: (0602) 861426

Park Royal: London NW10
Tel: (01) 961 6141

Penrith: Tel: (0768) 66826

Romsey: Tel: (0794) 512359

St. Austell: Tel: (072681) 5441

St. Neots: Howard Road, Eaton Socon, Cambs.
Tel: (0480) 213388

Sleaford: Tel: (0529) 302790

South Woodham Ferrers
Tel: (0245) 329881

Tyre Retreading (Scotland)
61 Napier Road, Ward Park North,
Cumbernauld, Glasgow.
Tel: (02367) 22204

Wakefield: Crigglestone Industrial Estate, Wakefield, Yorks.
Tel: (0924) 257341

Walsall: West Bromwich Road, Tamebridge
Tel: (0922) 20361

Wigan: Lamberhead Industrial Estate, Leopold Street,
Pemberton, Nr. Wigan
Tel: (0942) 214827